AF595862
ANZ·979
TG977
ARB
4X4 ACCESSORIES

NEW SOUTH WALES ATLAS

First published 2013

Updated 2022

Published and distributed by
AFN Fishing & Outdoors
PO Box 544 Croydon, Victoria 3136
Telephone: (03) 9729 8788
Email: sales@afn.com.au
Website: www.afn.com.au

ISBN: 9781 8651 3340 9

MAKE TRAX 4WD
NEW SOUTH WALES
ATLAS
THE BEST BUSH TREKS ACROSS THE STATE COVERING
• SYDNEY AREA • LOWER NORTH
• NORTHERN RIVERS • SOUTH EAST • OUTBACK
DETAILED MAPS
AFN FISHING & OUTDOORS
JENOLAN STATE FOREST
BLUE MOUNTAINS NATIONAL PARK
NATTAI NATIONAL PARK

LAND ROVER
XFB·655

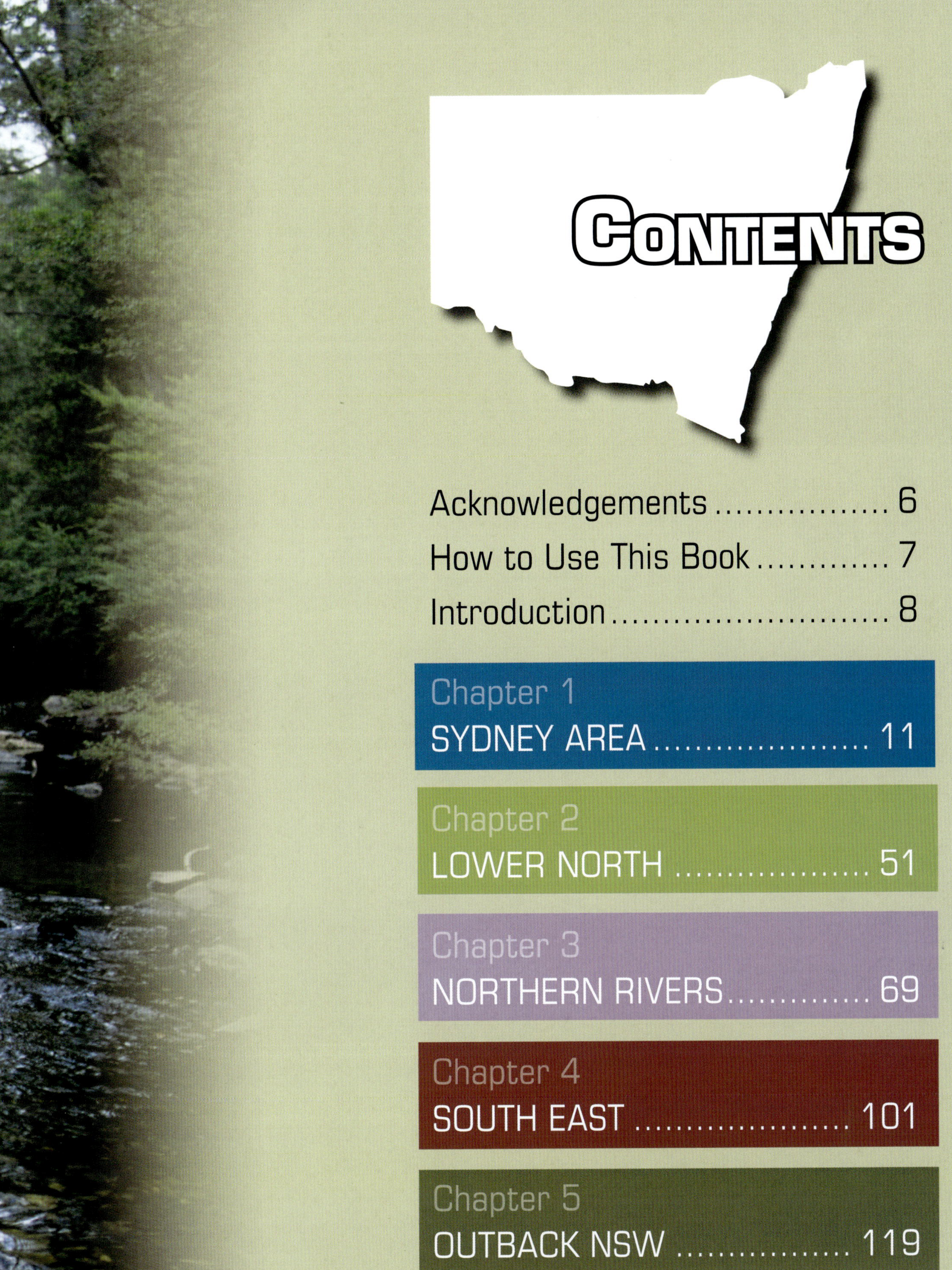

CONTENTS

ABOUT THE CONSULTANTS

John and Anne Morton, have been four-wheel driving for over 30 years clocking up nearly 700,000 kilometres around Australia.

John is a qualified mechanic while Anne is an editor and writer. Their knowledge of four-wheel driving tracks around Australia is comprehensive and in their home state of Victoria, they have pretty well covered every track and 4WD adventure.

In 1995 they started Lifestyle Video Productions, and produced their first video documenting their month-long adventure on the Canning Stock Route. Their videos now document the four-wheel driving, the route and track conditions, mud maps of daily travel, as well as the sights, history, landscapes, scenery and the camaraderie of travelling with others.

Over the years Lifestyle Video Productions has grown into an award-winning business. Together John and Anne have completed a multitude of 4WD adventures – they have travelled Cape York 4 times, Canning Stock Route 3 times, Simpson Desert 7 times, plus dozens of trips on tracks all over Australia and more recently trips in New Zealand and Africa.

They are currently planning further explorations in NSW and Queensland.

Travel Videos of Australia

Explore Discover and Experience using these videos as your guide

travelvideosofaustralia.com

Fraser Island and the Sunshine Coast | **Long Road to the Alice - Port Augusta to Alice Springs** | **Namibia Experience - African Adventure** | **Vistas to Valleys - High Country Adventures** | **Wild Southern Land - New Zealand's South Island**

The Old Ghan Heritage Trail | **Simpson Desert - 50 years on** | **Canning - Stock Route Adventures** | **Savannah Way - Across the top** | **High Country - The Victorian Alps** | **The Madigan Line - Crossing the Northern Simpson** | **Colours of The Kimberley**

The Binns Track - Savannah to Simpson | **Desert Highways - The Roads of Len Beadell** | **New Zealand - Down South** | **On the Track of Burke and Wills** | **Tasmania - The Devil's Playground** | **The Magic of the Flinders Ranges** | **Cape York - Still the Great Adventure**

HOW TO USE THIS BOOK

MAKE TRAX NEW SOUTH WALES presents all of the information that you will need to undertake a safe and enjoyable 4WD trip into the back blocks of this State.

Our TRACK SNAPSHOT identifies the vital requirements for each trek, listing them in a boxed format.

The detailed maps are all oriented with north to the page top, and an integral distance bar to give a sense of scale. Towns, together with the road and track network linking them are clearly displayed, with broken lines indicating unsealed surfaces. For the sake of clarity we have omitted contour lines, but have included waterways and State / National Park boundaries. Camping areas, lookouts and other points of interest are indicated by boxed captions, and the tour route and direction are highlighted in yellow with orange arrows.

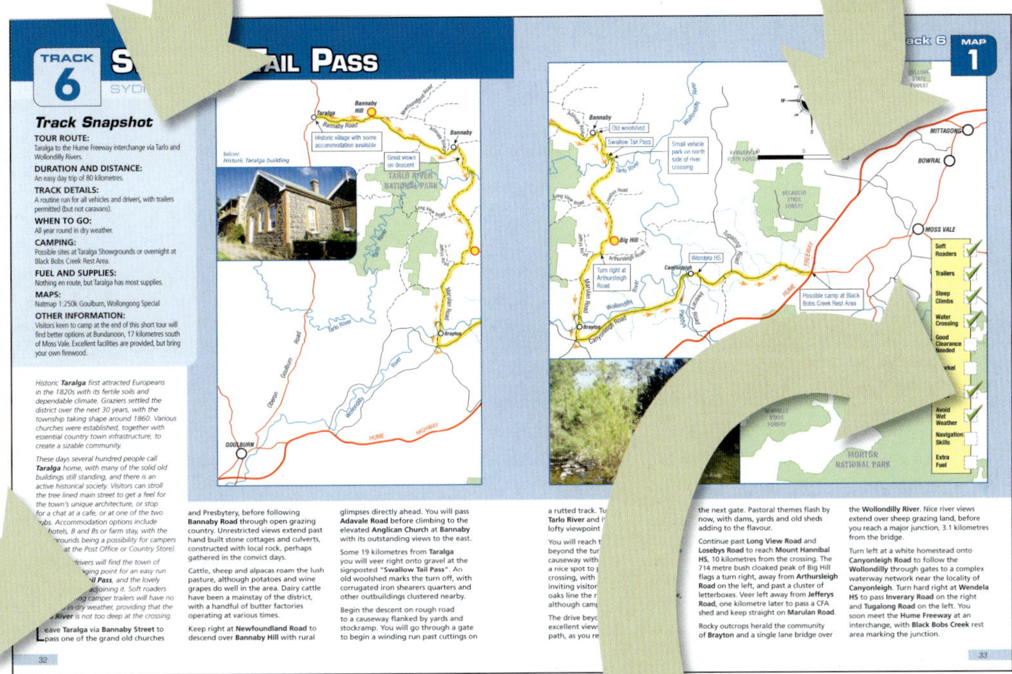

The text follows the vehicle journey using landmarks and intersections as stepping stones through the trek. The intermediate distances mentioned can be compared with your own progress, but it will be necessary to read ahead through the text to identify the next "stepping stone". Those running a GPS unit within the vehicle will have an advantage here, as they can easily compare their position in relation to the maps provided. (A GPS is recommended on any tours where the "Navigation Skills" box has been ticked). In any case, try to keep a record of your odometer readings as you reach the various landmarks described in the text.

A "tick the box" list of tour hazards and basic requirements is included with Map 1 of each trek. This list cannot account for every combination of driver, vehicle and weather combination, but rather attempts to provide a guide for what is likely on the tour. For example a tick in the "Steep Climbs" box cannot indicate how steep the climbs are, but if there is a tick in the "Soft Roaders" box as well, then they are likely to be climbs that will not require low range.

Similarly, a tick in the "Water Crossings" box, but without one in the "Snorkel" box would indicate relatively shallow crossings (although it is customary for travellers to check out an unknown water crossing on foot before plunging in – with the exception of waterways that may be the habitat of salt water crocodiles).

Introduction

MAKE TRAX NEW SOUTH WALES describes 33 of the best 4WD destinations and tours from across the state. From the station country "Back of Bourke" to shorter treks just out of Sydney, there is no time frame that cannot be satisfied. We will travel station country tracks to the major inland rivers, and return to the coastal fringe for some beach driving.

Each trek is graded, allowing travellers to choose a suitable tour matching their experience and vehicle's capability. Camping details, together with practical notes,

encourage you to plan your own itinerary, with one eye on the information presented here, and another on making the trek a personal adventure.

These tours visit many of NSW 's well known destinations, but broaden that appeal with some forays into the lesser travelled regions. Whether you are a local looking for something different, or an interstate visitor searching for new and exciting destinations, we know that you will find NSW to be the adventure state.

THE PRACTICALITIES

This book has been produced as a guide book and does not attempt to cover the technique of 4WDing in any detail. Some of the treks described require little more knowledge than that to drive a conventional car, but others will require a much greater level of skill. It is important to understand that a novice is unlikely to drive their new 4WD up a rocky climb with any more "natural ability" than somebody reversing a trailer for the first time.

Luckily practice does make perfect, and an experienced instructor can dramatically flatten the learning curve. Travel with such a person in the early days – or better still join a 4WD club or undertake a commercial training course. It is an unfortunate irony that most newcomers underestimate what their vehicle is capable of, but overestimate their ability to reach that limit.

VEHICLE CHOICE

These tours have been field checked in full sized conventional 4WDs, occasionally towing a trailer or boat, and regularly with a utility based camper outfit. I have also travelled to many of these destinations in an early "soft roader" with reasonable success.

Ground clearance, rather than gearing would be the limiting factor for soft roaders on most of these tours, so tactical driving can compensate for some dimensional restrictions. Choosing a suitable line over rough sections will elevate the underbody of any vehicle, while robust tyres and traction control assist in the grip department.

Each of these tours indicate whether a full size 4WD (with low range gearing) is necessary, or whether a soft roader could undertake the journey. In some cases a well driven AWD will complete the tour routinely, but recent rain for example can scour troublesome ruts into what may have been an easy track.

Equally, full size 4WDs are not automatically guaranteed easy travel. Driving experience and track conditions are variable, so always drive within you and your vehicle's

ability, and turn back (or exit via an easier track) if the conditions demand.

NAVIGATION

These trek notes and associated maps should be used in conjunction with a compass, and preferably a vehicle mounted GPS. Our maps provide the essential

information, but can be supplemented with the relevant 1:50K or 1:25K topographic maps if you need contour lines or more detail. A GPS is also invaluable for locating

your position quickly and allowing it to be plotted on a paper map.

It should be noted that the accompanying maps indicate more tracks than may be accessible to the travelling public. Follow the described route for each tour, and only use other tracks if they are known to be for general use, perhaps seeking local knowledge or permission.

The trek notes utilize fixed locations such as rivers, tee intersections, homesteads etc as the reference points for distances throughout the tour. By working with intermediate distances, rather than a cumulative distance from the trip start, a number of inaccuracies are reduced. Variables such as odometer changes due to worn or non-standard tyre sizes, or loose surface slippage can be significant, so follow the kilometre readings with a degree of caution, and lookout for other defining features as described in the notes.

TRACK ACCESS

Most of these tours follow public roads through national parks, state forests, and station country. In some cases (national parks, and less frequently, in state forests) a permit to traverse is required. Elsewhere access is generally both free and unrestricted – providing you stay on the designated tracks, and not venture onto management vehicle only tracks, which are usually locked or clearly signposted

In all cases it is essential to behave in a respectful manner. Do not drive on closed or rain affected tracks, obey all road signs, leave gates as found, and do not drive "off road" especially over vegetated sand dunes

CAMPING

Bush camping sites have been detailed in most of the treks and may be private or national park based. The former have all of the usual facilities, while the latter vary

from just a plot of dirt, to formal campgrounds with all facilities

Camping in national parks (if permitted) usually attracts fee that varies between parks and seasons. Ph 1300 361 967 or (02) 9585 6068 for current details or online at *www.environment.nsw.gov.au*

You may not camp on station property without permission, however informal camping occasionally occurs within the roadside reserve at some river crossings for example. Seek permission if an overnight stop is necessary (try using the station channel on your UHF) and respect restrictions mentioned. No shooting is a universal rule, and fishing / campfires may not be welcome. Always select a site well away from stock watering points, and leave no trace on departure.

TRAILERS
Trailers can be successfully towed along many of the tours presented (check our TRACKS SNAPSHOT for an overview), but will limit your progress in tight country (sharp creek crossings, overgrown tracks and obstacle bypasses etc) and are a particular burden on soft sand or muddy sections – while slippery descents and failed climbs can be disastrous.

If a trailer is considered essential, gain some experience on the easier treks, before undertaking a more difficult tour. Travel in company if possible, as vehicle recovery can be tedious when travelling solo and substantially more difficult with a trailer in tow. However it is sometimes possible to unhitch a bogged trailer / vehicle combination and continue to drive out without the additional weight hampering progress – it is a good idea to fit a skid plate underneath the trailer's leading "A" frame structural member to facilitate the subsequent trailer recovery.

It is very desirable to select a robust trailer with a similar track to the towing vehicle, and preferably riding on the same wheel / tyre combination. An extended articulation coupling is essential, and it is important to adjust the trailer lyre pressures in proportion to those needed by the towing vehicle. In soft sand for example, a typical front and rear pressure may be 18psi and 22psi in the vehicle, but the trailer may only require 16psi for the weight it is carrying.

SAFETY
Touring by 4WD is not without risk in itself, so travelers should minimise any hazards within their control. Always travel in a roadworthy vehicle, on good tyres and at a speed consistent with the terrain ahead. Full size 4WDs tend to be more top heavy and require longer braking distances than a conventional car (or soft roaders), so drive conservatively, particularly on side slopes and on wet bitumen.

Secure any load within the vehicle, preferably behind a cargo barrier, and use the roof rack for light weight items. Keep a fire extinguisher and first aid kit handy, together with a satphone or new generation EPIRB. A UHF radio is very desirable for convoy chatter, but can be a lifesaver in station country too. Regular outback travelers should consider fitting a HF radio for longer distance communications.

Recovery gear should always be carried, with shovel, axe and heavy duty jack being mandatory items. A snatch strap together with rated shackles and suitable anchor points (definitely NOT a tow ball or vehicle tie down point) may be useful when travelling in company. All items of recovery gear should only be used by experienced people, noting especially that snatch straps should not be joined together by any type of metal coupling.

Always carry adequate water, fuel and food on even the shortest of trips, a breakdown or accident can happen anywhere. On longer tours top up with water fuel wherever possible, as track closures can mean lengthy detours, and rain can close tracks for days at a time.

ABBREVIATIONS USED IN TEXT:

N.P. National Park
S.F. State Forest
H.S. Homestead
M.V.O. Management Vehicle Only

TOUR LISTINGS BY REGION:

SYDNEY AREA
Yengo • Hill End • Newnes • Kanangra • Yalwal • Swallow Tail Pass • Abercrombie River • Six Foot Track • Blue Mountains • Morton

LOWER NORTH
New England • Crowdy Bay • Coopernook • Bulga Plateau • Barrington Tops

NORTHERN RIVERS
Severn River • Old Grafton Road • Chaelundi • Nymboida River • Bundjalung • Yuraygir • Coffs Harbour Hinterland

SOUTH EAST
Major Clews Trail • Northern Kosciusko • Deua • South East Forests

OUTBACK NSW
Mutawintji • Paroo River • Corner Country • Darling River • Lachlan River • Macquarie Marshes • Mount Kaputar

CHANGING CONDITIONS:

Please be aware that track conditions, campsites, locations and many other aspects of access can change. It is the responsibility of individuals to ensure and enquire about the current status of these possible changes prior to departure.

DISCLAIMER:

The publisher and consultants cannot accept responsibility for any errors or omissions in this guide as track conditions can change overtime. Every effort has been made to ensure the information in this book was accurate at the time of publication. The representation of roads and tracks on maps is not evidence of right of way. This publication is

Chapter 1

SYDNEY AREA

◀ *Wolgan River*

TRACK 1 YENGO

SYDNEY AREA

Track Snapshot

TOUR ROUTE:
Broke to Yallambie via Yengo NP.

DURATION AND DISTANCE:
Nice day trip of 120 kilometres

TRACK DETAILS:
Routine, but full sized 4WDs with low range needed to negotiate Howes Valley Trail. Trailers OK.

WHEN TO GO:
All year round, avoiding sustained wet weather.

CAMPING:
Finchley Camp within the national park, and a water side camp at Broke offer basic facilities.

FUEL AND SUPPLIES:
Top up at Broke or Singleton.

MAPS:
Natmap 1:100K Howes Valley, St Albans

OTHER INFORMATION:
Travel to Wisemans Ferry via Mogo is an option at this tour's end. Historic culverts and additional camping opportunities are a feature of the scenic drive.

Above: *Mount Yengo from trig point*

Right: *Yengo NP*

*Hundreds of rock engraving sites etch the **Hunter Range**, as witness to Aboriginal history dating back some 12 000 years. Artwork, stone arrangements and scar trees provide further evidence of a once vital trade route through these sandstone hills.*

*Visitors of today can access a few of these important sites, while enjoying some scenic bushland close to **Sydney**. This trek follows the **Putty Road** into **Yengo NP**, before crossing the **Hunter Range**, and exiting on the convict built roads and culverts around **Yallambie**.*

We begin at **Broke**, a small township 15 kilometres south of **Singleton** on the **Wollombi Road**. Basic supplies can be obtained here, and there is a nice camp at **McNamara Park**. Plenty of shade is a feature of the terraced area, where basic facilities are provided on the banks of **Wollombi Brook**.

Take the **Milbrodale Road**, signposted **"Bulga"** on the south side of town, west over the **Wollombi Bridge**. Follow the blacktop past vineyards and hobby farms, skirting the **Hunter Range** on your left. A picnic stop and the turn off to **Balame Cave** marks the tee intersection on **Putty Road** at **Milbrodale**, about 13 kilometres from **Broke**.

Veer left, signposted **"Windsor"** to follow **Parsons Creek** through an opening in the range. The prominent formation of **Parsons Ridge** on the right flags the western boundary of **Yengo NP** on the left and the beginning of narrow winding road.

A couple of turn out lanes and wayside stops offer the only opportunity to pull over and enjoy this forested country. Steel mesh blankets provide some protection from falling rock within the cuttings, but drivers still need to remain alert, especially for motorbikes using the popular route.

The valley opens up closer to **Howes Valley** with broken views taking in some pleasant farmland scenes. You will pass **Settlers Trail** on the left, noting that permission is now required to follow the 4WD track over **Mount Murwin** to reach **Paynes Crossing** on **Wollombi Creek**.

Continue along **Putty Road** over **Howes Valley** and **Oaky Creeks** to **Howes Valley Trail**, some 2.5 kilometres from the **Settlers Trail** turn off. Access to **Howes Valley Trail** is not well marked, but a red painted gate marked **"Fire Trail"** just prior to a road crest marks the turn off.

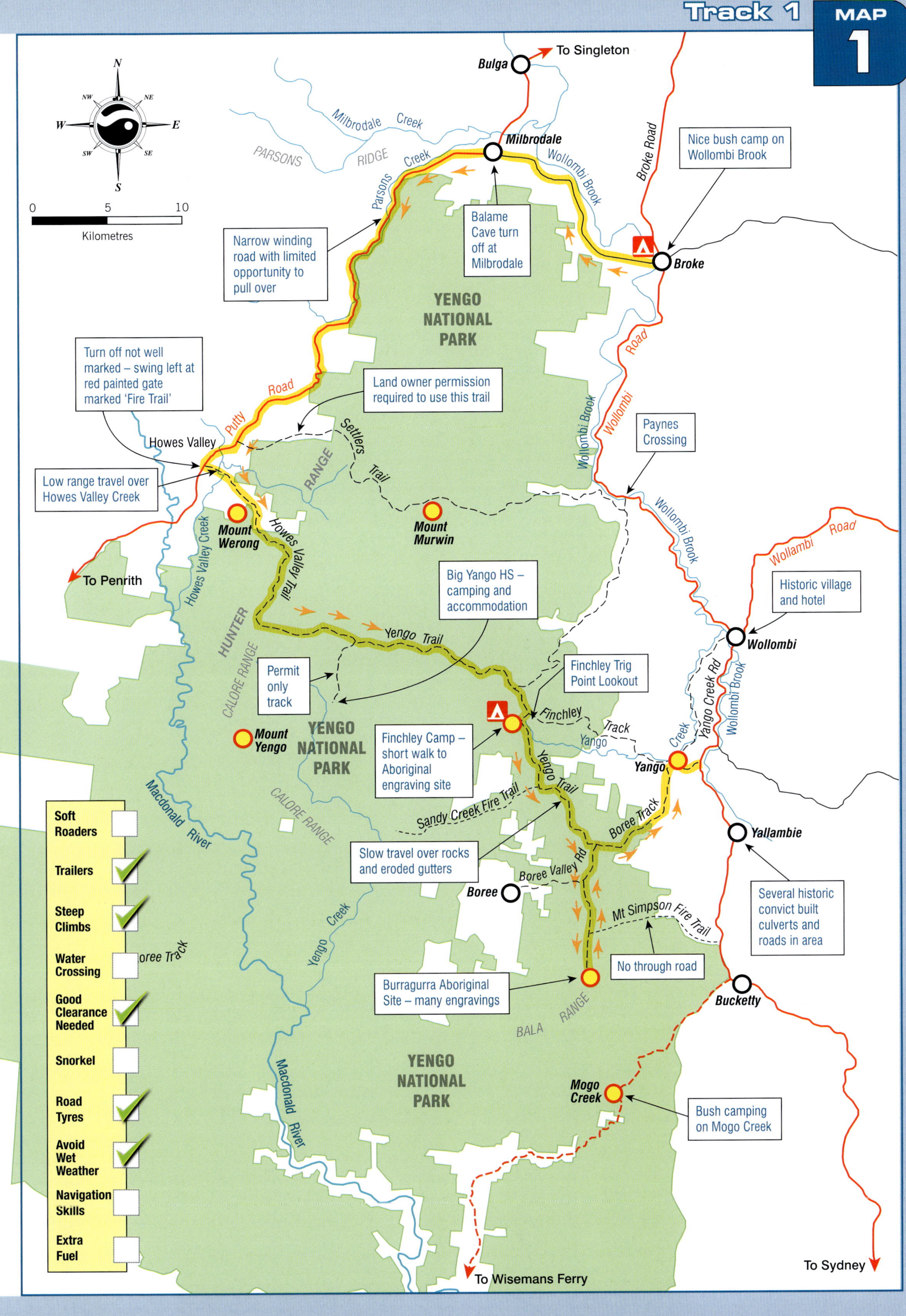

To Singleton
Bulga
Milbrodale Creek
PARSONS RIDGE
Parsons Creek
Milbrodale
Wollombi Brook
Broke Road
Nice bush camp on Wollombi Brook
Broke
Balame Cave turn off at Milbrodale
Narrow winding road with limited opportunity to pull over
0 5 10
Kilometres
YENGO NATIONAL PARK
Turn off not well marked – swing left at red painted gate marked 'Fire Trail'
Putty Road
Land owner permission required to use this trail
Settlers Trail
RANGE
Howes Valley
Low range travel over Howes Valley Creek
Wollombi Road
Paynes Crossing
Mount Werong
Mount Murwin
Howes Valley Trail
To Penrith
Howes Valley Creek
Big Yango HS – camping and accommodation
Wollombi Road
Historic village and hotel
Wollombi
HUNTER
CALORE RANGE
Yengo Trail
Permit only track
Finchley Trig Point Lookout
Finchley Track
Yango Creek Rd
Wollombi Brook
Mount Yengo
YENGO NATIONAL PARK
Finchley Camp – short walk to Aboriginal engraving site
Yango Creek
Yango
Yengo Trail
Macdonald River
CALORE RANGE
Sandy Creek Fire Trail
Boree Track
Slow travel over rocks and eroded gutters
Yallambie
Boree Valley Rd
Boree
Several historic convict built culverts and roads in area
Mt Simpson Fire Trail
Yengo Creek
No through road
Boree Track
Burragurra Aboriginal Site – many engravings
Bucketty
BALA RANGE
YENGO NATIONAL PARK
Mogo Creek
Bush camping on Mogo Creek
Macdonald River
To Wisemans Ferry
To Sydney
Soft Roaders
Trailers
Steep Climbs
Water Crossing
Good Clearance Needed
Snorkel
Road Tyres
Avoid Wet Weather
Navigation Skills
Extra Fuel

Swing left here through this gate, and keep left 20 metres later to follow an earthen track with fenceline on the right.

Access is permitted through this section of private land, but stay on the main track, as erosion control mounds slow progress. Continue through a second gate to a crossing of **Howes Valley Creek**, and a lurching climb out over sheets of sandstone.

Follow the fenceline through native pine at the foot of **Mount Werong** to just clip national park and descend to a paperbark forest and the roar of cicadas. A low range climb offers broken views through grass tree as you keep right to trace the **Calore Range** some 16.7 kilometres from **Putty Road**.

At 668 metres, the basalt dome of **Mount Yengo** is prominent on the right, as you balance atop the ridge with a drop off on either side. Boulders and sandstone formations punctuate the eroded track through flowering tea tree, as you reach the turn off to **Big Yango HS**.

Access to the historic homestead grounds is limited to permit holders (ph 02 4320 4260 for details and key) and there is a circuit drive with camping options that passes by the foot of **Mount Yengo**. We will keep straight at the junction however, taking advantage of the wider, smoother surface of **Yengo Trail**.

Sandy patches and the odd boghole pave the way past MVO tracks to the **Finchley Track** intersection, about 13 kilometres later. Veer left at the triangulated junction to make a short side trip to **Finchley Trig Point**. Banksia bushes frame a lookout here, with broad views extending to **Mount Yengo** and the surrounding ranges.

Return from the trig point to arrive in **Finchley Camp** at the southern corner of the triangulated intersection. Basic facilities are provided at a large camp site, where goannas and swamp wallabies are routinely sighted. A short walk from the camp will take you to an Aboriginal engraving site, where animal outlines and other motifs can be appreciated from an elevated platform.

Continue south on **Yengo Track** to pass **Sandy Creek Fire Trail**, and reach a tee

Right: *Burragurra Aboriginal site*

Below: *Yengo NP*

Above: *Boree Trail*

intersection on **Boree Track**, about 10 kilometres from **Finchley Camp**. Take note of this intersection, as we will leave **Yengo NP** via the left option.

However, travellers wishing to visit the **Burragurra Aboriginal site** can swing right here, to trace the **Hunter Range** to the **Old Boree Track** junction 2.6 kilometres later. Keep left away from the better surfaced **Boree Valley Road** (access to private property) and begin a low range amble through encroaching vegetation.

Eroded gutters and rocks pave the way past **Mount Simpson Fire Trail** on the left (no through road) to a minor track heading to **Little Boree Valley** (private road). Continue straight over a rocky shelf to an informal carpark on the right, about five kilometres from the **Mount Simpson** turn off.

The Burragurra Aboriginal site is reached on foot from here, following a short steep trail onto the **Bala Range**. An enormous sandstone cap projects several hundred metres from the underlying range, offering an excellent vantage point from which to take in the surrounding country. Caves and smaller rock holes perforate the sandstone, and dozens of Aboriginal engravings can be found by keen eyed visitors.

Return from this site to the **Boree Track** junction mentioned earlier, and keep right on good road to descend past broken views and reach the boundary of national park. Continue past the fishboning driveways into private allotments where post and rail fences restrain stock. Cottages fringing **Yango Creek** mark an old iron bridge and a fording of the waterway.

Veer right at a tee to continue along **Boree Track**, then turn right 800 metres later onto **Upper Yango Creek Road**. Cross a causeway into the **Yango** community with character rich houses and stockramp located right on the road. Veer right to climb through ironbark forest and reach the main **Yango Creek Road** and the conclusion of this tour.

Options beyond here include turning left to **Wollombi** (historic village and outlet for the infamous Dr Jurd's Jungle Juice) or swing right toward **Bucketty**. The latter option follows rural country over early hand built stone culverts to a wall constucted by convict labour on **Mogo Creek Road**. The unsealed drive from here to **Wisemans Ferry** passes camping opportunities at **Mogo Creek**, and some scenic winding travel through exotic trees beyond **St Albans**.

TRACK 2

Hill End

SYDNEY AREA

Track Snapshot

TOUR ROUTE:
Orange to Capertee via the old mining towns of Ophir, Hill End and Sofala.

DURATION AND DISTANCE:
Allow at least a weekend to travel the 190 kilometres at a leisurely pace – more if you plan to do some fossicking or fishing.

TRACK DETAILS:
A routine bush drive in the dry, but river levels at Long Point can easily stop vehicles with inadequate clearance, and possibly those without a snorkel. Assess the water flow and depth very carefully before proceeding. Trailers OK.

WHEN TO GO:
All year round, but avoid wet weather.

CAMPING:
Numerous options for bush camping on the Macquarie and Turon Rivers. Serviced camping areas are found at Ophir and Hill End.

FUEL AND SUPPLIES:
Orange offers all services with basic supplies available at Hill End, Capertee and Sofala (no fuel at Sofala).

MAPS:
Natmap 1:100K Orange, Bathurst

OTHER INFORMATION:
Avoid the busy holiday periods to really enjoy this historic piece of the state.

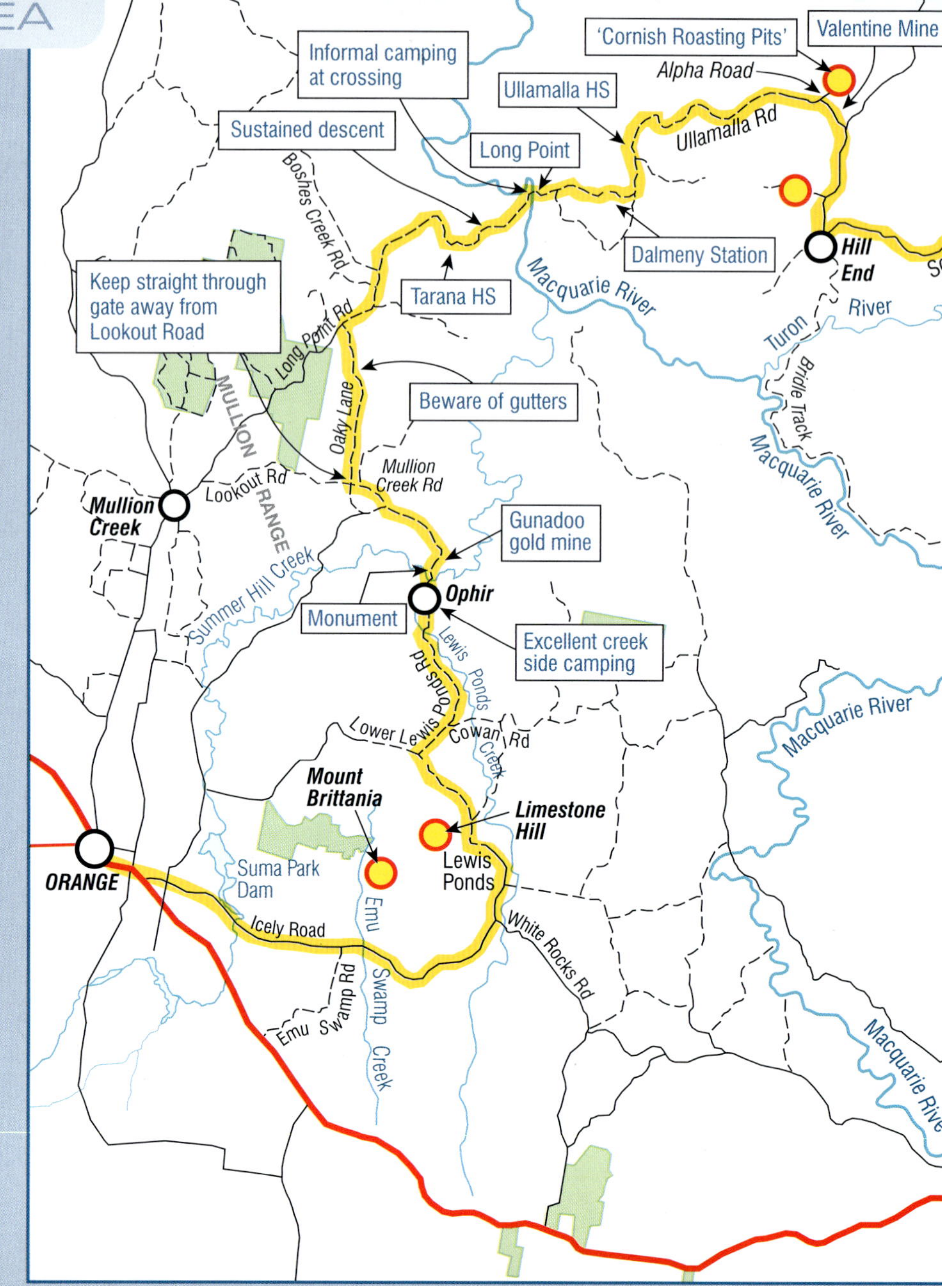

__Hill End__ was the hub of gold mining activity in central NSW for over two decades. A few flecks of the precious metal seen in the __Macquarie River__ in 1851, drew thousands of hopefuls to the district almost overnight. The subsequent discovery of reef gold renewed the rush, with Hill End growing to become NSW's second largest inland town. However, like many other gold towns of the day, the decline began just as suddenly, as disillusioned prospectors drifted elsewhere.

This tour follows the most profitable diggings from __Ophir__ to __Sofala__, crossing the __Macquarie__ at __Long Point__. We then continue the trek by following the __Turon River__ along its upper reaches, before meeting the __Castlereagh Highway__ at __Capertee__.

We begin the tour at **Orange,** heading east via **Icely Road** (the town centre is split by **Summer Hill Creek**, making the route through town a dogleg path – McLaughlin, then Summer

Ophir Camping Area

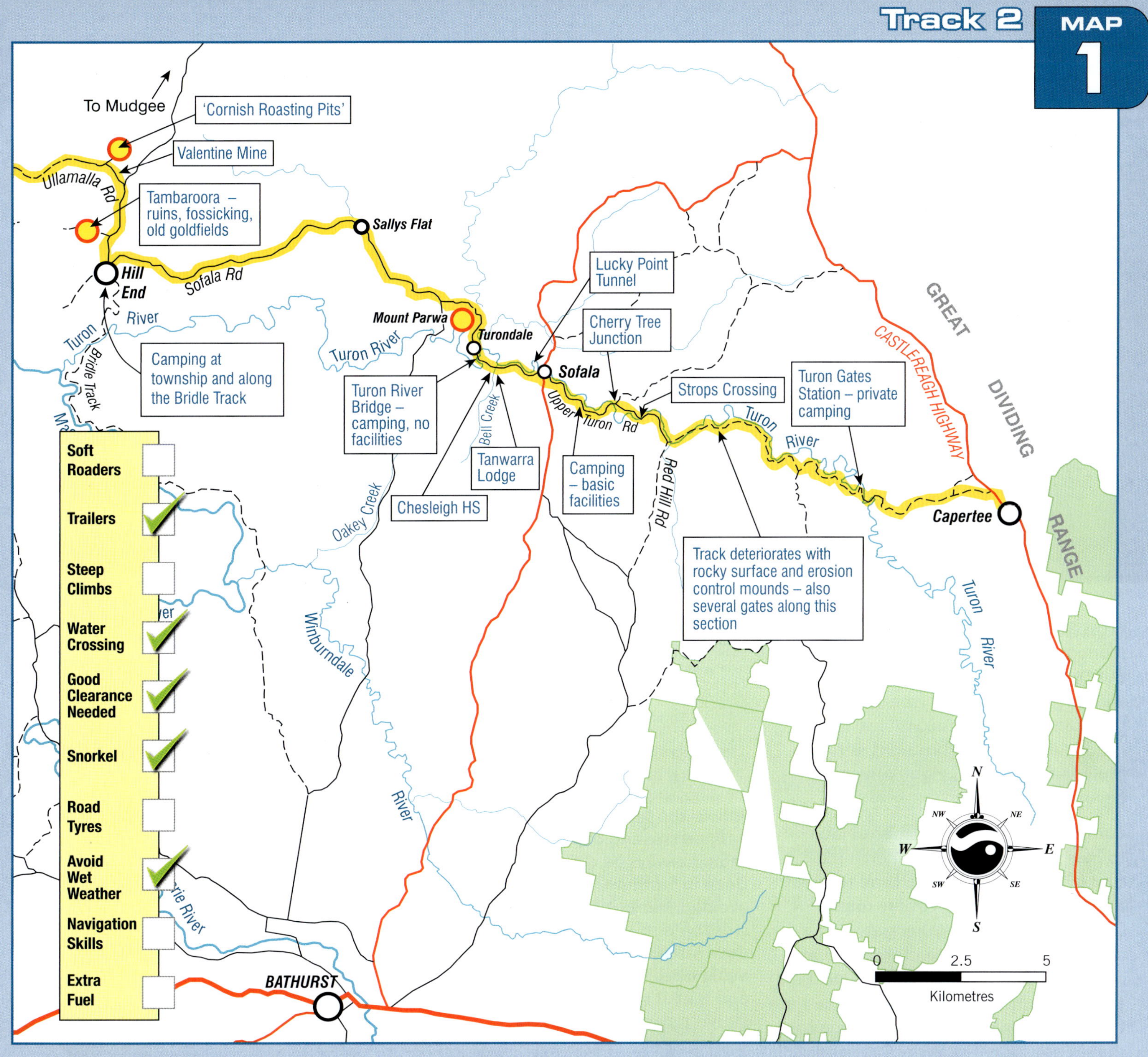

Street eventually lead you to Icely Road). Continue east past **Conobolus High School** and the exotic tree fringe of **Suma Park Dam**, some six kilometres out of town.

You will pass **Emu Swamp Road** on the right, then the willow lined creek of the same name, as the grazing lands become rockier. Follow the main road past several more side roads, where rolling hills extend to the skyline. Keep left at **White Rocks Road**, about 22 kilometres from Orange, to reach the locality of **Lewis Ponds** shortly after.

A cluster of character cottages mark a floodway and the beginning of gravel road. Several private mine sites flag **Mount Brittania** and **Limestone Hill**, before you reach a tee intersection, 32 kilometres from Orange.

Turn right onto **Lower Lewis Ponds Road**, keeping left at **Cowan Road** 1.7 kilometres later. Follow the deciduous trees of **Lewis Ponds Creek** to cross the waterway 4.6 kilometres further on. Continue through a gate into the **Ophir Reserve** – the site of Australia's first viable goldfield in 1851.

Yorkies Corner, as it was known then, proved relatively productive, and the vestiges of both reef and alluvial mining remain evident to this day. Numerous walking tracks lead to some well preserved relics (take care with children near the numerous open shafts and drives) while enthusiastic visitors can try to find some colour left behind.

Some commercial operations are still underway in the locality, so respect their claims and associated "Keep Out" signs. Rutted road winds through the 560 hectare reserve, to a cleared creekside camping area, where poplars and river oaks shade the crossing. It is a lovely area to stop for a night or two, with a modest (honesty box) fee to cover maintenance and basic facilities.

TRACK 3 NEWNES

SYDNEY AREA

Wolgan River

Track Snapshot

TOUR ROUTE:
Lidsdale to Lithgow via Newnes and the Maiyingu Marragu Trail.

DURATION AND DISTANCE:
This 50 kilometre run can be done as a day trip, or camp overnight to more fully explore the area.

TRACK DETAILS:
An easy drive for all vehicles and trailers, with some slippery patches around Blackfellows Hand Cave.

WHEN TO GO:
All year round in dry weather.

CAMPING:
Bush camping with basic facilities at Newnes and Bungleboori.

FUEL AND SUPPLIES:
Lithgow has all services and supplies.

MAPS:
Natmap 1:100K Wallerawang

OTHER INFORMATION:
The abandoned mine and processing plant at Newnes is surprisingly complex and well worth the two hour walk.

*A strong demand for kerosene used in 19th century lighting, saw shale mining begin at **Newnes** in the late 1800s. Kerosene extraction expanded into a range of products including paraffin, naphtha, and lubricating oils, overseen by the **Commonwealth Oil Corporation**. Spasmodic production continued over three decades before mining was abandoned, and the town dismantled.*

*Prior to closing down, the enterprise gave life to a township of many hundreds at **Newnes**, and an impressive piece of railway infrastructure that linked the mining outpost with **Newnes Junction**. Visitors of today can appreciate some aspects of the work here, together with some impressive landscape within **Wollemi NP**, an indigenous art site, and even some glow worms.*

We begin the trek at **Lidsdale** on the **Castlereagh Highway**, some 14 kilometres north of **Lithgow**. Veer right on **Wolgan Road** to pass the **Centennial Coal Colliery**, and follow the **Cox River** valley to **Blackfellows Hand Trail** on the right.

This track is more correctly known as **Maiyingu Marragu Trail**, but not all of the signage has been updated as yet. We will use this track as our exit into **Newnes SF** later in the tour, but at this stage, continue straight to **Wolgan Gap Lookout** for some spectacular views. If you disregard the prominent power lines, you will appreciate a swathe of range country extending from the **Wolgan River** over **Sunnyside Ridge** to the **Gardens of Stone** and **Wollemi National Park**.

An initially sealed drop off begins the narrow winding run (no stopping permitted), before gravel begins at a set of old yards just a few kilometres later. Wider road weaves through a conservation reserve, where sandstone ramparts dominate the bush foreground.

Watch out for oncoming traffic on the corrugated corners, as the **Wolgan Valley** begins to narrow, with **Mount Wolgan** on the right. Walk in access to **Donkey Mountain** is reached about 14 kilometres from the lookout, with the turn off to **Wolgan Valley Resort and Spa**, three kilometres later.

Keep straight at the junction to cross a causeway onto narrower road, with **Barton** and **Tunnel Creeks** merging into the **Wolgan**. You will reach a walking track to the **Glow Worm Tunnel**, about 1.5 kilometres from the causeway, where walkers face an eight kilometre, four hour return hike.

The **Glow Worm Tunnel**, known as **Bells Grotto**, is one of two tunnels hewn

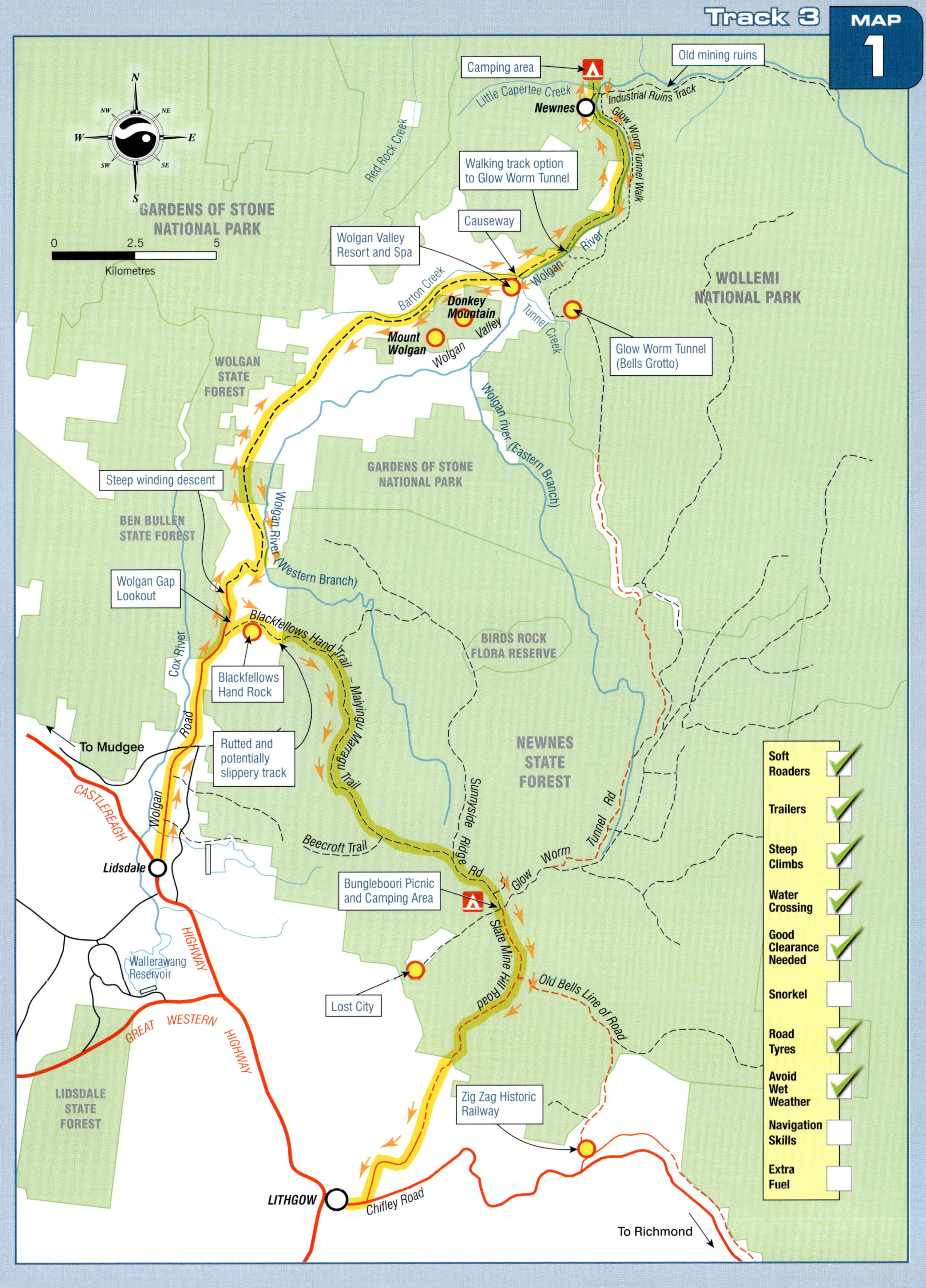

N
NE
E
SE
S
SW
W
NW
0
2.5
5
Kilometres
GARDENS OF STONE NATIONAL PARK
Camping area
Old mining ruins
Little Capertee Creek
Industrial Ruins Track
Newnes
Glow Worm Tunnel Walk
Red Rock Creek
Walking track option to Glow Worm Tunnel
Causeway
Wolgan Valley Resort and Spa
Wolgan River
Barton Creek
Donkey Mountain
Mount Wolgan
Wolgan Valley
Tunnel Creek
Glow Worm Tunnel (Bells Grotto)
WOLLEMI NATIONAL PARK
WOLGAN STATE FOREST
Wolgan river (Eastern Branch)
GARDENS OF STONE NATIONAL PARK
Steep winding descent
BEN BULLEN STATE FOREST
Wolgan River (Western Branch)
Wolgan Gap Lookout
Blackfellows Hand Trail
BIRDS ROCK FLORA RESERVE
Cox River
Blackfellows Hand Rock
Maiyingu Marragu Trail
To Mudgee
Rutted and potentially slippery track
NEWNES STATE FOREST
Sunnyside Ridge Rd
Glow Worm Tunnel Rd
CASTLEREAGH
Wolgan Road
Beecroft Trail
Lidsdale
Bungleboori Picnic and Camping Area
HIGHWAY
State Mine Hill Road
Wallerawang Reservoir
Lost City
Old Bells Line of Road
GREAT WESTERN HIGHWAY
LIDSDALE STATE FOREST
Zig Zag Historic Railway
LITHGOW
Chifley Road
To Richmond
Soft Roaders
Trailers
Steep Climbs
Water Crossing
Good Clearance Needed
Snorkel
Road Tyres
Avoid Wet Weather
Navigation Skills
Extra Fuel

through rock to facilitate the **Newnes Rail Line**. Following the rail closure in 1934, glow worms invaded the moist, dark central sector of the tunnel, and visitors using a torch to walk into **Bells Grotto**, can turn off the light to see countless blue pin heads of luminescence all around. There is a full day walk (22 km return) to the tunnel via the old rail route from near the shale plant at **Newnes**, or an alternative two kilometre return walk detailed later in this trek.

For now continue into the locality of **Newnes** to find the relocated hotel standing as the lone reminder of a once bustling village. Now a private residence, the pub does open to the public on weekends and holiday periods as a kiosk, and offers private cabin accommodation.

Campers continue straight ahead, crossing **Little Capertee Creek** to reach an open grassy area at the foot of

Left: *Old Newnes Hotel*

Below: *Abandoned mining relics, Newnes*

Sandstone Range, Wollemi NP

some grand sandstone range country. Alternative camping is possible along the signposted "**Industrial Ruins**" track. In this case swing right to ford the sandy base of the **Wolgan River**, and swing left (away from the longer **Glow Worm Tunnel** walk) to reach a creekside camp with basic facilities and shaded or open areas.

The side track continues past a couple more secluded camping areas, before finishing at a carpark adjoining the industrial ruins. Walkers should allow a couple of hours to roam the complex site, where informative plaques give an insight into the processing plant. Some steep sections will be encountered, but inquisitive folk will find the walk well worthwhile.

You leave **Newnes** via the only road in and out, and return to **Blackfellows Hand Trail** to swing left onto dirt, and bumpy beginnings to the track. A camping area 700 metres later (no facilities) marks a short, but steep walking track to **Blackfellows Hand Rock**. A log book heralds the 20 metre wide gallery of hand stencils – some perhaps many hundreds of years old.

Continue east beyond the camping area along a rutted and potentially slippery track peppered with bog holes and some bypasses, to a bracken adorned break in the **Blue Mountains Range**. An eerie sandstone amphitheatre of mosses, ferns and greenery is well worth a stop, just one kilometre from the gallery.

You will swing right at the rocky grotto to negotiate scoured sandstone steps, before the drive levels out on better road. A few side tracks radiate from the main arterial – the notorious **Spanish Steps** and others are difficult and potentially dangerous, so stick to the main track.

A patchwork forest of stringybark and mountain gum are habitat to brush tailed rock wallabies and koalas, while the rare Regent Honeyeater may be spotted in the bush. Banksias colour the roughish drive over potholes and uneven country, to a tee intersection, some 8.7 kilometres from the gallery. Swing left onto better track, keeping straight at **Beecroft Trail**, then veering right onto **Sunnyside Ridge Road**.

You again reach a tee at **Bungleboori Picnic and Camping Area**, some 17.3 kilometres from the gallery. (Just prior to the tee is an unsignposted track on the right that leads to the **Lost City**. If you follow the main track you will reach a carpark 2.8 kilometres later, from where walkers can access these amazing formations of layered sandstone, known as pagodas).

Camping at **Bungleboori** offers basic facilities, and we will turn right at the camp to continue the trek. However **Glow Worm Tunnel Road** branches to our left and offers the closest walking access to **Bells Grotto**.

(Follow good gravel past **Waratah Ridge**, veering left 5.2 kilometres beyond **Bungleboori**. Narrow road paves the way along sections of the old **Shale Oil Rail** as you negotiate the first rail tunnel 14.5 kilometres later. You will reach the final, small carpark 24.8 kilometres from **Bungleboori**, from where a one hour return walk takes you into the **Glow Worm Tunnel**).

Slate Mine Hill Road heads south from **Bungleboori** through pine plantation on good gravel. Keep right from **Old Bells Line of Road** 2.2 kilometres later, as interesting rock formations crowd in on the road. You will descend quickly to the outskirts of **Lithgow**, where poppet heads and mine workings stand witness to the town's heritage. This tour finishes at the terraced houses near **Chifley Road**.

TRACK 4 KANANGRA

SYDNEY AREA

Kanangra Walls

Track Snapshot

TOUR ROUTE:
Jenolan Caves to Yerranderie via the Kanangra Range and Mount Werong.

DURATION AND DISTANCE:
This 150 kilometre trek will take two days at a leisurely pace, and more if you wish to linger at the caves or hike within Kanangra Boyd NP.

TRACK DETAILS:
Some steep and rocky country limits this trek to full sized 4WDs, and trailers are not permitted along the access road to Yerranderie.

WHEN TO GO:
All year round, providing rain has not closed the tracks.

CAMPING:
Good camping with basic facilities at Boyd River, Dingo Dell, Mount Werong, Batsh Camp and Yerranderie.

FUEL AND SUPPLIES:
No fuel or supplies along this route – arrive at Jenolan Caves with plenty of fuel as there are no services at Yerranderie, and you must retrace your steps to Oberon (or beyond) on the return journey.

MAPS:
Natmap 1:100K Oberon, Taralga, Burragorang

OTHER INFORMATION:
The once popular exit from Yerranderie via Limeburners Flat is currently closed, making The Range Fire Trail your only option for travel south through Blue Mountains NP.

*While much of **Kanangra – Boyd National Park** lies off limits to 4WDers, those tracks open for use more than compensate. There are some stunning destinations within the **World Heritage** ranges, and a ghost town well off the beaten track.*

We will climb mountains, descend into caves, fish the wild rivers, and follow in the footsteps of loggers and miners. Appealing camp sites allow visitors to appreciate the range of environments across this region, and a network of walking tracks that extend the opportunity further.

Jenolan Caves marks this tour's beginning and is an ideal place to regroup before hitting the tracks. More than 300 caves pock the subterranean karst geology, with some open to the public. Self guided walks provide access to **Blue Lake** and the surrounding bushland, while guided cave tours vary from easy to adventurous. No camping facilities are provided, but a range of formal accommodation possibilities can be booked ahead (ph 02 6359 3911 or *www.jenolancaves.org.au*)

Leave the caves and head west on narrow bitumen for a steep and winding journey, with views at every turn. Switchbacks and old chain mesh guarding keep the driver alert, as you reach **Kanangra Road** on the left, five kilometres later.

Turn left onto gravel for a sustained descent through tall forest and into **Kanangra – Boyd NP**. A number of fire trails fishbone off the main arterial, but are restricted to management vehicles and walkers only.

At 1286 metres, **Mount Empress** flags the turn off to **Kowmung River Fire Trail** on the right, 20 kilometres beyond the caves. We will exit the **Kanangra Range** here on our return, but for now continue past the junction to a crossing of the **Boyd River** five kilometres later.

Basic facilities are provided at the **Boyd River Camping Area**, with segregated parking for trailers or tents. The shady sites are appealing, and the trickling **Boyd River** waters are nearby. A grassed open area forms the plateau hub, and the beginnings of **Morong Creek** – to be visited later in the trek.

Continue south past **Morong Creek Fire Trail**, to follow a line of Blue Mountains Mallee to a carpark, 7.4 kilometres from the camp. A number of extended walks begin from here, but the shorter walk to **Kanangra Walls Lookout** is a must. Visitors gaze over **Kanangra Creek Valley** to see a 100 metre high sandstone ridge capping the range. Take care near the unguarded rocky viewpoint.

Return from the lookout to **Kowmung River Fire Trail** and turn left onto a narrow track piercing brown barrel and ribbon gum bushland. Swampy lowlands four kilometres into the drive support colourful heathland, but present some slippery sections in wet weather. Keep left at an unmarked fire trail 500 metres later, to reach **Morong Creek Fire Trail** under the shadow of **Boyd Hill**.

Our trek continues to the right here, but those who choose to swing left onto **Morong Creek Fire Trail** will bounce over ruts and humps to reach a clearing on **Morong Creek**. Camping is possible here (no facilities) with the **Boyd River Fire Trail** (MVO) tracing a path back to the **Kanangra Range**.

High clearance vehicles can cross **Morong Creek** via a rocky and eroded approach (check your line on foot before

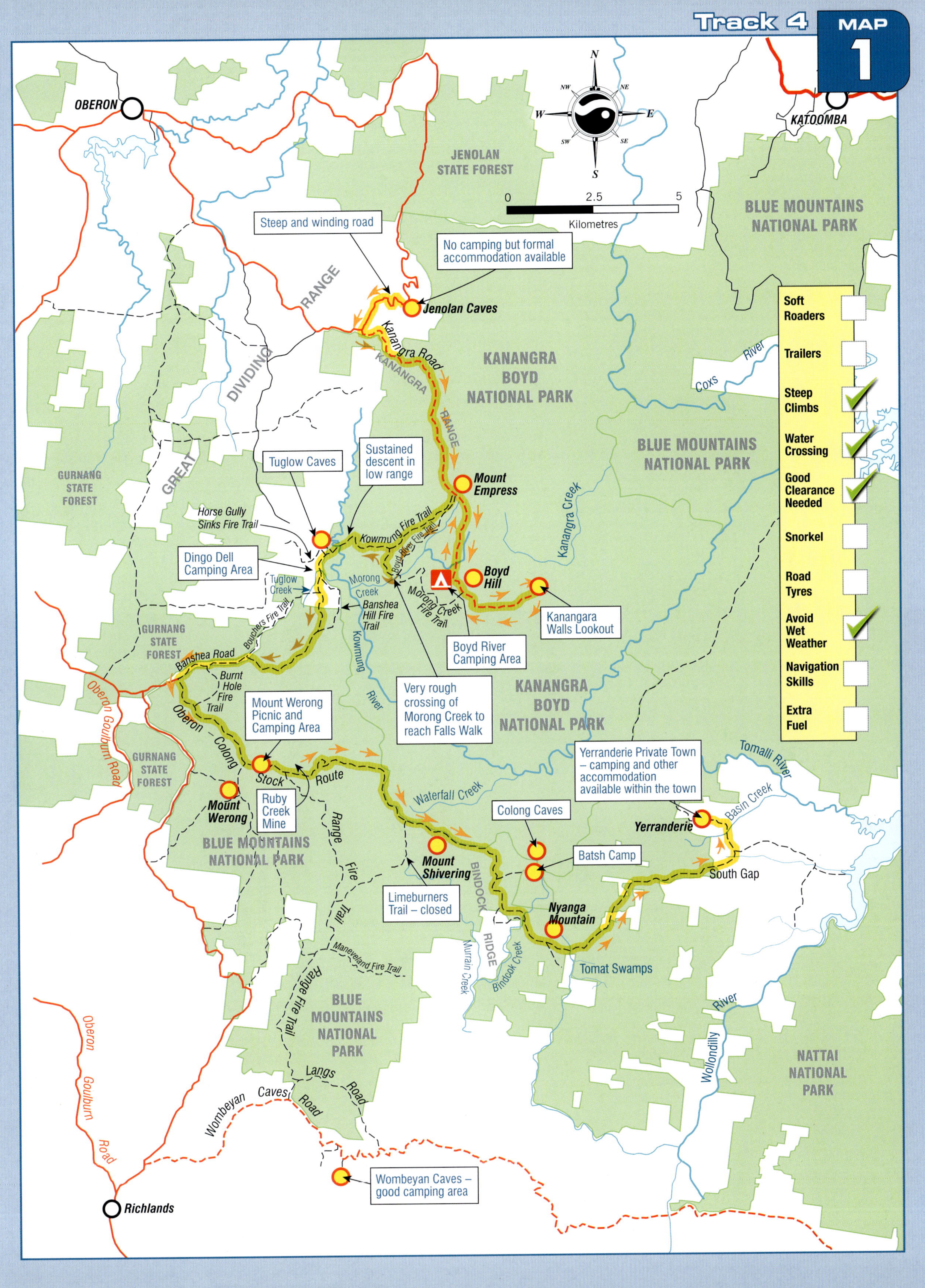

OBERON
KATOOMBA
JENOLAN STATE FOREST
BLUE MOUNTAINS NATIONAL PARK
0 2.5 5
Kilometres
Steep and winding road
No camping but formal accommodation available
Jenolan Caves
Kanangra Road
KANANGRA RANGE
KANANGRA BOYD NATIONAL PARK
GREAT DIVIDING RANGE
Coxs River
BLUE MOUNTAINS NATIONAL PARK
Soft Roaders
Trailers
Steep Climbs
Water Crossing
Good Clearance Needed
Snorkel
Road Tyres
Avoid Wet Weather
Navigation Skills
Extra Fuel
Tuglow Caves
Sustained descent in low range
Mount Empress
GURNANG STATE FOREST
Horse Gully Sinks Fire Trail
Kowmung Fire Trail
Boyd River Fire Trail
Kanangra Creek
Dingo Dell Camping Area
Tuglow Creek
Morong Creek
Banshea Hill Fire Trail
Morong Creek Fire Trail
Boyd Hill
Kanangara Walls Lookout
Boyd River Camping Area
Bouchers Fire Trail
Banshea Road
GURNANG STATE FOREST
Kowmung River
Very rough crossing of Morong Creek to reach Falls Walk
Burnt Hole Fire Trail
KANANGRA BOYD NATIONAL PARK
Oberon Goulburn Road
Oberon – Colong Stock Route
Mount Werong Picnic and Camping Area
Yerranderie Private Town – camping and other accommodation available within the town
Tomalli River
GURNANG STATE FOREST
Mount Werong
Ruby Creek Mine
Waterfall Creek
Colong Caves
Basin Creek
Yerranderie
Range Fire Trail
BLUE MOUNTAINS NATIONAL PARK
Mount Shivering
Batsh Camp
South Gap
BINDOCK RIDGE
Limeburners Trail – closed
Nyanga Mountain
Maneveland Fire Trail
Murrain Creek
Bindook Creek
Tomat Swamps
Range Fire Trail
BLUE MOUNTAINS NATIONAL PARK
Wollondilly River
Oberon Goulburn Road
Langs Road
Wombeyan Caves Road
NATTAI NATIONAL PARK
Wombeyan Caves – good camping area
Richlands

driving down, or have a spotter give you directions), to reach **Morong Falls Fire Trail**, 400 metres later. Walkers can continue from here, to a series of falls amid a jumble of granite. The eight kilometre return walk takes four hours, with some demanding rock hopping across pools and cascades.

Retrace your steps to **Kowmung River Fire Trail** and turn left to begin a sustained descent. Broken views open through the tree tops, as you reach a turn table 3.4 kilometres later. A 4WD only sign keeps the soft roaders out now, as erosion control mounds limit vehicles to low range.

You reach the pebbly banks of the **Kowmung River** 1.6 kilometres later, where day use parking is available on both sides of the waterway (the western bank offers walk in camping – 500 metres away). A steep climb exits the river to a walking track for **Tuglow Caves** (permit holders only – ph 02 6336 1972 in advance for details), and the beginnings of a descent.

You will pass **Horse Gully Sinks Fire Trail** on the right (private) to cross **Tuglow Creek** at **Dingo Dell Camping Area**. This lovely clearing offers basic facilities amid the tussock grasses, although camping is a walk in affair, with fences restricting vehicle access.

Gravel topping paves the way south from **Dingo Dell**, as you keep right at **Banshea Hill Fire Trail** (private) and follow a fenceline. A low range climb passes **Bouchiers Fire Trail** for broken views one kilometre later, then descend to a junction marking the other end of **Banshea Hill Fire Trail**.

Keep right at this junction and exit the **Blue Mountains NP** some 10.5 kilometres from **Dingo Dell**, veering left to remain on **Banshea Road**. Harvested pine plantation offers a desolate view to the right as you follow native bushland on the left.

Turn left 2.3 kilometres from the national park exit (**Bicentennial National Trail** diamond at junction) to pass **Burnt Hole Fire Trail** on the left, keeping left

Left: *Frosty morning, Boyd Plateau*

Below: *Boyd River*

1.6 kilometres after that. You will reach a tee intersection 800 metres later, where you turn left onto the historic **Oberon – Colong Stock Route** (right turn takes you to the main **Oberon – Goulburn Road**, and is one option for the return drive at the conclusion of this trek).

Return to the **Blue Mountains NP** to follow good gravel past a number of firetrails, reaching the **Mount Werong Picnic and Camping Area** 9.2 kilometres later. A lovely stone cottage is the centrepiece of this well appointed camping area, and there is a walking track to the ruins of **Ruby Creek Mine**.

Mining and logging of this area dates to the late 1800s, when pastoralists were moving stock along the **Murruin Range**. (Local aboriginal groups had been using this route for generations, and significant sites still remain). A township was envisaged at **Mount Werong** to cater for workers on the **Ruby Creek** silver and lead mines, but little came to fruition.

Head east from **Mount Werong** for one kilometre to reach **Range Fire Trail** on the right. (This is another option for travellers at the conclusion of this tour – a reasonably easy drive climbs to good views, and descends through bracken and tree ferns, over erosion mounds and some rocky sections. Turn right at **Maneveland Fire Trail**, veering left 5.7 kilometres later. Turn right onto **Langs Road** 4.5 kilometres beyond that to reach **Wombeyan Caves Road**, shortly after. There is good camping at the caves reserve, or turn right to **Taralga**.)

For now we continue into the **Warragamba Catchment Area** (Sydney area water supply) and pass **Big Plain** with swamp vegetation and ringed with snowgums. **Limeburners Trail** on the right (currently closed) is passed, as you reach **Mount Shivering** and the **Bindock Ridge**.

Deep Saddles looks over **Waterfall Creek** with rounded peaks and dissected valleys on your left, some 18.5 kilometres from **Mount Werong**. The turn off to **Batsh Camp** is found 3.5 kilometres later, where basic facilities are provided. Permit holders can walk from here to **Colong Caves** (warmer months only) to explore limestone caverns that are habitat for bent wing and horse shoe bats (ph 02 6336 1972 in advance for details).

Veer left 2.5 kilometres beyond **Batsh** turn off to cross **Bindock Creek**, with **Nyanga Mountain** on the left. Several waterways mark the **Tomat Swamps** area, and punctuate travel for the next 10 kilometres. You will pass **Colong Station** and reach narrower road, with glimpses of the surrounding sandstone ranges at **South Gap**.

Turn left at a tee, two kilometres beyond the gap to ford **Basin Creek** and enter the **Yerranderie** township area. Turn right into **Yerranderie Street** to reach the **Government Town** site with camping at the junction and basic facilities. The town's cemetery is found further along this road, with historic graves dating from the pioneering days.

Yerranderie Private Town is found directly ahead from the first township junction, and is well worth a visit. A small fee is payable for day visitors to wander the old shops and buildings, while the remains of an abandoned silver / lead mine lie walking distance away. Camping and other accommodation is available within the town (ph 02 4659 6165 or *www.yerranderie.com*).

Yerranderie marks the conclusion of this tour as it is a no through road, and many side tracks are now closed. You can return to main roads by retracing your steps to **The Range Fire Trail** (4WD option to **Wombeyan Caves**), or continue beyond **Mount Werong** to the **Oberon – Goulburn Road**.

Right: *Old shop, Yerranderie*

Below: *Mt Werong Hut*

TRACK 5

Yalwal

SYDNEY AREA

Hylands Lookout

Track Snapshot

TOUR ROUTE:
Wandandian to Yalwal via Jerrawangala Lookout, Tianjara Falls and Hylands Lookout.

DURATION AND DISTANCE:
This 60 kilometre run can be done as a day trip, with camping at Yalwal to extend the time frame if needed.

TRACK DETAILS:
Routine driving conditions suitable for all vehicles and trailers.

WHEN TO GO:
All year round in dry weather, although the falls are best seen following local rain, and spring is ideal to appreciate the heathland colour.

CAMPING:
Camping with basic facilities at Yalwal.

FUEL AND SUPPLIES:
All services and supplies at Nowra.

MAPS:
Natmap 1:250K Wollongong Special

OTHER INFORMATION:
Fantastic views from the lookouts are best seen in clear weather.

*Now encompassing nearly 200 000 hectares, **Morton National Park** is one of this state's largest conservation areas, with high value wilderness as its centrepiece. The mighty **Shoalhaven River** pushes a contorted path through the sandstone maze, while the **Ettrema Creek** has cut a gorge up to 400 metres deep.*

*Few vehicle tracks penetrate the heart of **Morton**, but a network of fire trails and forestry roads allow us to visit the fringes of this outstanding country. We will stop at a few commanding viewpoints, marvel at one if its best waterfalls, and find excellent water front camping at an old gold mining town.*

We begin at the community of **Wandandian**, 26 kilometres south of **Nowra** on the **Princes Highway**. Head west along **Wandean Road**, keeping left at **Maddens Road**, 2.6 kilometres later. You will cross **Gnatilia Creek** at a causeway before reaching gravel near the boundary of **Jerrawangala NP**. Keep left some 1.1 kilometres later to pass **Gnatilia Creek Road**, as heathlands burst out with spring colour.

You will pass a couple of side tracks, and keep right at **Hawthorn Road** some six kilometres beyond the **Gnatilia Creek** causeway. Follow **Wandean Fire Trail** past a couple more forestry roads, keeping right as a sealed section paves the way up onto the **Turpentine Range**.

A sandstone escarpment flags the turn off to **Jerrawangala Lookout**. Swing left through a potentially locked gate, noting that caravans and trailers are not permitted between here and the lookout (unhitch, or walk the extra 900 metres).

You will reach a small carpark near **Wandean Gap**, where a boardwalk leads to a fenced vantage point. Views extend east over **Jervis Bay** and the **Beecroft Peninsula**, through **St Georges Basin**, and west to **Mount Tianjara** and the receding **Galbraith Plateau**.

Return from the lookout, and continue west on the sandy track through orange coloured banksia. You will exit **Jerrawangala NP** and reach a tee on the sealed **Braidwood – Nowra Road**, some 3.8 kilometres from the lookout.

Turn left here to follow good bitumen through **Morton NP** along a section of the **Old Wool Road**. The original road was cut in 1841 with convict labour, to enable selectors of the **Braidwood**

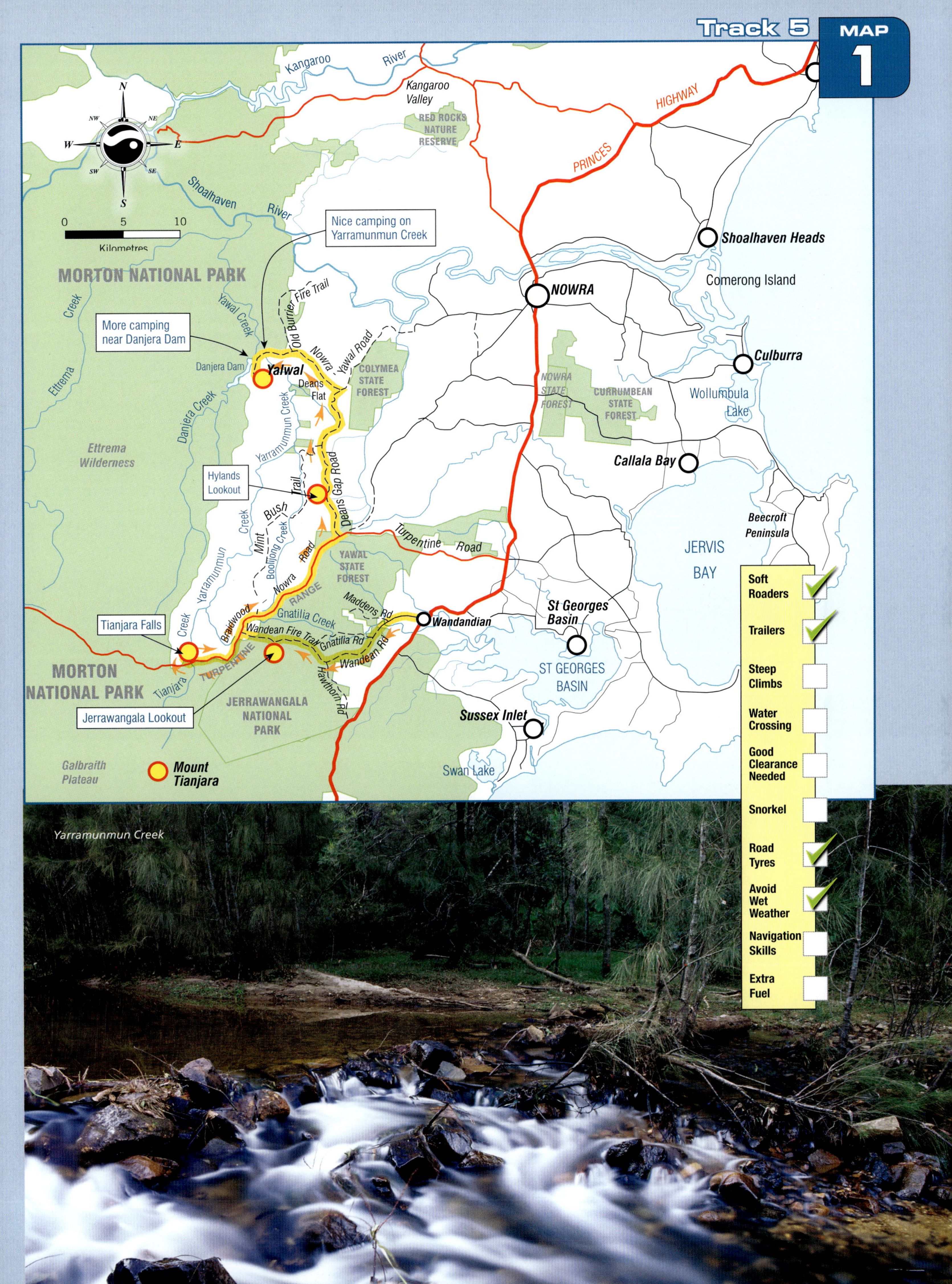

Yarramunmun Creek

Yarramunmun Creek

area to get their wool clip to the port of **Jervis Bay**. Local wool production proved unviable however, and poor soils kept agricultural development from the **Morton** area, hastening its national park status in 1938.

One of the jewels in this protected area is **Tianjara Falls**, and you will reach its turn off on the right, some five kilometres from the **Wandean Fire Trail** junction. Turn into a carpark and picnic area, where **Tianjara Creek** tumbles over the **Turpentine Range**. A short walk takes you to a viewpoint overlooking the sheer 64 metre drop, where water from the **Tianjara Plateau** contributes to the northern flowing **Yarramunmun Creek**.

We will parallel this waterway into **Yalwal**, so retrace your steps to the **Wandean Fire Trail** junction, and continue along the bitumen for a further 10.8 kilometres. Turn left at an unmarked intersection onto **Deans Gap Road**

Yalwal Road

(**Turpentine Road** is on the right, 200 metres beyond this turn off if you miss it, although the approach from the opposite direction is difficult, because of double white lines).

Follow the gravel back into **Jerrawangala NP**, and past a couple of clearings (potential bush camps). Stay on the main track, avoiding other side tracks on an untidy surface punctuated with potholes. You will cross under powerlines and turn left on an unmarked track, 3.6 kilometres from the **Nowra Road** turn off.

A turn table 800 metres later allows parking for the short walk to **Hylands Lookout**. An informal rock ledge provides a vantage point high above **Boolijong Creek**, with exceptional views down the valley. Take care near the sheer drop off, especially in company with children.

Return to **Deans Gap Road** and continue north, keeping right away from the powerline track, 1.8 kilometres later. Keep right at **Mint Bush Trail** some two kilometres further on to follow rutted track on a winding run into **Deans Flat**.

You will reach a tee intersection on the **Nowra – Yalwal Road**, where you turn left and follow good gravel on a serpentine path through mixed forest. Keep left at the **Old Burrier Fire Trail** some 4.6 kilometres later, to reach a small parking area on the left 800 metres beyond that.

Good views take in the complex topography over **Yalwal** and **Yarramunmun Creeks** from a couple of informal lookouts. Vehicles descend from here through a corridor of sandstone formations, adorned with mosses, ferns and stands of macrozamia.

Glimpses of the **Ettrema Wilderness** continue to a lovely picnic and camping area with basic facilities on **Yarramunmun Creek**, just a couple of kilometres later. Several grassy sites (beyond bollards) offer shade and shelter, with a sandy beach on the creek, only 100 metres away.

A timber bridge spans the waterway with larger camping areas found a few hundred metres further on. Basic facilities are provided, and there is a much larger choice of sites suitable for groups or camper trailers. Access to the **Danjera Dam** is close by, with canoeing or electric powered boats permitted on the small catchment.

Tianjara Falls

Constructed in 1971, the **Danjera** collects its water from a catchment of 114 square kilometres, before it is released into **Yalwal Creek**, and the **Shoalhaven River** beyond that. Both the **Yalwal** and the dam's feeder creek, the **Danjera**, have cut a gorge through volcanic rock, exposing some gold bearing mineral.

Alluvial gold was found here in the 1870s, but the much richer deposits found in deeper quartz veins proved more viable. A town was established in the 1880s, and miners maintained a presence up until WW2. Visitors can get a feel for its history at the nearby cemetery, or walk to abandoned mine workings near the dam.

Vehicles are not permitted beyond the dam, so it is necessary to retrace your steps back to **Deans Gap Road**, past the **Colymea State Forest**. You will meet the **Shoalhaven River**, and veer right to **Yalwal Road** into **Nowra**.

TRACK 6

Swallow Tail Pass

SYDNEY AREA

Track Snapshot

TOUR ROUTE:
Taralga to the Hume Freeway interchange via Tarlo and Wollondilly Rivers.

DURATION AND DISTANCE:
An easy day trip of 80 kilometres.

TRACK DETAILS:
A routine run for all vehicles and drivers, with trailers permitted (but not caravans).

WHEN TO GO:
All year round in dry weather.

CAMPING:
Possible sites at Taralga Showgrounds or overnight at Black Bobs Creek Rest Area.

FUEL AND SUPPLIES:
Nothing en route, but Taralga has most supplies.

MAPS:
Natmap 1:250k Goulburn, Wollongong Special

OTHER INFORMATION:
Visitors keen to camp at the end of this short tour will find better options at Bundanoon, 17 kilometres south of Moss Vale. Excellent facilities are provided, but bring your own firewood.

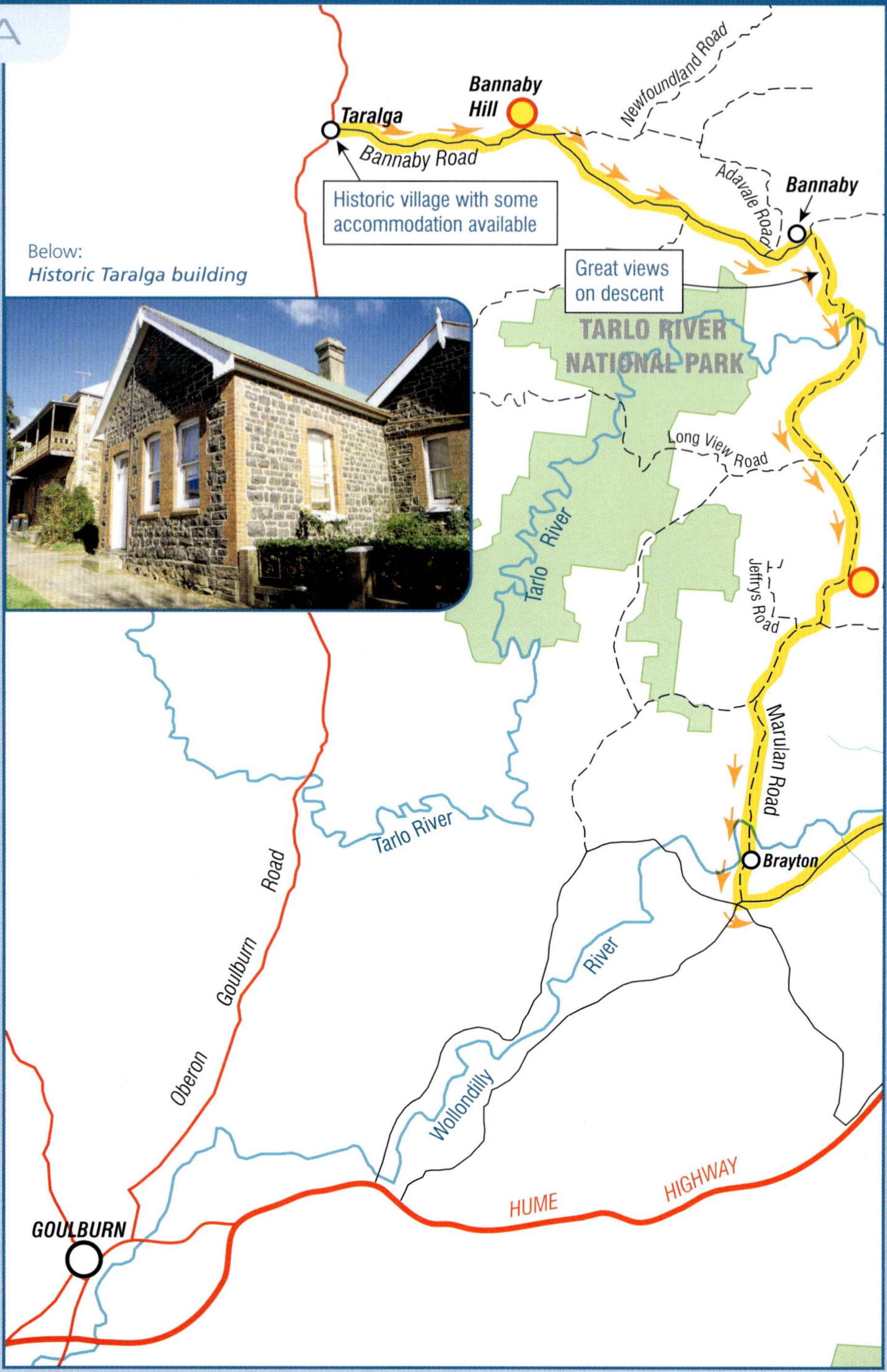

Below:
Historic Taralga building

Historic village with some accommodation available

Great views on descent

Historic ***Taralga*** *first attracted Europeans in the 1820s with its fertile soils and dependable climate. Graziers settled the district over the next 30 years, with the township taking shape around 1860. Various churches were established, together with essential country town infrastructure, to create a sizable community.*

These days several hundred people call ***Taralga*** *home, with many of the solid old buildings still standing, and there is an active historical society. Visitors can stroll the tree lined main street to get a feel for the town's unique architecture, or stop for a chat at a cafe, or at one of the two pubs. Accommodation options include the hotels, B and Bs or farm stay, with the Showgrounds being a possibility for campers (enquire at the Post Office or Country Store).*

Four wheel drivers will find the town of interest as a staging point for an easy run over ***Swallow Tail Pass****, and the lovely pastoral country adjoining it. Soft roaders or those towing camper trailers will have no problems in dry weather, providing that the* ***Tarlo River*** *is not too deep at the crossing.*

Leave **Taralga** via **Bannaby Street** to pass one of the grand old churches and Presbytery, before following **Bannaby Road** through open grazing country. Unrestricted views extend past hand built stone cottages and culverts, constructed with local rock, perhaps gathered in the convict days.

Cattle, sheep and alpacas roam the lush pasture, although potatoes and wine grapes do well in the area. Dairy cattle have been a mainstay of the district, with a handful of butter factories operating at various times.

Keep right at **Newfoundland Road** to descend over **Bannaby Hill** with rural glimpses directly ahead. You will pass **Adavale Road** before climbing to the elevated **Anglican Church** at **Bannaby** with its outstanding views to the east.

Some 19 kilometres from **Taralga** you will veer right onto gravel at the signposted "**Swallow Tail Pass**". An old woolshed marks the turn off, with corrugated iron shearers quarters and other outbuildings clustered nearby.

Begin the descent on rough road to a causeway flanked by yards and stockramp. You will go through a gate to begin a winding run past cuttings on

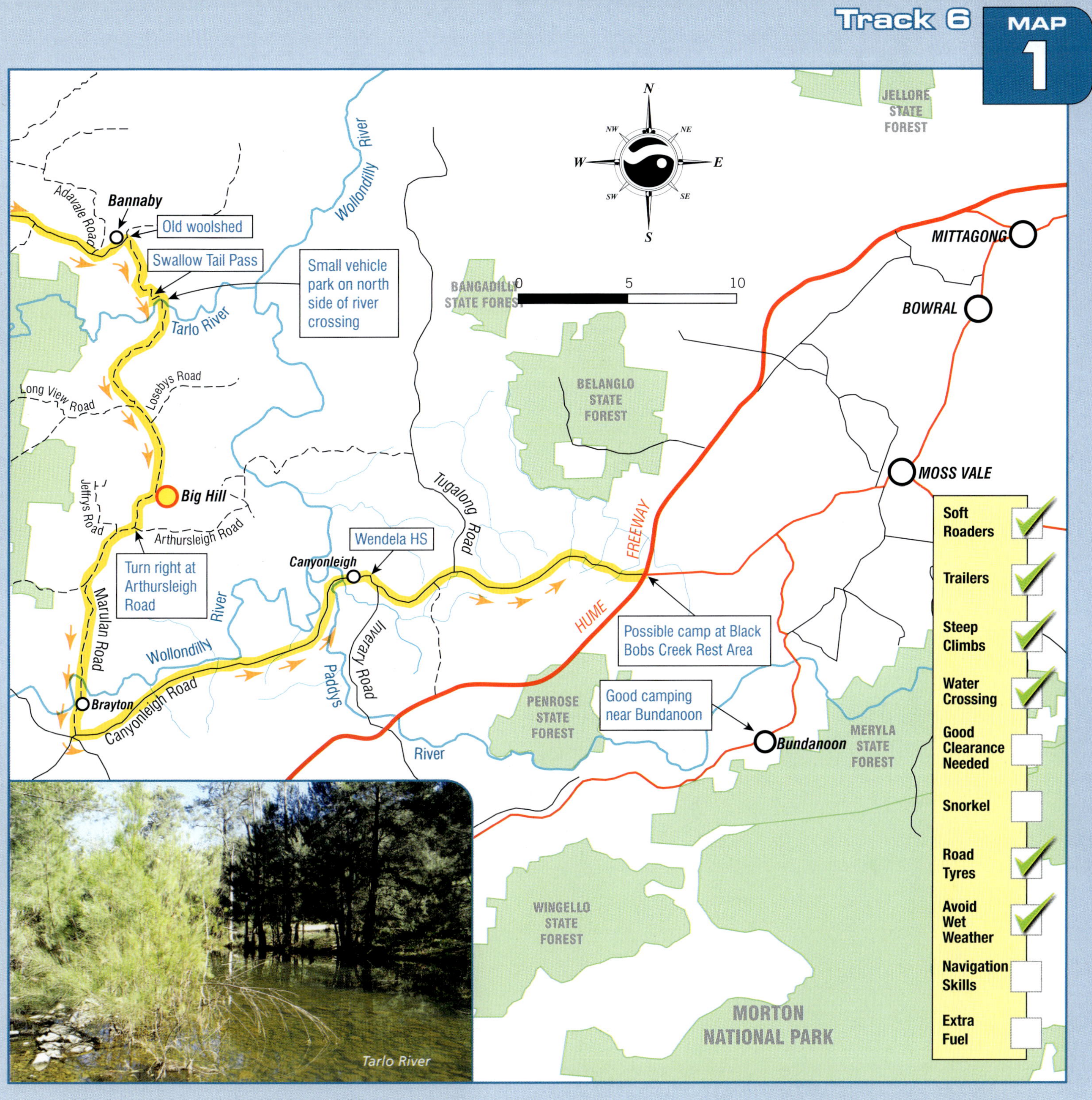

Tarlo River

a rutted track. Tussock grasses frame the **Tarlo River** and its rocky choke from a lofty viewpoint mid descent.

You will reach the river, five kilometres beyond the turn off, to cross a concrete causeway with a rocky exit. There is a nice spot to pull over prior to the crossing, with the tranquil waters inviting visitors for a dip. Dense river oaks line the river offering some shade, although camping is not permitted.

The drive beyond the **Tarlo** features excellent views of its craggy, forested path, as you reach better road beyond the next gate. Pastoral themes flash by now, with dams, yards and old sheds adding to the flavour.

Continue past **Long View Road** and **Losebys Road** to reach **Mount Hannibal HS**, 10 kilometres from the crossing. The 714 metre bush cloaked peak of Big Hill flags a turn right, away from **Arthursleigh Road** on the left, and past a cluster of letterboxes. Veer left away from **Jefferys Road**, one kilometre later to pass a CFA shed and keep straight on **Marulan Road**.

Rocky outcrops herald the community of **Brayton** and a single lane bridge over the **Wollondilly River**. Nice river views extend over sheep grazing land, before you reach a major junction, 3.1 kilometres from the bridge.

Turn left at a white homestead onto **Canyonleigh Road** to follow the **Wollondilly** through gates to a complex waterway network near the locality of **Canyonleigh**. Turn hard right at **Wendela HS** to pass **Inverary Road** on the right and **Tugalong Road** on the left. You soon meet the **Hume Freeway** at an interchange, with **Black Bobs Creek** rest area marking the junction.

TRACK 7 ABERCROMBIE RIVER

SYDNEY AREA

*The **Abercrombie River** headwaters gather on the western face of the Great Divide, before undertaking a lazy cross country meander to meet the **Lachlan River** at **Lake Wyangala**. Several pockets of a 1900 hectare national park combine to protect these infant waters, with the major holding being criss crossed by a network of 4WD tracks. This tour takes in some pleasant back country terrain, together with a number of bush camping opportunities, and the chance to pull in a trout for dinner.*

*There are two entry points for access into the major block of national park, with **Arkstone Road** offering access from the west, and **Felled Timber Track** entry from the north east. We will use the latter option and undertake a circuit drive via some of the numerous waterways,*

Our journey kicks off at Taralga; an historic town 45 kilometres north of Goulburn. Stone and character weatherboard dwellings frame the main street, with several eateries and a historical museum beckoning those with time to spare. Fuel and other supplies are also available here – your only chance to top up on this trek.

Leave town via the **Richlands Road** following the poplar lined avenue north past wind turbines and a rustic woolshed on the left. You will cross **Woolshed Creek** and its small carpark with grassy rest stop several kilometres from town.

Snipes Flat Road branches to the left as you reach the locality of Richlands and the **Wombeyan Caves Road** on your right. Keep left heading for Oberon over a potential floodway, and past a pocket of pine plantation.

Track Snapshot

TOUR ROUTE:
Taralga to Porters Retreat via tracks within Abercrombie River NP.

DURATION AND DISTANCE:
Allow at least two days to travel the 130 kilometre route as described, with a further 45 kilometres to reach Oberon at the tour's conclusion.

TRACK DETAILS:
Steep grades require vehicles equipped with low range gears, and good clearances are needed for the creek fordings. Trailers not permitted on Silent Creek Fire Trail.

WHEN TO GO:
The tracks are only closed for very wet weather or days of extreme fire danger. Spring visits are pleasant, but water levels in the rivers and creeks can be very low by autumn. Summer is hot and winter can be freezing. No access in wet weather.

CAMPING:
Excellent vehicle based camping at Bummaroo Ford, Silent Creek, The Beach and The Sink. Possible camping at the Taralga Showgrounds (enquire at Post Office or Store).

FUEL AND SUPPLIES:
Taralga and Oberon

MAPS:
Natmap 1:100K Taralga

OTHER INFORMATION:
Fires are only permitted within the steel rings provided, and drinking water must be carried. Avoid visiting the park in wet weather as many tracks will be slippery.

Scrambling climbs and descents are part of Silent Creek Fire Trail.

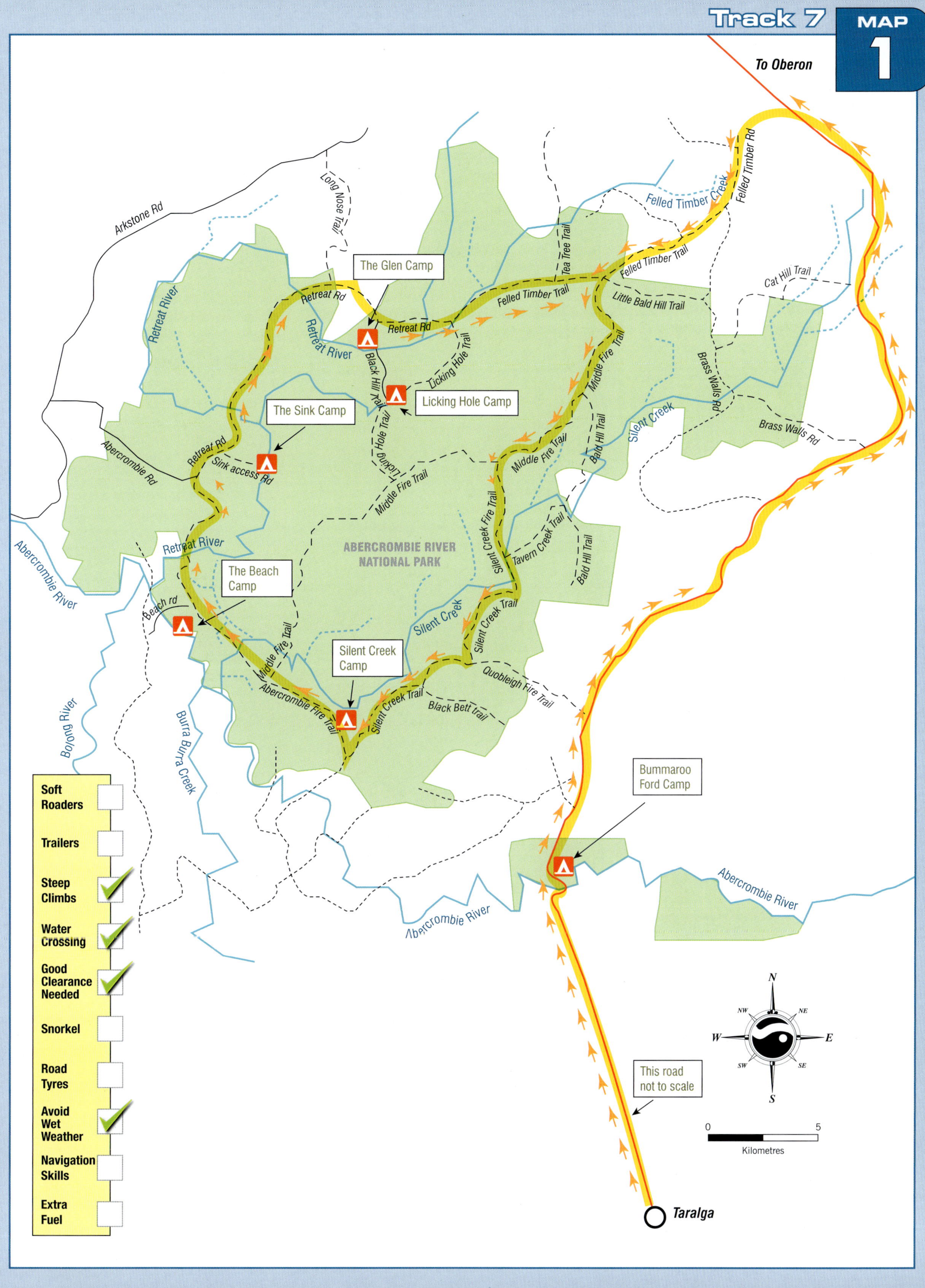
To Oberon
The Glen Camp
Licking Hole Camp
The Sink Camp
The Beach Camp
Silent Creek Camp
Bummaroo Ford Camp
ABERCROMBIE RIVER NATIONAL PARK
Arkstone Rd
Long Nose Trail
Retreat River
Retreat Rd
Black Hill Trail
Licking Hole Trail
Felled Timber Creek
Felled Timber Rd
Felled Timber Trail
Tea Tree Trail
Little Bald Hill Trail
Cat Hill Trail
Middle Fire Trail
Brass Walls Rd
Silent Creek
Bald Hill Trail
Abercrombie Rd
Sink access Rd
Silent Creek Fire Trail
Tavern Creek Trail
Abercrombie River
Beach rd
Silent Creek Trail
Quobleigh Fire Trail
Abercrombie Fire Trail
Black Bett trail
Bolong River
Burra Burra Creek
This road not to scale
Taralga
N
NE
E
SE
S
SW
W
NW
0
5
Kilometres
Soft Roaders
Trailers
Steep Climbs
Water Crossing
Good Clearance Needed
Snorkel
Road Tyres
Avoid Wet Weather
Navigation Skills
Extra Fuel

Grazing cattle mark the locality of Curraweela with **Craigs Road** on the left. Thicker bush is more evident now as you cross **Curraweela Creek** on a single lane bridge and around Toms Corner – a sharp right bend. Minor roads branch left and right as you reach Cobodong HS and its picturesque dam fringed with autumnal trees.

Views of the **Abercrombie Valley** open up on the right, with a complex crumpled landscape backing up to the the **Blue Mountains NP**. A sustained winding descent snakes its way to a small parcel of national park, about 30 kilometres from **Taralga**. A single lane timber bridge spans the Abercrombie here, with vehicle access prior to the crossing on the left. Fishers can try their luck here, and in quieter times you may see a Gippsland water dragon or even one of the resident platypus.

Camping with basic facilities is available across the bridge at the signposted Bummaroo Ford. With 2WD access it is a popular destination for campers, and home to some of the local wildlife including kangaroos, wombats and feral goats. Domestic pets are not permitted at Bummaroo Ford, as well as the other two blocks of **Abercrombie River NP**.

Beyond the camp, vehicles begin a very steep climb around tight bends to Quobleigh Station about 3.5 kilometres later. Elevated views around the locality of Paling Yards take in much of the Abercrombie headwaters. **Mingary Park** flags the crest of the range with winter grasses and wattle marking a transition back to bushland.

High voltage powerlines and a patch of pine plantation herald a more northerly heading as you enter **Gurnang SF**. Unnamed private tracks branch to the left before you reach the **Yerranderie Road**, signposted "Mt Werong" on your right. Keep straight and pass a second road on the right, signposted "**Gurnang Road**" 1.3 kilometres later. Mount Bathurst HS flags the locality of Porters Retreat on a sweeping bend, and a left turn onto **Felled Timber Road**, some 2.2 kilometres beyond Gurnang Road.

Gravel now paves the way south past an alpaca stud and private side tracks. Keep straight to skirt state forest on the right and cross back under the high voltage power lines to reach a junction 2.7 kilometres from the bitumen. Keep right here away from **Brass Walls Road** on the left and follow the signposted "New entrance to **Abercrombie River NP**". Keep left 1.3 kilometres beyond that to cross a grid and follow an old fenceline on the left. Beware of grazing stock as you cross two more grids and enter national park.

View from the heights

Veer right shortly after into superb thick forest dotted with ant hills and creamy mountain gums. You will reach **Northern Boundary Trail** on the right, one kilometre from the last grid, where you keep heading straight past a 4WD only sign. Earthen tracks, leaf litter and erosion control mounds are a regular feature of the drive now.

You pass another link to **Brass Walls Fire Trail** on the left (no longer publicly viable) and reach the junction of **Felled Timber Fire Trail** on the right and **Middle Fire Trail** on the left. (Felled Timber Fire Trail will be our exit route from the national park, and it is from this point that you will need to retrace your steps to Porters Retreat). However at this stage, keep left on Middle Fire Trail to negotiate a series of erosion control mounds and some rocky intrusions. Broken views open up through recently fire damaged bush, from a relatively elevated location in the park.

Keep right at the Bald Hill Fire Trail junction, to remain on Middle Fire Trail. **Silent Creek Fire Trail** is reached 2.9 kilometres later, when you swing left past a sign indicating "Not Suitable For Trailers". A sustained descent passes the other end of Bald Hills Fire Trail with broken views to the west.

Low range will be essential to hold back the vehicle on what would be an uphill scramble in the opposite direction, and not at all viable in wet weather. The drop off finishes at **Silent Creek** – a lovely wilderness of strewn rocks and seasonal bubbling waters that irrigate some enormous river sheoaks.

Remain in low range for the climb out, reaching a tee intersection, with **Quobleigh Fire Trail** on the left (locked gate on the boundary of national park). Turn right at this junction to negotiate an especially steep uphill pinch for 700 metres, before again tackling a sustained descent.

Back Creek with the usual casuarinas and rocky ford signals the next climb to **Black Bett Fire Trail** some 700 metres later. Keep right at this junction to follow better track surface to the **Oaky Creek** crossing, 2.4 kilometres beyond that.

Continue south to the next junction and turn right onto **Abercrombie Fire Trail** (closed gate in 300 metres if you continue straight ahead). You now head north west through the park and reach a tee 700 metres later. You will turn right here to continue the trek, but creek access and potential campsites are found along a 400 metre stretch of Silent Creek to the left. Pit toilets, shade, fire pits and grassy fenced off areas mark the designated **Silent Creek Camp** nearby, where lots of debris has been washed downstream. Indeed in times of flood, Silent Creek would be anything but!

Slightly better track heads north west now following a roller coaster ride over the spine of the range. Middle Fire Trail is reached three kilometres from Silent Creek Camp, where you keep left for excellent views in all directions. A turn off to **"The Beach"** is reached three kilometres from Middle Fire Trail, where you can turn left to a camping area on the **Abercrombie** itself.

The Beach on the Abercrombie River

The one kilometre long access track drops steeply to a small terraced camp with fireplaces, toilet and river access. Again sheoaks line the waterway, and fishers could pull in trout or blackfish, bearing in mind that other fish species are protected, and should be released if hooked. The vulnerable trout cod is an especially endangered species.

Fishing the **Abercrombie** has occurred here for thousands of years, with indigenous groups using the river as a trading route for stone tools and possibly shells. The area now known as Macs Flat, near the **Abercrombie** and Retreat River's confluence, remains a site of significance to Aboriginal people.

Beyond The Beach, **Abercrombie Fire Trail** continues to a rock paved ford of the Bolong River. Just beyond the crossing, a track to the right leads to a nice camp with fireplace, and shaded by massive sheoaks. Continue north past pine plantation on both sides of the road to a tee three kilometres later. The Abercrombie Fire Trail forks to the left here (signposted "Emden Vale main access road" and is a 2WD exit from the park), while **Retreat Road** forks to the right.

We turn right, signposted "The Sink", and find The Sink turn off 800 metres later. Head down to the camp on **Retreat River** to enjoy a shady red peppermint forest and easy river access. Redgum and yellow box also grows on these western slopes – an ideal home for some of the 14 types of bat found within the park, and for the 90 native bird species that call the Abercrombie home. Basic facilities are located nearby, with camping restricted to a fenced off area.

Return to Retreat Road and turn right to again reach the Retreat River at a bush shack. The private residence is home to an old truck, vegetable patch and some exotic trees. Its owner may well use the rather rickety old suspension bridge nearby from time to time, but it is probably best left as a talking point.

Cross the river and begin the low range climb to **Gate Tunnel Trail** on the left four kilometres later. Keep straight and avoid other side tracks until you reach **Black Hill Fire Trail** on your right, about eight kilometres from the Retreat crossing.

Turn right here and drop down through native pines framing broken views, to an old fenceline. You will reach **Licking Hole Creek** at an old cattleman's hut 2.4 kilometres later. The track becomes indistinct around this site, and potentially boggy to boot, so follow previous wheel marks to your left, and check for really soft ground on foot if necessary.

The old hut still features an interior that dates from the early 1900s with other relics from more recent times. A decaying stockyard is located nearby together with rusting 44s, and a rather elaborate gate. Stock grazing occurred in the area from around 1820, and at its peak the **Abercrombie** carried up to 3000 sheep.

Head in a north easterly direction from the hut to cross the creek and follow it upstream along **Licking Hole Fire Trail**. Outcrops of quartz shine from the forest floor, and although gold prospecting was undertaken on the **Abercrombie** over many years, it was largely a futile endeavour.

You will return to **Retreat Road** at a tee, with Felled Timber Fire Trail on the right, some three kilometres from the hut. Turn right and pass several tracks that fan off to the left, before you reach a major junction 4.8 kilometres later. This is the junction at which you first entered the national park. Retrace your steps from here to Porters Retreat on the **Taralga-Oberon Road**, with Oberon just 45 kilometres away by sealed road to the north.

TRACK 8

SIX FOOT TRACK

SYDNEY AREA

Cox's River Reserve sign

Track Snapshot

TOUR ROUTE:
Hampton Halfway Hotel and return via Six Foot Track, Black Range and Cox's River.

DURATION AND DISTANCE:
This trek of 70 kilometres could easily be done as a day trip.

TRACK DETAILS:
Easy travel in the main, with minor water crossings on Little River and some rough sections. Suitable for soft roaders and trailers.

WHEN TO GO:
Open all year round, but avoid wet weather when the waterways can rise and some sections of track become very slippery. Will be busy during holiday periods over the warmer months.

CAMPING:
Millionth Acre Camp and Cox's River Camp are the best choices if you need basic facilities. Some bush camping possibilities along tour route.

FUEL AND SUPPLIES:
None along tour route, stock up at Oberon, Lithgow or Katoomba.

MAPS:
Natmap 1:100K Katoomba

OTHER INFORMATION:
Watch out for other track users along this entire tour, especially for walkers using the Black Range Road and Six Foot Track.

__The Six Foot Track__ was originally cut in the late 1880s to link __Katoomba__ with the increasingly popular destination of __Jenolan Caves__. Pioneering tourists who previously needed to undertake a demanding expedition to reach the caves system, could now follow the six foot wide bridle trail on horseback in about a day's ride.

These days the __Six Foot Track__ is no longer a viable general tourist route to the __Jenolan Caves__, although energetic hikers can still tackle the hard 44 kilometre one way walk, on a three day slog from near __Katoomba__ to the caves. This trek follows part of that journey, with some scenic rural country to be enjoyed and plenty of bush camps enroute.

We begin the trek at the **Hampton Halfway Hotel**, located some 20 kilometres south of the **Great Western Highway** from Hartley along the **Jenolan Caves Road**. We will return to Hampton at the trek's conclusion. Drive in a southerly direction with wind turbines on your right, and past some grand Blue Mountain views to the left. **Rydal Road** on the right marks the rural community of **Hampton** as you pass the now closed servo, on good sealed road that can be ice affected over the colder months.

Trace the Great Divide's spine to begin a sustained descent through pine plantation at various stages of growth. The **Duckmaloi Road** branches to the right (signposted "Oberon"), with a camping area located on the junction. **The Millionth Acre Camping** and **Picnic Area** has fireplaces, toilets and tables, with camping on a grassed area beyond bollards. Access is off the Duckmaloi Road.

A steep descent ramps down the range beyond the Millionth Acre Camp, with pine forest access tracks fanning to either side, and the possibility of log trucks using the road. **Mini Mini Road** branches to the left some 10 kilometres

Rural views are very pleasant along Marsden Swamp Road.

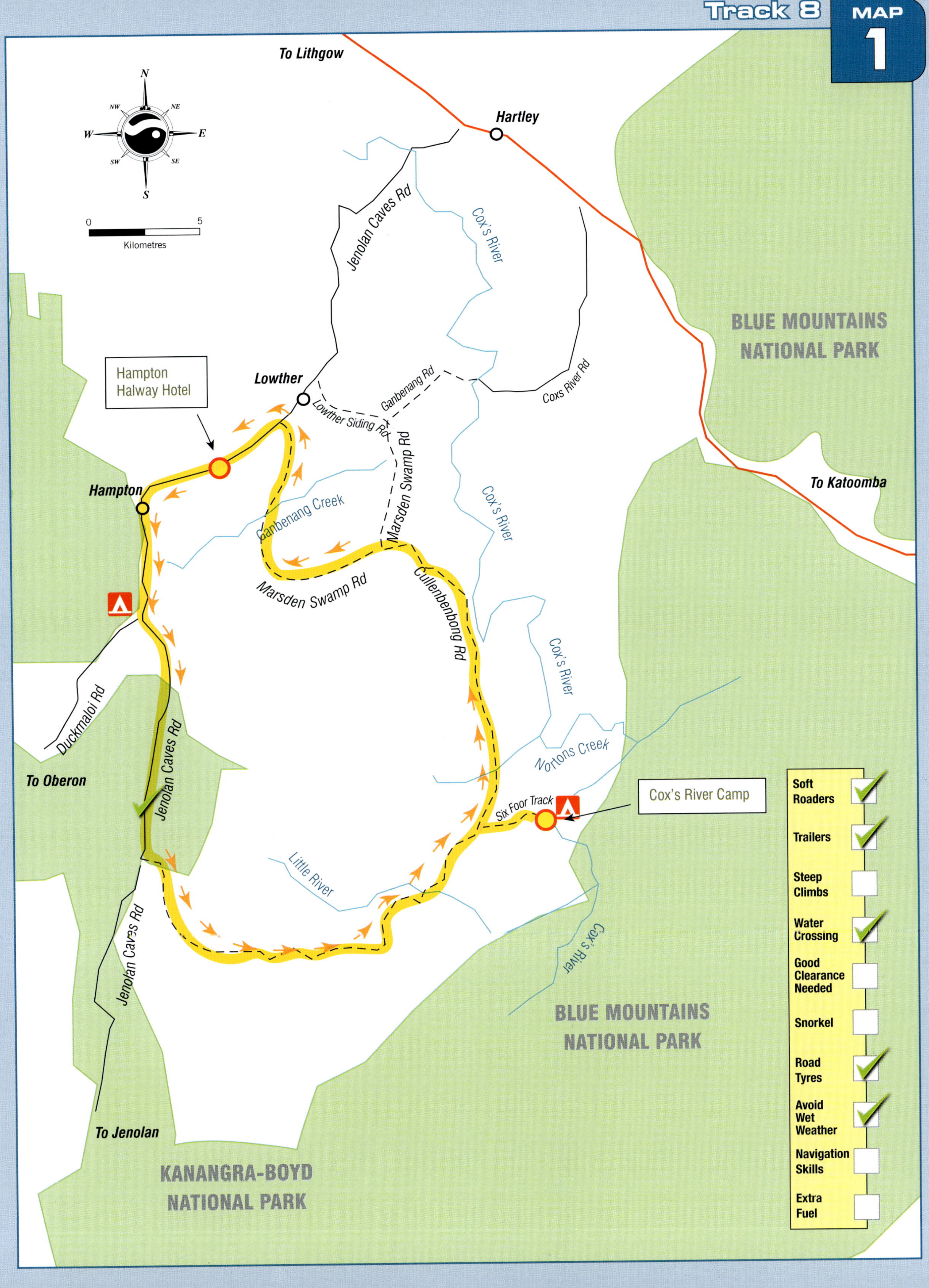

To Lithgow
Hartley
N
NE
E
SE
S
SW
W
NW
0
5
Kilometres
Jenolan Caves Rd
Cox's River
Hampton Halway Hotel
Lowther
Ganbenang Rd
Coxs River Rd
Lowther Siding Rd
Marsden Swamp Rd
Hampton
Ganbenang Creek
Cox's River
To Katoomba
BLUE MOUNTAINS NATIONAL PARK
Marsden Swamp Rd
Cullenbenbong Rd
Cox's River
Duckmaloi Rd
Jenolan Caves Rd
Nortons Creek
To Oberon
Six Foor Track
Cox's River Camp
Little River
Jenolan Caves Rd
Cox's River
BLUE MOUNTAINS NATIONAL PARK
To Jenolan
KANANGRA-BOYD NATIONAL PARK
Soft Roaders
Trailers
Steep Climbs
Water Crossing
Good Clearance Needed
Snorkel
Road Tyres
Avoid Wet Weather
Navigation Skills
Extra Fuel

SIX FOOT TRACK

Cox's River

beyond the Halfway Hotel, with the unsign posted **Black Range Road** on the left 4.3 kilometres later, and the now publicly closed **Boggy Creek Road** peeling off to the right.

Turn left at this intersection to pass plantation pines on the left and native bushland on the right. Avoid minor tracks on the left and right to reach a five way junction 1.2 kilometres later. The left track heads into pines, the right track is a powerline access track, with the remaining fork veering left to the **Six Foot Track**, and right to a camping area.

Those looking to camp will find a tiny carpark 100 metres later, but a very nice grassy clearing with toilet, shelter shed, water tank and walk in camping. Fires are not permitted at this site or at any other camps along the **Six Foot Track**, which is primarily intended for bushwalkers. Hikers and those who spend a little time exploring this trail will find flannel flowers, boronias and iris in the open bushland, and catch a glimpse of at least some of the 150 bird species that call this area home.

Vehicles follow the **Six Foot Track** signage past this camp, turning right 200 metres later to remain on the signposted track. The route follows powerlines, with a plantation of younger pines on the left. Bushwalkers and trail bike riders regularly use this track, especially on weekends and holiday periods, so keep your speed down and drive with caution looking out for other track users.

Head south into **Kanangra Boyd NP** and follow the signposted **Black Range Track** past a number of side tracks (generally no vehicle access into the national park). You will follow the spine of the Black Range along an earthen track which is rutted, potholed and sometimes boggy. This trek is not suitable in wet weather when it becomes very slippery.

Beefsteak Creek Fire Trail branches to the left three kilometres from the five way junction, and **Warlock Fire Trail** branches to the right 400 metres later. Keep straight to enjoy broken views of the Blue Mountains through a forest of grey gum, stringybark and peppermint,

Creek crossing on Six Foot Track

with a local understorey of grass trees, bracken, and reedy tussock grasses. A noticeable descent drops to **Cronje Mountain Fire Trail** (walkers only), where you keep left and begin a north easterly route, maintaining the descent past cuttings and a somewhat rougher section of track.

You will reach a tee intersection 1.3 kilometres beyond the **Cronje Mountain Fire Trail**, with **Waterfall Creek Fire Trail** branching to the left. Swing right here past a potential bush camp site 800 metres later, then reach a lovely fern gully on a subsequent hairpin bend. The transition from open wooded plateau to moist verdant lowland is both sudden and captivating as the **Little River** reveals itself.

You ford this trickling waterway several times in 200 metres before reaching a clearing near the confluence of **Alum Creek** and **Little River**. Old fenceline and exotic trees mark one of the pioneering rural outposts in this area that sprang up in the late 1800s. You then cross **Alum Creek** to reach an excellent camp 100 metres later. A new toilet and bench seats cater for bushwalkers, but very limited parking and walk in only access reduces its value for vehicle based travellers.

Climb up from the creek via a new track alignment to leave **Kanangra Boyd NP** at a flat area on Mini Mini Saddle. Fenceline and rampant blackberry usher your journey to a large junction three kilometres later, where kangaroos often graze. Other animals regularly seen include echidnas and wallabies, while lizards and snakes are quite common. We will exit via the signposted "Glen Chee" road to the left, but for now turn right past a stockyard and cross a grid to descend into a valley ringing with bellbirds.

Cox's River Camping Area marks the end of vehicle travel three kilometres later at a set of gates and some private property. There is good camping here with toilet, shelter and easy access to the river, which is lined with sheoak and manna gum. Fires are not permitted and tent campers must walk their gear past bollards. **The Six Foot Track** continues toward Megalong from here, but short term vehicle bound walkers can undertake the 1.5 kilometre hike to Bowtells Swing Bridge – a lofty wire structure strung up in 1992 that allows walkers to cross the **Cox's River** in times of flood.

Return to the large stockyard junction and take **Glen Chee Road** over a rock filled causeway and short piece of bitumen. Side tracks and gateways punctuate the drive north, so stick to the main road and follow the high voltage powerlines, which basically trace the route out. It is a smooth and well surfaced gravel road with good drainage.

Broad views open up on the right overlooking the Cox's valley with an especially nice vantage point found 3.2 kilometres from the stockyard junction. Cross a grid (one of many along this road) and descend to an unsignposted tee intersection, 5.4 kilometres from the stockyard.

Turn right here and reach a short section of bitumen around the locality of **Cullenbong** about 1.8 kilometres later. Lovely casuarinas line the Cox's River here, where the waterway has cut a sizable horseshoe bend into the landscape.

Table Rock D Road branches to the left as you continue to follow the Cox's River on scenic road around sweeping bends. Poplars and willows colour the undulating drive, with some stock roaming the valley. You will reach a tee intersection, about seven kilometres from Cullenbong where you turn left onto **Marsden Swamp Road**, signposted "To Jenolan Caves".

The unsealed road winds through undulating pasture and bushland with excellent views opening up at every bend. Pass by Mycumbene Station on a sustained climb with corrugated corners to a tee intersection on the Jenolan Caves Road at the community of Lowther. Turn left here to return to the Halfway Hotel (4.4 kilometres), or swing right to Hartley and the Great Western Highway (16 kilometres)

The Cox's River marks the end of vehicle travel.

TRACK 9

BLUE MOUNTAINS

SYDNEY AREA

Jamison Creek drops into the Kedumba Valley near Wentworth Falls.

Track Snapshot

TOUR ROUTE:
Wentworth Falls to McMahons Lookout via the Tableland Road and return.

DURATION AND DISTANCE:
Allow a full day or weekend to make the 50 kilometre return trek (70 kilometres for those camping at Ingar) if you intend to undertake some of the walks at Wentworth Falls.

TRACK DETAILS:
Easy unsealed roads suitable for all vehicles and trailers.

WHEN TO GO:
Spring and early summer will see impressive water flow over Wentworth Falls, with very cold conditions likely in Winter. Busy in holiday periods.

CAMPING:
Basic facilities and free camp at Ingar. Commercial possibilities at the township of Wentworth Falls.

FUEL AND SUPPLIES:
Lawson and Wentworth Falls can provide for all needs.

MAPS:
Hema Blue Mountains

OTHER INFORMATION:
There are a number of walking tracks beginning at Wentworth Falls Picnic Area. Most are well formed and offer spectacular waterfall access and great views down the Kedumba Valley.

Very little of the ***Blue Mountains National Park*** *is available for 4WDing, so this trek should be put on your "to do" list while access remains available. It is a very easy run over the* ***King's Tableland*** *to* ***McMahons Lookout****, and not that much rougher on the* ***Ingar Camp Fire Trail****, so the drive is suitable for all vehicles and drivers.*

Outstanding views of ***Lake Burragorang (Warragamba Dam)*** *are a fitting reward for travel here, but nice bushland and a quiet camp in the off peak season are equally enjoyable. Nearby* ***Wentworth Falls*** *are very popular all year round, but should be visited as part of the package for this area.*

To visit the **King's Tableland**, turn south off the **Great Western Highway**, four kilometres west of Lawson, at the top of Bodington Hill. The signposted **Tableland Road** begins as a sealed suburban street with numerous houses and some concealed driveways. Just 1.7 kilometres later, **Queen**

Diamond pythons sun themselves on the King's Tableland.

Elizabeth Drive (later to become Ingar Camp Fire Trail) heads to the left where bush camping with basic facilities and a superb waterfall fed pool is found at the end of a 10 kilometre unsealed track.

For now continue straight through scrubby bush following high voltage powerlines to a major fork in the road, some four kilometres from the highway. Keep left at this junction with the private grounds of the Queen Victoria Memorial Hospital on your right. Established as a country estate in the 1890s, the residence was later used to house sufferers of tuberculosis. This need all but ended in 1958, when the facility was converted into a nursing home. It finally closed in 1999 leaving empty buildings and exotic trees to mark the site.

Much earlier use of this area was made by local indigenous groups, who have left stone arrangements and tool sharpening grooves across the tableland: most notably near the hospital grounds. The Queen Victoria site marks the transition to gravel as single lane roadway funnels you through a forest of banksia and hakea. Other ecosystems of note on the tablelands include the **Blue Mountains'** largest expanse of heathland – especially evident on the western boundary, and due in part to the consistently high prevailing winds.

You will enter **Blue Mountains NP** one kilometre later, and pass **Camp Cave Hill** on your right as taller trees dominate, including numerous angophoras – eucalypts which shed their bark

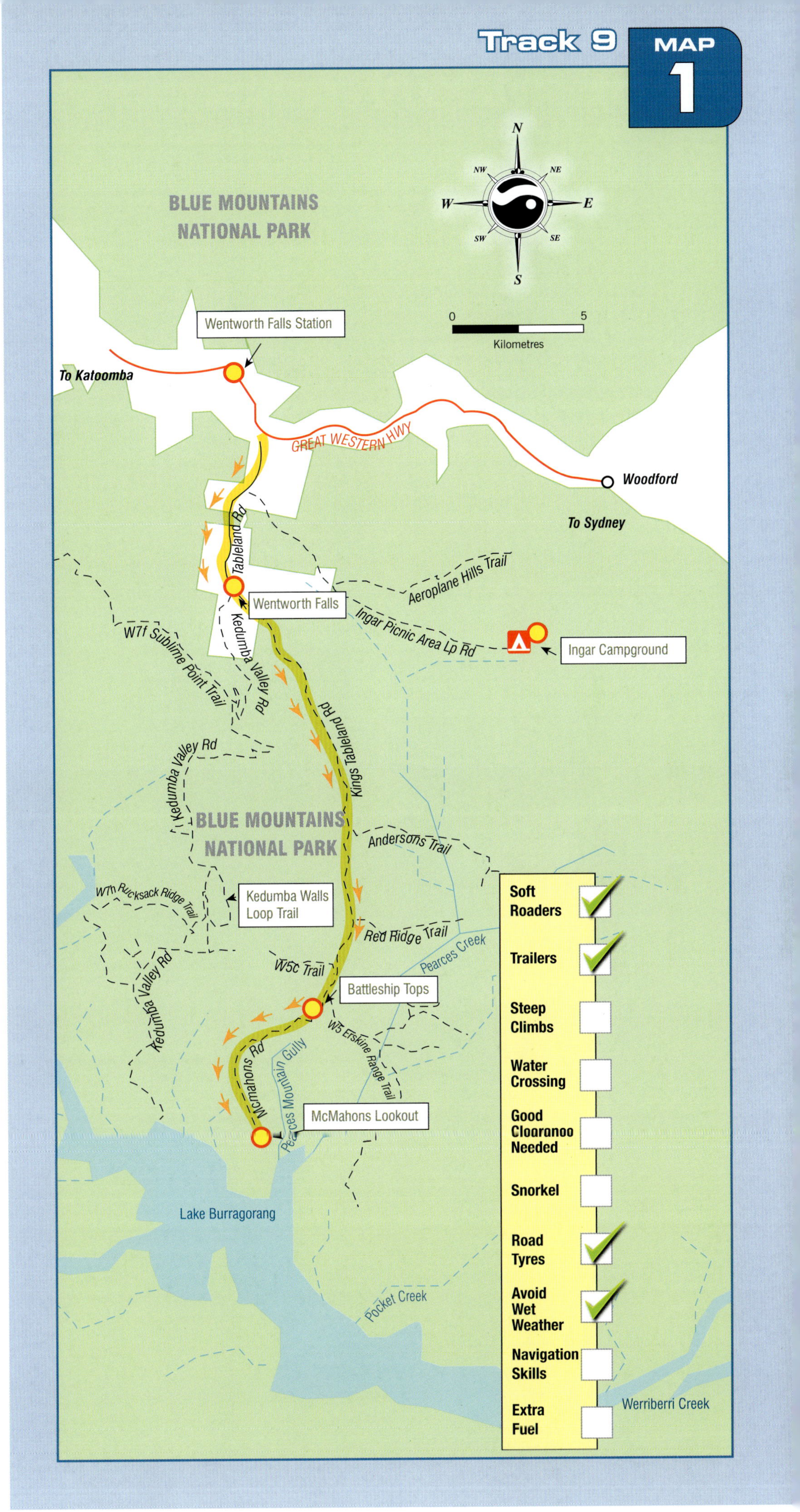

Track 9 MAP 1

BLUE MOUNTAINS NATIONAL PARK
N
NE
E
SE
S
SW
W
NW
0
5
Kilometres
Wentworth Falls Station
To Katoomba
GREAT WESTERN HWY
Woodford
To Sydney
Tableland Rd
Aeroplane Hills Trail
Wentworth Falls
Ingar Picnic Area Lp Rd
Ingar Campground
W7f Sublime Point Trail
Kedumba Valley Rd
Kings Tableland Rd
Kedumba Valley Rd
BLUE MOUNTAINS NATIONAL PARK
Andersons Trail
W7h Rucksack Ridge Trail
Kedumba Walls Loop Trail
Red Ridge Trail
Pearces Creek
W5c Trail
Battleship Tops
Kedumba Valley Rd
W5 Erskine Range Trail
Mcmahons Rd
Pearces Mountain Gully
McMahons Lookout
Lake Burragorang
Pocket Creek
Werriberri Creek

Soft Roaders	✓
Trailers	✓
Steep Climbs	
Water Crossing	
Good Clearance Needed	
Snorkel	
Road Tyres	✓
Avoid Wet Weather	✓
Navigation Skills	
Extra Fuel	

in autumn to reveal a striking rose coloured skin.

Andersons Fire Trail (locked gate) branches to the left just prior to High Valley – a private parcel of land marking Notts Swamp and the head of **Reedy Creek**. A forest of scribbly gums blotched in yellow and grey stand together with correas and flowering banksia in season.

Red Ridge Fire Trail flags the Erskine Range to the east and a potentially closed gate. Fern adorned rocky outcrops stand guard at the foot of Harris Hill, about two kilometres from **Red Ridge Fire Trail**, where you will find a small parking area. Several more side tracks fan off **Kings Tableland Road** before you reach Erskine Range Track on the left. Keep right at this junction to arrive at a carpark at **Battleship Tops** 1.6 kilometres later.

These abrupt sandstone formations sit adjacent to the main track and once featured indigenous artwork perhaps 25 000 years old. Unfortunately fire and

Lake Burragorang from McMahons Lookout.

Wentworth Falls can be reached via a short walking trail.

years of recent vandalism has almost entirely destroyed this gallery, and today it is only the curious formations themselves that make the stop worthwhile.

Minor sand drifts punctuate the last of the drive as the track merges to within 100 metres of the sheer **Kedumba Walls**. A parking area and toilet signal the end of vehicle travel, with **McMahons Lookout** 800 metres away.

Walkers will take 20 minutes to descend to a steel platform overlooking **Lake Burragorang**. The waters of the **Cox's** and **Kedumba Rivers** join way underneath your feet, with islands jutting up from the placid surface. Sandstone walls of the more distant ranges etch creamy lines across a landscape that really earns its regal title.

Stunning eucalypts line the drive to McMahons Lookout

Return by the same route to the **Great Western Highway**, with bush camping at Ingar Camp as previously mentioned. It is also well worth taking a look at the **Wentworth Falls** area nearby. Short and long walks take in a grand piece of the Blue Mountains that never fails to impress .

Bushland view on King's Tableland.

TRACK 10 Morton

SYDNEY AREA

Track Snapshot

TOUR ROUTE:
Bundanoon to Fitzroy Falls via Meryla State Forest and Morton National Park

DURATION AND DISTANCE:
Allow at least one day to undertake the 50 kilometre tour with sufficient time to look around.

TRACK DETAILS:
Routine state forest tracks in the main with no substantial grades. A rough section on Meryla Fire Trail would put most soft roaders out of their depth, with deepish ruts and some low rock shelves. Trailers OK behind full sized 4WDs.

WHEN TO GO:
All year round, but avoid wet weather.

CAMPING:
Excellent camping with facilities at Gambells Rest, and some bush camping within Meryla State Forest.

FUEL AND SUPPLIES:
Bundanoon and Nowra can supply all of your needs.

MAPS:
Natmap 1:100K Mossvale

OTHER INFORMATION:
Travel slowly and take extreme care along Red Hills Fire Trail between Renown Lookout and Fitzroy Falls Visitors Centre – walkers of all ages also use this track, and it can be very busy on weekends and holiday periods.

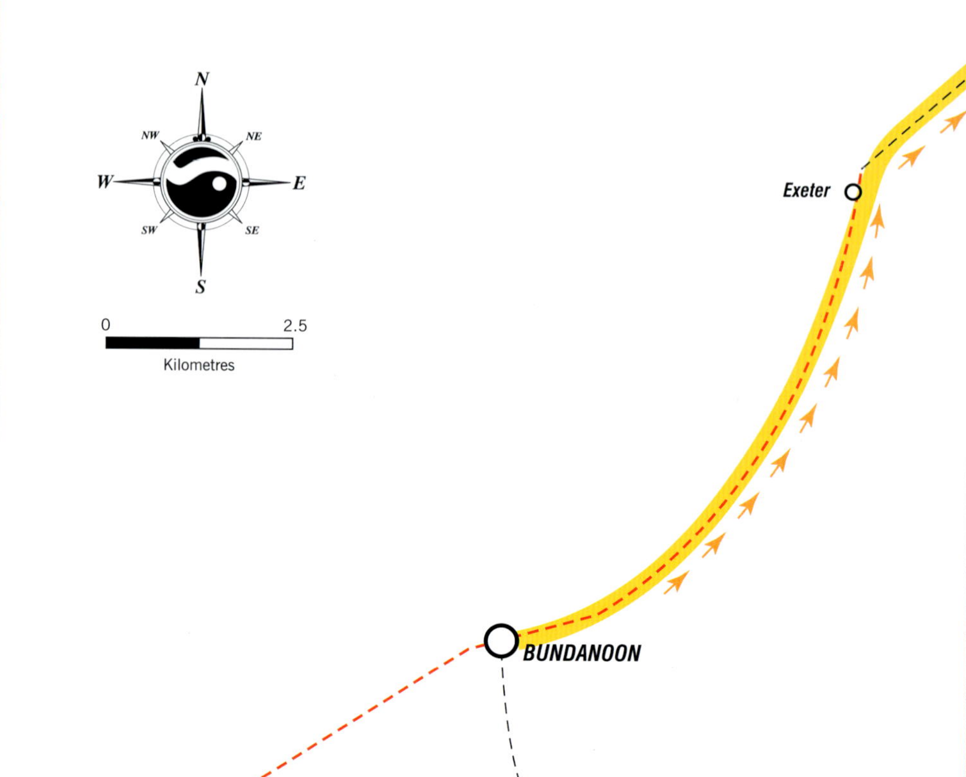

***The Shoalhaven River** and **Ettrema Creek** have sliced massive gouges into the sandstone of **Morton NP**, effectively annexing most of the central region from the perimeter escarpments. Fractured remnants of this major erosion can be seen all around this large national park, where other waterways continue to do their work.*

*Knobbly fingers of highland and open bluffs are especially accessible in the north where **Bundanoon** and **Yarrunga Creeks** drain into the soft **Kangaroo River valley.** Vehicle access to the national park is limited here, but very short walks will take you to some lofty lookouts that lord over all of the unfolding drama.*

This tour begins at **Bundanoon**, a usually quiet town that cuts loose in April every year to pay homage to its Scottish roots. Bagpipes, caber tossing and an influx of visitors disturb the peace for a weekend before the party ends and the village can relax again.

Check out the general town attractions at Bundanoon at the start of this tour.

A clearing at Gales Flat is a popular destination for walkers.

To Moss Vale
NOWRA RD
NOWRA RD
Fitzroy Falls
Fitzroy Falls
Yarrunga Creek
Yarrunga Creek
Gunrock Creek Firetrail
Gunrock Creek Firetrail
Gunrock Creek Firetrail
Red Hill Rd
Red Hill Firetrail
Meryla Rd
Meryla Firetrial
Link Firetrail
Spring Hills Rd
MERYLA STATE FOREST
MORTON NATIONAL PARK
Meryla Pass
To Nowra

Requirement	
Soft Roaders	
Trailers	✓
Steep Climbs	
Water Crossing	✓
Good Clearance Needed	✓
Snorkel	
Road Tyres	
Avoid Wet Weather	✓
Navigation Skills	
Extra Fuel	

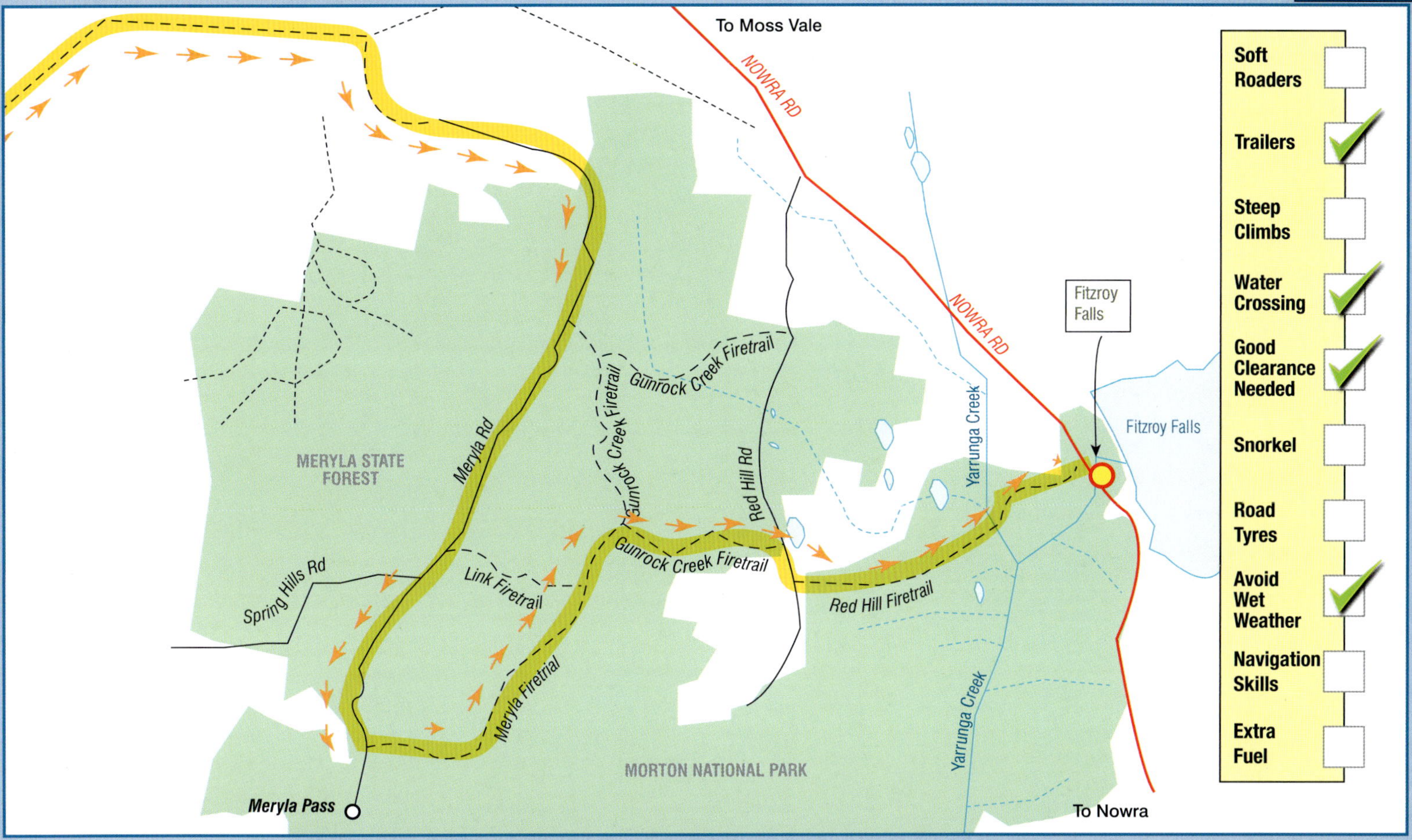

Left:
The headwaters of Bundanoon Creek gather before dropping into Morton NP.

Below:
Ferns and wetland vegetation spill over into Morton's waterways.

It is a great town to spend a night or two with historic buildings aplenty, nice eateries and a garden setting of autumnal trees. B&B and hotel accommodation is popular, but so too is the excellent national park camping at the south end of town.

Gambells Rest has a number of defined camping bays with toilets and hot showers. A shelter shed houses electric BBQs, sinks and table and chairs. Open fires are not permitted and there is a three week maximum stay – such is the camp's popularity. You must prebook to stay here, and fees apply for both camping and local entry into Morton NP.

Access to the local lookouts and walks is via a short drive and section of one way loop track. The Grand Canyon is especially appealing in the morning light, while Gambell's Lookout and Echo Point take in other aspects of the sandstone belt country. Longer walks are possible with only your fitness and experience dictating the options.

Leave Bundanoon via the main street heading north east past William Street (access to Glow Worm Glen carpark and one kilometre return nocturnal walk). Follow the rail line past several side roads to the hamlet of **Exeter**. Neat hedges, tudor style houses and formal gardens are part of the townscape, as you reach the town centre, 6.6 kilometres from Bundanoon.

Fitzroy Falls plunge into Morton's Yarrunga Valley.

Below:
Creek crossing in Meryla State Forest.

Take the Nowra exit from town, signposted **"Badgery's Way"**, turning off at the footy oval and driving under the rail line. Turn left immediately on the **Werai Road**, signposted "Nowra" at a clutch of character rich cottages.

Follow the rail on your left to pass Rockleigh Road and reach a sweeping bend to the left, signposted "Fitzroy Falls". Keep left here and continue through rural grazing land to a tee intersection on **Yarrawa Road**. Turn right at this tee, signposted "Nowra", and drive a further 2.5 kilometres to the signposted **"Meryla Road"**, where you turn right.

Drive in a southerly direction past farmlets and an atmospheric set of timber stockyards at the locality of **Werai.** Pines and a number of properties around Manchester Square flag a descent into bushland and the boundary of Meryla SF, 6.3 kilometres from the turn off.

Gravel paves the way now as you reach a single lane timber bridge well above **Bundanoon Creek**. A small parking area and old waterway ford are located near the permanent cascades which bubble around a jumble of boulders and irrigate masses of ferns.

Continue along the forestry road looking out for log trucks, trail bike riders, mountain bikers and horse riders who also frequent this area. Many tracks and some private driveways fishbone off the main arterial, as you reach another bridge three kilometres beyond the first.

A stand of exotic trees fringe the private holding of Midway Park on the right before you reach more dense bushland one kilometre later. The predominant stringybark and peppermint is coloured with banksia and seasonal heathland, with the occasional grass tree and sheoak. Kangaroos are regularly spotted with lyrebirds in good numbers, together with many other bird species.

Spring Hill Forestry Road branches to the right 3.3 kilometres from the last bridge, marking a transition to a more rutted trail with less stone topping. You will cross a creek 700 metres later where intricate lime/yellow ferns dangle over the banks. There is possible bush camping just over the ford, with a flat clearing, but no facilities.

You will reach an unsignposted intersection one kilometre later, with **Meryla Fire Trail** branching to the left, and **Meryla Pass** directly ahead. We will take the left turn here, but for now continue straight ahead for another 1.2 kilometres to arrive at a locked gate and walk in picnic area.

Several walks originate from here, but a number of informal lookouts can be reached if you follow the track uphill to some natural rock platforms (take extreme care near the edges and always supervise children). Other viewpoints are located on the Meryla Road 400 metres back the way you have come.

Other longer walks begin at Meryla Pass; one popular option follows **Griffens Fire Trail** downhill through a locked gate to an historic coal seam worked in the 1860s, with subsequent views over **Yarrunga Creek**. Energetic and experienced hikers who continue past the pioneering farm at Gales Flat, can follow the Old Meryla Road to Lake Yarrunga on a 16 kilometre return slog.

Return to Meryla Fire Trail junction and turn east onto the most demanding section of the track. Its uneven beginnings of sandstone steps and rutted bogholes may have you reaching for low range to control the lurching, but it is only a short stretch and better track appears one kilometre later at the site of a potential camp.

Clouds settle into Morton from Meryla Pass lookout.

Follow the boundary of national park past broken views of Mount Carrialoo and the Yarrunga Creek escarpment on a track peppered with bogholes. Cross a powerline track that heads left and right, to reach a tee intersection on **Gunrock Creek Fire Trail**, 900 metres later.

Turn right here on a boggy track filled with rubble to pass a locked gate and stockramp on the right. Tree ferns usher a more northerly drive past private property with pine plantation marking the corner. Keep left at another gate to climb past ferny wetland to another tee intersection on **Red Hill Road.**

Swing right and head south on good unsealed road past the turn offs to Redfern and Gunrock Springs (both private holdings). Then turn left onto **Red Hill Firetrail**, some 4.6 kilometres from the tee. This turn is not signposted but property numbers are screwed to a tree at the junction. Follow an avenue of deciduous trees and veer right back into national park 200 metres later. Avoid side tracks until you reach signposted West Rim Track, 2.9 kilometres from the Red Hill Road junction.

You will continue straight north from here, but **Renown Lookout** carpark is just 200 metres away on the right, and from there a 230 metre walk brings you to a viewing platform that takes in the triple drop of **Fitzroy Falls**. From this point it is essential to look out for walkers using this fire trail to access various viewpoints. Travel slowly and with considerable caution.

Bogholes are a hazard of Meryla Fire Trail.

Beyond Renown Lookout (and back on Red Hill Firetrail), cross a creek 400 metres later and keep right 100 metres beyond that. You will reach **Paynes Lookout** 400 metres later (80 metre walk to viewing platform) at a creek crossing (short walk also follows creek upstream).

Keep left 100 metres beyond the creek (right track is walkers only) to reach a tee intersection 100 metres later. Turn right here onto **Gwen Road** to arrive at another tee 400 metres further on. This is the **Bowral-Nowra Road**, where you turn right onto bitumen for 200 metres reaching the **Fitzroy Falls** turn off on your left.

An information centre, cafe and developed walking tracks provide plenty of opportunities for tourists and more energetic bush enthusiasts alike. The short walk to the top of Fitzroy Falls is popular and a great way to end the trek. From here it is a 16 kilometre drive to Moss Vale or 34 kilometres to Nowra, all on sealed road.

Chapter 2

LOWER NORTH

◀ *Bulga Forest view*

TRACK 11 NEW ENGLAND

LOWER NORTH

Macleay River valley

Track Snapshot

TOUR ROUTE:
Ebor to Bellbrook via Cathedral Rock, New England NP and the Styx River.

DURATION AND DISTANCE:
Allow two days for the 160 kilometre run; more if you wish to fully explore New England NP or fish the Macleay river.

TRACK DETAILS:
Easy travel in the main with a routine 4WD descent into the Styx Valley. Suitable for most vehicles, but trailers are not permitted on the Macleay River descent.

WHEN TO GO:
Avoid wet weather and possible snow in New England NP.

CAMPING:
Camping with basic facilities at Cathedral Rock and New England NP. Other opportunities at Styx River, Georges Creek and Blackbird Flat.

FUEL AND SUPPLIES:
Ebor and Bellbrook.

MAPS:
Natmap 1:100K Ebor, Carrai

OTHER INFORMATION:
New England NP offers some excellent walking trails and is well worth exploring for a day or two.

***New England NP** encompasses more than 70 000 hectares of bushland, etched by rivers and creeks that spill over from a simply stunning alpine plateau. The **Guy Fawkes**, **Styx** and **Bellinger Rivers** gather momentum on the contoured **Snowy Range** peaks, before rushing to the lowlands on a spirited journey through cool temperate rainforest and eucalypt clad slopes.*

*This tour begins at **Ebor** on the **Guy Fawkes River**, to trace the **Styx River** into the **Macleay Valley** on an easy run suitable for all 4WDs. Anglers will appreciate some productive waters, while a primeval world lurking within the plateau amazes most walkers.*

Start this tour at **Ebor** – a small town high on the **Waterfall Way**. (The **Waterfall Way** links **Armidale** with coastal NSW, just south of **Coffs Harbour**. It is a popular bitumen run taking in several major falls and rural themes from the beef cattle of **New England** to the dairying valleys of **Bellingen**.)

A general store, fuel outlet and cafe feature at **Ebor** as you pass the hotel and a bridge over the **Guy Fawkes River**. Turn right at the historic cemetery to visit **Ebor Falls** just off the main road. An upper and lower parking area give access to separate drops of the river as it exits the tableland in spectacular fashion.

Back in 1845 selectors ran stock on the grassy high plains here, reputedly in response to European exploration the year before on 5th of November – Guy Fawkes Day. A village sprang up to capitalise on the grazing lands, although today much of the area has been claimed as national park or state forest.

Return to the main road and turn right to cross **Rigney Creek**, swinging left at a rest area, sign posted **"Waterfall Way"**. Turn right 8.4 kilometres from **Ebor** onto **Cathedral Rock NP** access road. Follow the gravel past grazing stock into national park, for a boggy heathland run coloured with wildflowers in spring.

You will reach **Borokee Camping Area** eight kilometres later to find shady sites and basic facilities. A 5.8 kilometre circuit walk begins here weaving through eucalypt forest, and past a jumble of granite tors. You will haul yourself over car sized boulders on the final climb to the locally unrivalled 1586 metre summit of **Round Mountain**. The hike will take at least a couple of hours, but rewards walkers with panoramic views over the **New England** tablelands.

Return to the **Waterfall Way** and turn right for a couple of crossings of **Bullock Creek**. Turn left onto **Point Lookout Road** 5.2 kilometres later, reaching gravel just beyond an environmental conference centre.

Serpentine Creek flags **Duttons Trout Hatchery** (open to the public daily 8.00 – 3.30, with a self guided walk) and nearby private accommodation options. Continue through cleared grazing land to descend into **Styx River SF**.

There is camping near **Hyatts Flat** on the **Little Styx River**, with a toilet and pleasant water side sites. Swing left just beyond the camp signposted **"Point Lookout"** to cross a grid into **New England NP**. **Thungutti Camp** marks the entrance, along side the **Little Styx River**, where basic facilities and sheltered area are provided, although vehicle based camping can be difficult if you arrive to a full house.

Continue under lichen streaked trees toward **Point Lookout**, to find ample parking and a 20 minute walk to a lookout platform. Views extend for 100 kilometres on a clear day, with the ocean visible beyond range after range in the foreground.

Other walks in this area of national park vary from short and easy to more lengthy hikes involving steep climbs. This is superb country to explore though, with antarctic beech giants

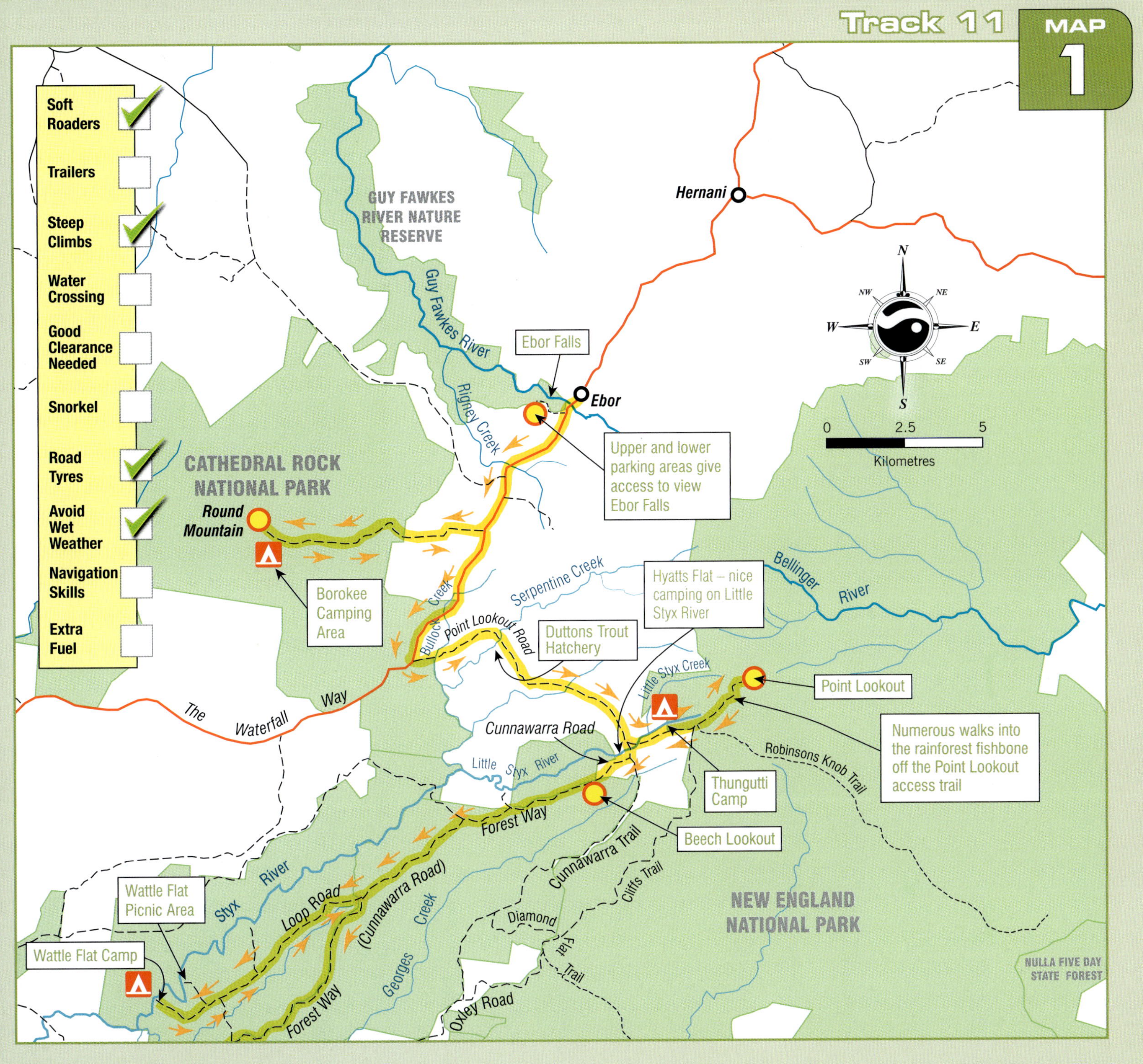

towering over king fern and mossy rock overhangs. Countless cascades spray water over the verdant rainforest, where lyre birds are regularly spotted.

When you are ready, return to the **Little Styx River Camp** just outside the national park, to turn left onto **Kempsey Road**, signposted "**Wattle Flat**". Veer right 100 metres later to follow **Cunnawarra Road** with state forest on the right, and national park on the left.

Beech Lookout is reached two kilometres later, with a vantage point just off the track taking in a southerly aspect of **Georges Creek** and the **Macleay Valley** more than one vertical kilometre below. Table, benches and fireplace allow visitors to linger for a while – perhaps to boil the billy while you wait for the regular mist and low cloud to disperse.

Continue to follow good gravel (although still slippery in places when wet) avoiding side tracks. Keep right at **Loop Road** about ten kilometres from **Beech Lookout**, for a lesser used road leading to **Wattle Flat** (left track will be our exit on return). Earthern track topped with some rock follows a sustained descent through tree fern toward the **Styx River**.

Several tracks radiate from **Loop Road** to the waterway itself: **Sleepy Fire Road** is the first, dropping suddenly via a rugged and little used track to a rough and deep fording of the **Styx** with no parking to speak off – this one is best avoided. **Wattle Flat Picnic Area** branches off **Loop Road** two kilometres later, to a wide river crossing with bathing possibilities. Toilet, table and fireplaces are located near the shade of two mature maple trees. **Wattle Flat Camp** is found one kilometre further down **Loop Road** with a grassy clearing and river side camps extending for a few hundred metres.

Return to the first **Loop Road** junction and turn right (south) to continue along **Cunnawarra Road**. Avoid any side tracks as you penetrate tall ribbon gum forest

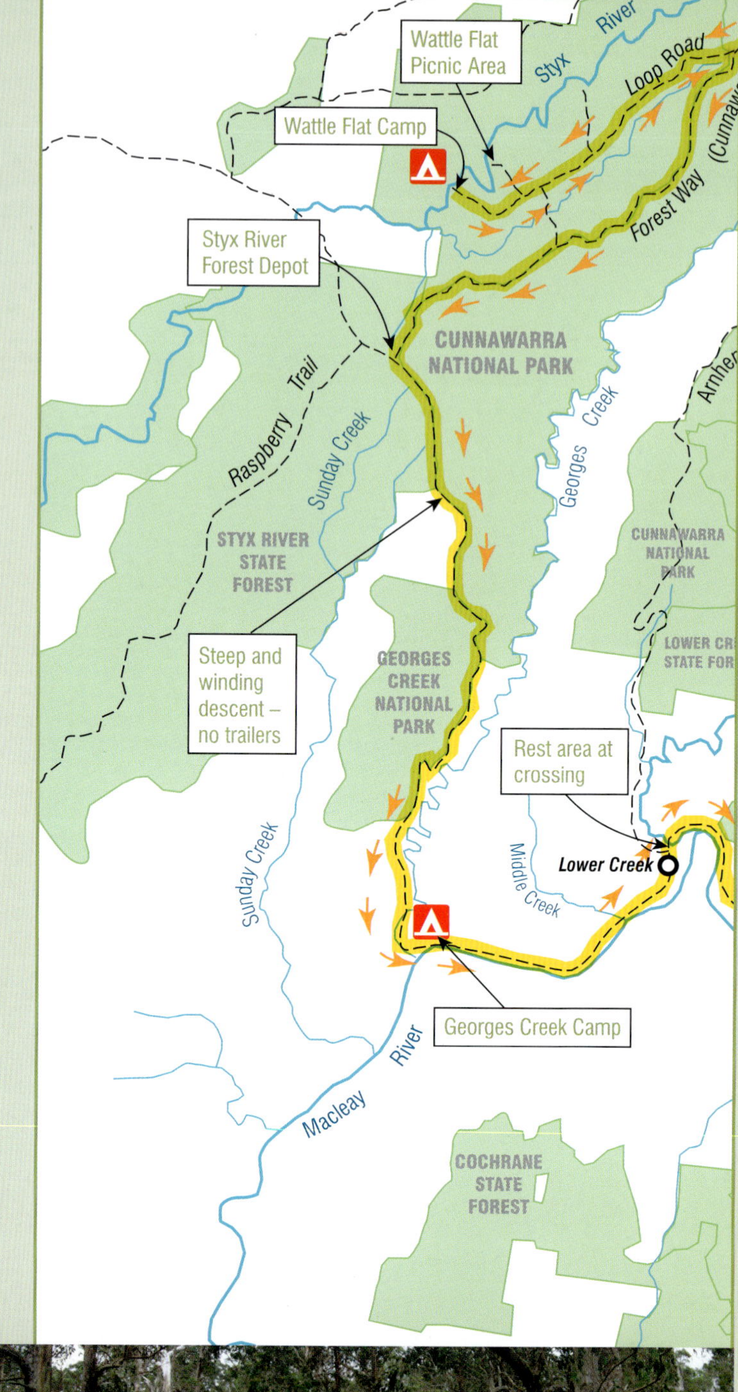

Above:
Lower Ebor Falls

with coachwood filling in the wetter gullies.

You will reach a tee about 7.6 kilometres from the **Loop Road** junction, where you swing left to reach another tee 5.6 kilometres after that. Turn left at the tee (right option leads to the old weatherboard cottages of the **Styx River forest depot**, and the beginnings of **Raspberry Trail** – permission and keys needed) to follow the boundary of **Cunnawarra NP**.

This is the beginning of a steep and winding descent to the **Macleay River**. Towing is not permitted, although logging trucks use this road, so travel with extra caution. Use the gears rather than rely on brakes to hold you back, and take it slowly on the narrow gravel switchbacks.

You will parallel **Georges Creek** and its nature reserve about seven kilometres into the journey, as broken views of the **Macleay Valley** open up. Look out for rockfalls on the numerous cuttings and

Below:
Cathedral Rock NP

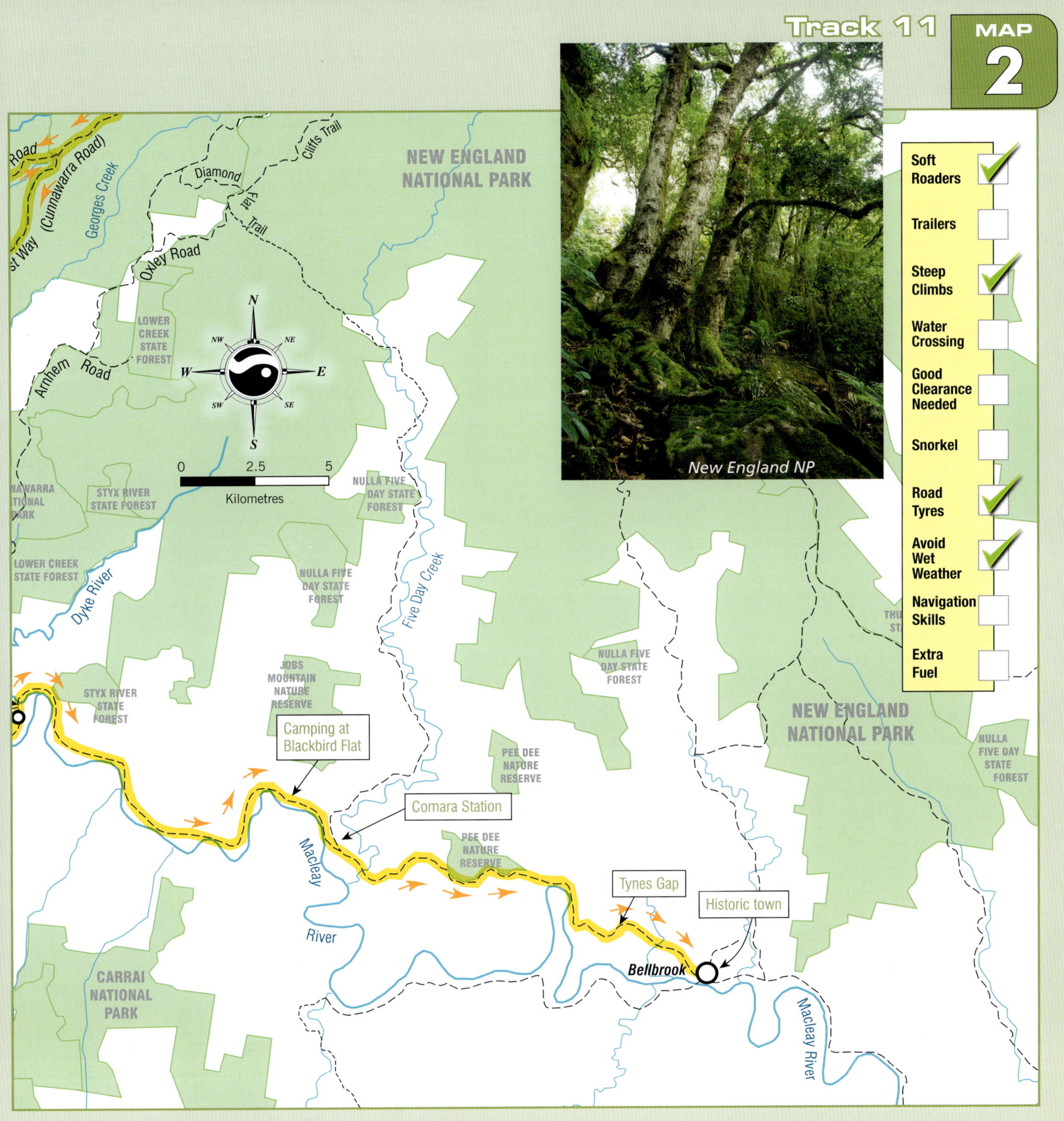

New England NP

listen for bellbirds as you reach **Little Georges Creek**.

Gibbs Gully offers access into the nature reserve as even narrower road flags a single lane bridge over **Georges Creek** with its nearby farm house. You will reach a camping area with toilet on the **Macleay River – Georges Creek** confluence where cattle graze near an otherwise pleasant piece of water.

Follow the **Macleay** downstream over **Middle Creek** then **Lower Creek**, where stockyards and farming infrastructure flag increasing rural activity. You will reach **Blackbird Flat** about 25 kilometres east of the **Georges Creek Camp**, and find toilet and shelter shed on the broadening river.

The river road breaks away from the **Macleay** at **Comara Station** to skirt **Pee Dee NR** and a scenic horse shoe bend in the river. Sealed road paves the way through **Tynes Gap** to reach **Bellbrook** shortly after.

This National Trust classified town marks the conclusion to this tour, but visitors can undertake a walking tour of its notable buildings, or get a meal from the original Cobb and Co pub. Formal accommodation can be arranged in town, and the general store caters for most basic needs.

TRACK 12 Crowdy Bay

LOWER NORTH

It was sand mining in the 1960s that first gave prominence to ***Crowdy Bay****. Local silicates and titanium oxides were in strong demand, before national park status in 1972 returned the coast to fishers and a few naturalists. These days 4WDers enjoy beach access, with good surfing and a variety of camping possibilities.*

This easy short trek follows the coastline from ***Kew*** *to* ***Crowdy Head****, with the opportunity to drive on the beach (permits required), or follow some routine unsealed roads instead. Several bush walks and a couple of unrivalled lookouts will extend your time at* ***Crowdy Bay****, or you can simply use the tour as a scenic alternative run south, instead of the busy* ***Pacific Highway****.*

You will exit the **Pacific Highway** at the small town of **Kew**, where you will need to obtain a permit from the Visitors Centre if you wish to undertake beach driving along **Dunbogan Beach**. Take the sign posted **"Laurieton"** road east toward **Queens Lake**, then follow bitumen for 5.5 kilometres to the **North Brother Mountain Lookout**. Turn right for a winding run through **Dooragan NP** to a summit lookout on **North Brother**.

The viewpoint encompasses **Watson Taylors Lake**, the **Crowdy Bay** beaches and the **Camden Haven River** system, with the twin towns of **Dunbogan** and **North Haven** standing guard over the heads. Hang glider pilots launch themselves from a summit ramp to land on one of the nearby beaches.

Return to the main road and turn right to follow a residential corridor through **West Haven**. Keep right at the **North Haven** turn off, and turn left over a bridge 1.7 kilometres later. Keep right at the **Camden Head** junction just over the river (although **Kylies Beach** travel hopefuls will need to obtain a permit from the marina at **Dunbogan**).

(**Camden Head**, together with **Dunbogan** and **North Haven** are situated very close geographically and are collectively known as **Camden Haven**. The region is a fishing hotspot, with oysters, shellfish and flathead commercially harvested. Bream are also a prized catch, and amateur anglers share in the bounty.)

A caravan park at **Dunbogan Beach** marks the entrance into **Crowdy Bay NP** and the beginning of corrugated gravel. **Diamond Head Road** limits vehicles to 60 kph as you pass three picnic areas on the left. **Blackbutt**, **Cheesetree**, and **Geebung** are all 200 metres or so off the main road, with a carpark, and short walking track to the beach. Toilets are available at all stops, but camping is not permitted.

You will reach the turn off to **Diamond Head** 7.6 kilometres into the national park, where you swing left to a camping area and beach access. This campground is very popular, and you may need to book ahead for the peak season.

A two kilometre walk to **Mermaid Lookout** begins at the campground with a longer 4.8 kilometre loop walk being a better option, as it takes in a variety of coastal views. Silica crystals glisten in the sun, giving rise to the name **Diamond Head**, while low growing heath frames the shoreline coves and the **Brothers** triple peaks.

Return to the main road and turn left to **Indian Head**, arriving at its camping area two kilometres later. **Indian Head** is quieter than **Diamond Head** – due in no small part to a lack of beach access by vehicle, however a walking track to the rocky headland offers some compensation. Fortunately the camp still provides basic facilities together with cold showers in a sheltered setting. The main loop walk can also be undertaken from here.

Return to **Diamond Head Road** and turn left at a tee intersection two kilometres later. Travel over corrugated road through flooded paperbark forest to another junction one kilometre beyond that. Turn left to **Kylies Beach Camping Area** with beach access available for vehicles (Taree City Council permit required).

Kylies Beach offers basic facilities and is also more popular than **Indian Head**; probably because of ready beach access for vehicles and people. Kylie Tennant (after whom this beach was named) lived in a swamp mahogany hut here while authoring her book "The Man on the Headland". You can follow a 300 metre walk from the camp through black wattle to reach her rustic shack.

The beach drive runs from rocky headland just north of **Kylies Beach** access to **Crowdy Head** in the south. Beach driving restrictions include a 40 kph limit on the sand, reducing to 15 kph in proximity to pedestrians, and no access to the south corner at **Crowdy Head** from 8.00am to 6.00pm during school holidays (June/July break excluded).

If the tide is not in your favour (beach travel is best within two hours either side of low tide) you can follow **Kylies Beach** south on an inland track with walk in beach access at **Mermaid** and **Figtree**. The six kilometre access track stops at **Figtree Parking Area**, and you must return to **Kylies Beach Camp**.

Retrace your steps to **Diamond Head Road** and turn left (south) past an avenue of taller trees. You will pass pockets of private land backed by **Johns River SF** with some beautiful mahogany gums to admire.

Continue past **Stuarts Road** on the right to turn left 2.5 kilometres later onto **Crowdy Bay Road**. Drive over a creek back into national park for more paperbark wetlands and the turn off to **Abbey Creek Picnic Area**. Table and seats mark a beach access walk here, but there is no vehicle entry over the sand dunes.

Return to **Crowdy Bay Road** to pass **Sand**

Track Snapshot

TOUR ROUTE:
Kew to Crowdy Head via Kylies Beach.

DURATION AND DISTANCE:
At 55 kilometres, this easy beach run can be done in a day, but surfers and fishers will definitely want more.

TRACK DETAILS:
Pleasant driving with beach access possible to drivers who feel confident.

WHEN TO GO:
All year round.

CAMPING:
Camping opportunities at Dunbogan Beach, Diamond Head, Indian Head, Kylies Beach and Crowdy Head.

FUEL AND SUPPLIES:
Dunbogan and Crowdy Head

MAPS:
Natmap 1:100K Camden Haven

OTHER INFORMATION:
Beach driving requires a Council permit and includes some restrictions. Try to time your drive to within two hours on either side of low tide.

Below: *Indian Head*

Track on the right 2.7 kilometres later (MVO, but good walking access into the 8000 hectares of **Crowdy Bay** heathland, where nectar feeding birds congregate for a feast in autumn).

Turn left 100 metres later to a lovely camping area with basic facilities and gas BBQ provided. There is no vehicular access to the beach from here either, but visitors can follow a 300 metre walk through littoral rainforest to a beach sheltered from the south easterly weather.

Return to **Crowdy Bay Road** and turn left to reach a tee intersection on the **Harrington – Crowdy Head** bitumen road. Turn left to reach **Crowdy Head**, with houses and beach shacks lining the main road. A breakwater shelters jetty moorings and adjacent boat ramp, with most services available.

TRACK 13 COOPERNOOK

LOWER NORTH

Vincents Lookout

Track Snapshot

TOUR ROUTE:
Coopernook to Moreland via Coorabakh NP.

DURATION AND DISTANCE:
This 70 kilometre trek can be done comfortably in a day, while still allowing for plenty of stops.

TRACK DETAILS:
Easy travel for all vehicles and trailers.

WHEN TO GO:
All year round, avoiding sustained wet weather.

CAMPING:
Coopernook Forest Park.

FUEL AND SUPPLIES:
Coopernook.

MAPS:
Natmap 1:100K Camden Haven

OTHER INFORMATION:
A great day trip offering views, swimming hole and bushland variety.

The ***Manning River*** *and its floodplain make for great viewing from the* ***Lansdowne Escarpment*** *within* ***Coopernook SF****. A trio of basalt extrusions dominate the northern limits of the volcanic escarpment, where national park has now captured a number of scenic attractions. Sub tropical rainforest and pockets of drier woodland are supplemented with picturesque creeks and waterfalls.*

Coorabakh NP *was established in 1999 to protect these features, while neighbouring* ***Coopernook SF*** *encompasses logging country, with some stands of blackbutt now into their second century of regrowth. This leisurely tour follows old forestry roads into the hills, before looping back to the* ***Pacific Highway****.*

We begin our run at **Coopernook**, a small township north of **Taree**, just beyond the **Lansdowne River bridge**. Take the highway exit to the town's north west, to follow **Bangalow Road** and its gravel beginnings.

Follow the signposted **"Picnic Area"** access into **Coopernook SF** and cross the rail timber bridge to reach a tee intersection 2.5 kilometres from **Coopernook**. Turn left onto signposted **"Coopernook Forest Way"** and continue straight through the next intersection 1.5 kilometres later (signposted **"Vincent Lookout"**).

An old homestead and banana plantation mark some taller timber and the **Langley Vale Road** intersection some 7.8 kilometres from **Coopernook** – where we will keep straight ahead on the signposted **"Coopernook Forest Way"**. (Good camping at **Coopernook Forest Park** can be found a few kilometres away on the right, while the hamlet of **Langley Vale** on the left, saw horse drawn trams pulling tallowood and iron bark logs to its mill in the 1870s.)

Narrow road passes the recently harvested areas on **Pipeclay Creek Road** (keep straight) to palm trees on the climb into **Lansdowne SF**. Avoid side tracks until you reach the **Vincents Lookout** turn off, some 4.8 kilometres beyond **Langley Vale Road**.

Turn left here for a short run to a trig point and radio tower. An expansive view over the **Lansdowne Valley** extends to the **Manning River** floodplain and **South Pacific Ocean**. Return to the main forest drive and turn left for a steepish pinch into **Coorabakh NP** and a tee intersection.

Swing left here (signposted **"Newbys Cave"**) for a short descent through coachwood and tallowood forest to **Newbys Cave Walking Track**. Park just prior to the creek for a 10 minute walk to a rock overhang - named after local pioneering trader, John Newby. While the caves are of some interest, it is the lovely tannin stained waters of **Newbys Creek**, and its rainforest flora, that makes this a worthwhile stop.

Continue the drive beyond **Newbys Cave** for 2.7 kilometres to reach **Newbys Lookout** carpark and a short boardwalk. Sweeping views to the west take in the forest canopy foreground and a patchwork of rural properties, framed by receding mountain ranges.

Two kilometres beyond the lookout you will reach a junction back on Coopernook Forest Way where you veer left to the signposted **"Big Nellie Picnic Area"** (right option leads to **Hannam Vale**). You will descend through macrozamia and bangalow palms, with glimpses of **Little Nellie**, to a sharp right turn onto **Starrs Creek Road**.

The descent continues under rainforest canopy to a timber bridge spanning **Starrs Creek**. A carpark here allows visitors to stretch their legs on a short rain forest boardwalk, with picnic facilities on the walk. Stinging trees and yellow carabeen are festooned by a maze of vines in this quiet pocket of national park.

Vehicles follow **Starrs Creek** to the **Big Nellie Picnic Area** turn off, and a 200 metre side trip. A parking area and shelter shed (no fires permitted) mark the track's end under the shadow of **Big Nellie**. Experienced climbers can rock hop to the 542 metre summit of the volcanic plug, as no formal path is blazed. Less capable visitors will appreciate the monolith from its adjacent viewing platform, then return to the main forestry road.

Continue for another 2.8 kilometres to arrive at a parking area near **Flat Rock Lookout**. A boardwalk leads to a prominent viewpoint with range country

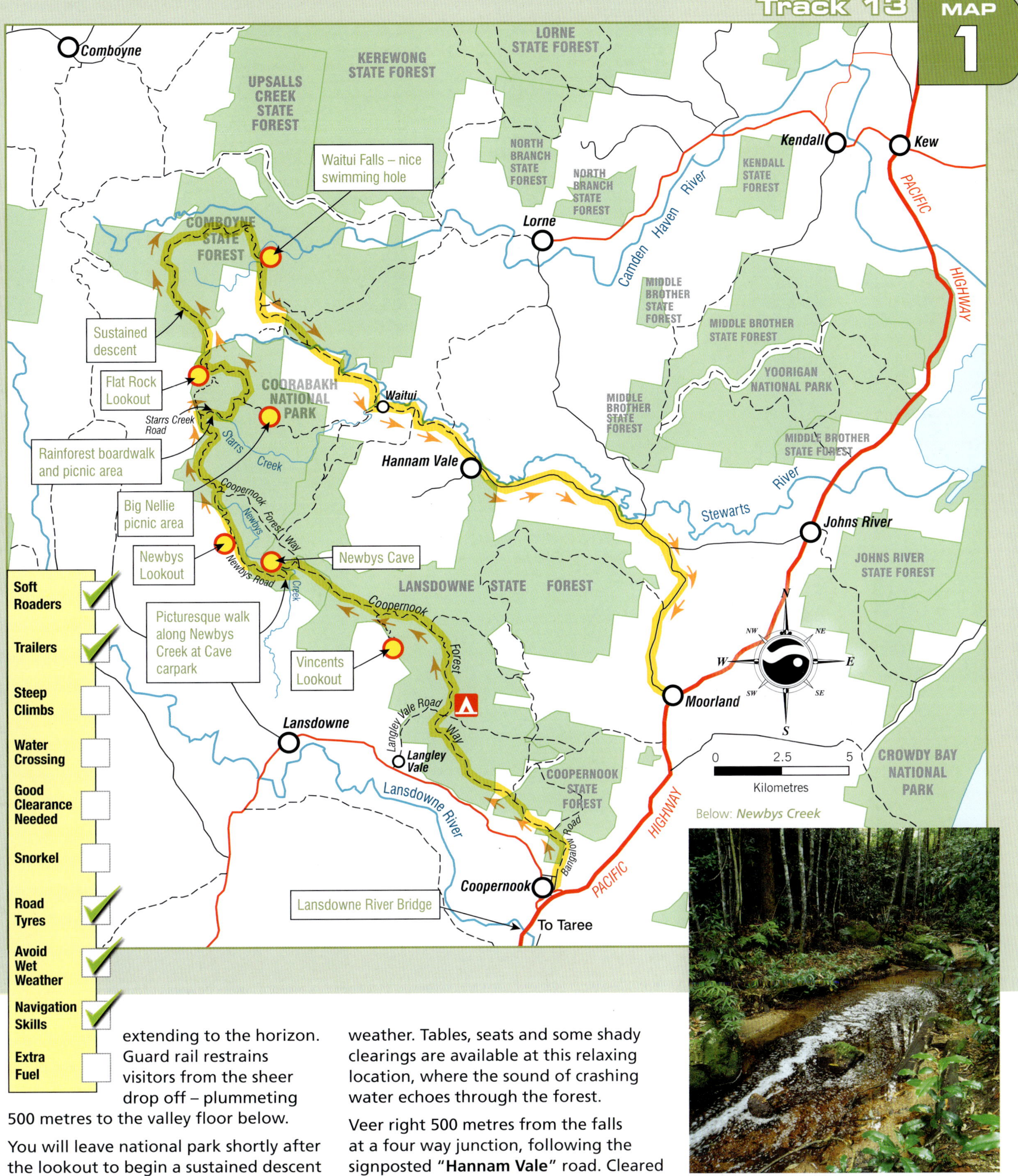

Below: *Newbys Creek*

extending to the horizon. Guard rail restrains visitors from the sheer drop off – plummeting 500 metres to the valley floor below.

You will leave national park shortly after the lookout to begin a sustained descent through tree fern cuttings. Pass **Slater Road** on the left, then broken views over the **Camden Haven Valley**, to reach **Waitui Falls** some 8.8 kilometres beyond **Flat Rock Lookout**.

It is a short walk to the small falls, but the swimming hole at its base is welcome (and popular) in warmer weather. Tables, seats and some shady clearings are available at this relaxing location, where the sound of crashing water echoes through the forest.

Veer right 500 metres from the falls at a four way junction, following the signposted "**Hannam Vale**" road. Cleared grazing land and lilly fringed dams mark our exit from the forest, as you reach a tee intersection 3.3 kilometres from the falls. Turn left on **Waitui Road** (**Timber Ridge Road** on the right) to begin a run past cottages and hobby farms.

A timber bridge spans the **John River** as dairy farms and a strip of older houses back onto **Middle Brother SF** and its centrepiece hill. Sealed road heralds the hamlet of **Hannam Vale**, where you swing right just prior to the prominent peak of **South Brother**. **Moorland** marks this tour's end on the **Pacific Highway**, only eight kilometres from where you began.

TRACK 14

Bulga Plateau

LOWER NORTH

Track Snapshot

TOUR ROUTE:
Wingham and return via Ellenborough Falls and Dingo Tops.

DURATION AND DISTANCE:
You will probably take two days to drive the 130 kilometres and see what is on offer, although those staying at Wingham could do it in a day.

TRACK DETAILS:
Routine 4WDing on gravel and unsurfaced tracks, but suitable for soft roaders and trailers.

WHEN TO GO:
Avoid wet weather, bearing in mind that the falls will be pumping following a dump of local rain.

CAMPING:
The Dingo tops area offers basic facilities, but it is a "walk in" grassed area.

FUEL AND SUPPLIES:
Arrange all supplies at Wingham prior to leaving.

MAPS:
Natmap 1:100K Wingham

OTHER INFORMATION:
Numerous side trips offer potential for further exploration within this area.

Top of Ellenborough Falls

***Tapin Tops** and the **Bulga Plateau** are quiet retreats from the bustling coastal strip of this state's lower north. Pockets of dense rainforest can be found within the former logging country, and the southern hemisphere's second highest waterfall spills over to eventually meet the **Hastings River**.*

Secluded camping can be found within the region, with bushwalking opportunities and a couple of commanding viewpoints. Amateur naturalists will have a ball identifying birds and plants within the various ecosystems, and there are crystal clear waterways trickling across the plateau.

Wingham, just west of **Taree** is our start and finish point, and a good place to top up on supplies. The **Manning River** skirts this historic town, where interested visitors will find a 10 hectare block of rainforest sandwiched between its waters and the shopping strip. Subtropical flowers colour the understorey, and mature moreton bay figs are home to migratory flying foxes.

Leave town via the signposted **"Elands"** road taking **Tourist Drive #8** past farms with horses and deer. Keep right at **Wherrol Flat Road** 7.5 kilometres later (we will return via this road) and proceed into the community of **Marlee**.

Cross the clunking timber bridge over **Dingo Creek** with patchy views over Red Tail vineyards to reach the character general store at Marlee. Another crossing of **Dingo Creek** and a procession of innovative letter boxes (varying from the ubiquitous milk can to beer kegs, and even a complete compressor) provide interest on this bitumen run.

A small school and scattered houses mark the locality of **Bobin** and the beginning of gravel about 28 kilometres from Wingham. Winding road begins in earnest now, with substantial cuttings held together by steel mesh. Falling rock is still a concern however, together with oncoming log trucks, so drive accordingly.

You will reach a tee intersection at the "alternative" community of **Elands** where you turn left toward signposted **"Ellenborough Falls"**. Follow the signs for a few kilometres to the parking area and adjoining cafe.

Ellenborough Falls is a magnificent sight from the upper viewing platform, with a single drop of almost 200 metres crashing to the rocky ravine below. A demanding walk follows a formed stairway to a lower viewpoint, but less energetic travellers may prefer the short walks to **Tallowood Grove** or **The Knoll Track** – both invade dimly lit rainforest with delicate mosses and ferns adorning the walkway.

Leave the falls, turning right (north) at the tee, signposted **"Tapin Tops NP"**. Keep straight on **Glen Warrin Road** to pass **Beech Road** on the left, and cross

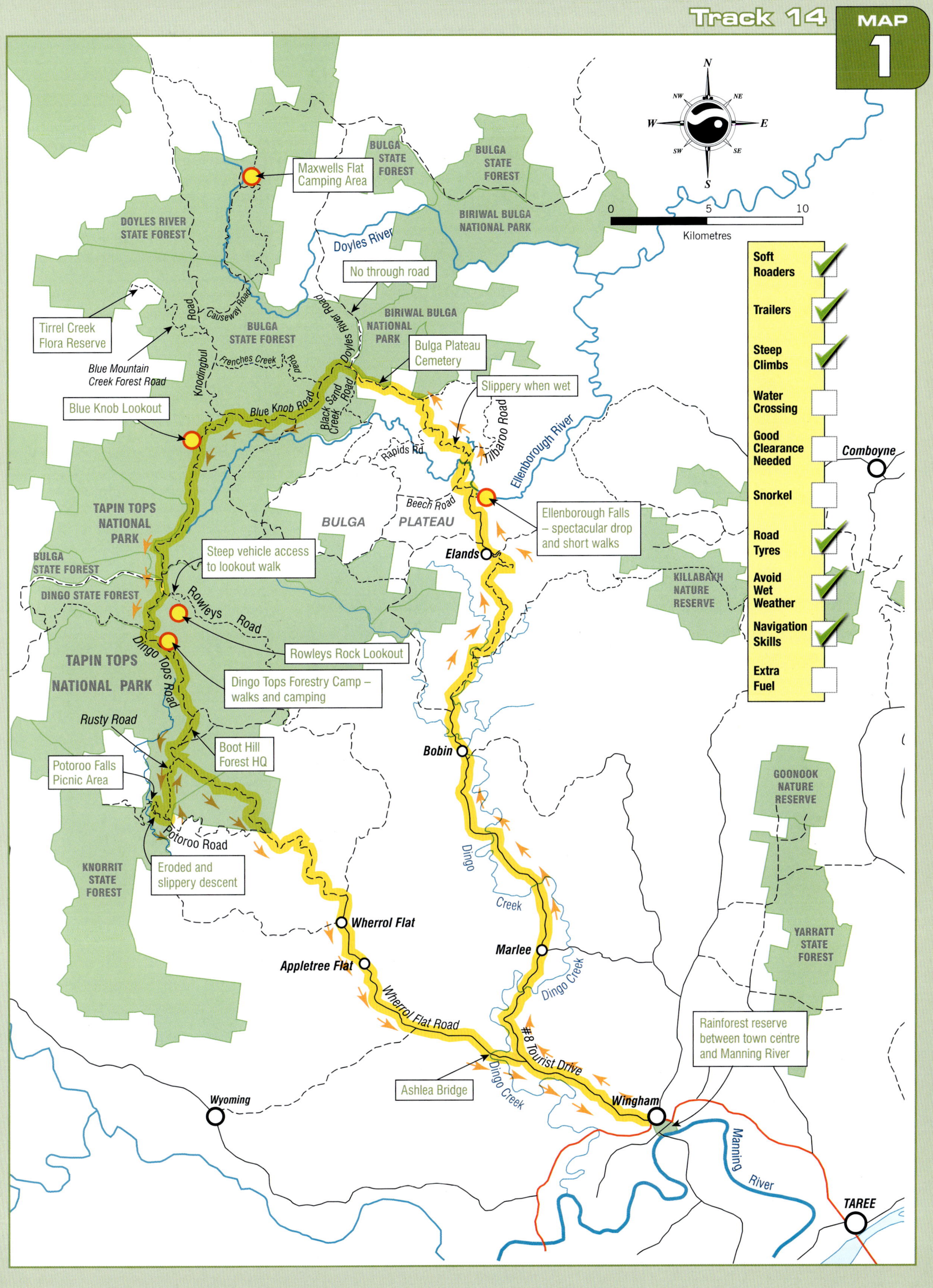
Maxwells Flat Camping Area
BULGA STATE FOREST
BULGA STATE FOREST
BIRIWAL BULGA NATIONAL PARK
DOYLES RIVER STATE FOREST
Doyles River
No through road
Tirrel Creek Flora Reserve
Blue Mountain Creek Forest Road
Causeway Road
Road
BULGA STATE FOREST
Doyles River Road
BIRIWAL BULGA NATIONAL PARK
Bulga Plateau Cemetery
Knodingbul
Frenches Creek Road
Black Sand Creek Road
Blue Knob Road
Blue Knob Lookout
Slippery when wet
Tibaroo Road
Ellenborough River
Rapids Rd
Beech Road
Ellenborough Falls – spectacular drop and short walks
BULGA PLATEAU
TAPIN TOPS NATIONAL PARK
BULGA STATE FOREST
DINGO STATE FOREST
Steep vehicle access to lookout walk
Rowleys Road
Elands
KILLABAKH NATURE RESERVE
Rowleys Rock Lookout
TAPIN TOPS NATIONAL PARK
Dingo Tops Road
Dingo Tops Forestry Camp – walks and camping
Rusty Road
Boot Hill Forest HQ
Potoroo Falls Picnic Area
Potoroo Road
Eroded and slippery descent
KNORRIT STATE FOREST
Bobin
Dingo Creek
Wherrol Flat
Appletree Flat
Marlee
Dingo Creek
Wherrol Flat Road
#8 Tourist Drive
Ashlea Bridge
Dingo Creek
Wingham
Wyoming
Rainforest reserve between town centre and Manning River
Manning River
TAREE
Comboyne
GOONOOK NATURE RESERVE
YARRATT STATE FOREST
N
NE
E
SE
S
SW
W
NW
0
5
10
Kilometres
Soft Roaders
Trailers
Steep Climbs
Water Crossing
Good Clearance Needed
Snorkel
Road Tyres
Avoid Wet Weather
Navigation Skills
Extra Fuel

Dingo Tops steam engine

the **Ellenborough River**. Keep left at **Tilbaroo Road** some 2.9 kilometres from the falls and follow a clay topped road (slippery when wet) past farm stay opportunities to a tee 3.1 kilometres later.

Turn right away from **Rapids Road** following the signposted **"Tapin Tops"** to **Biriwal – Bulga NP** on the right. Dense forest is flanked by dairying country on the left and the **Bulga Plateau Cemetery** on the right.

Continue past **Black Sand Creek Road** as you enter **Bulga SF** with **Doyles River Road** on the right (no through road). Keep straight on **Blue Knob Road**, avoiding MVO tracks to either side (although **Frenches Creek Road** offers 4WDing across the upper reaches of **Doyles River** to exit on **Knodingbul Road**). You will reach a tee intersection about 19 kilometres from **Ellenborough Falls**, where you turn left to signposted **"Tapin Tops"**.

(**Knodingbul Road** on the right heads north to the **Oxley Highway** through

Potoroo Falls area

Potoroo Falls area

Bulga Forest view

Doyles River SF. There is a turn off to the left six kilometres in, that leads to **Tirril Creek Flora Reserve** via **Blue Mountain Creek Forest Road**. This bubbling waterway irrigates a sheltered pocket of delicate rainforest, adjacent to the picnic area. **Maxwells Flat Camping Area** is reached further north along **Knodingbul Road**, on the **Causeway Road** turn off. Self contained campers will find a shady grassed river flat on the banks of the **Doyle River**.)

Head south on a climb past fern encrusted cuttings to the **Blue Knob Lookout** turn off 1.5 kilometres later. Swing right here to reach an old fire tower just over one kilometre later. Table and seats mark a rather exposed picnic area, but on a clear day the 1014 metre vantage point offers 360 degree views.

Return to **Knodingbul Road** and turn south into **Tapin Tops NP**. Avoid side tracks; although **Rowleys Road** may interest energetic visitors – steep vehicle access leads to a parking bay and even steeper walking access to **Rowleys Rock Lookout**, for more uninterrupted views.

You will enter the **Dingo Tops** area 2.5 kilometres from **Rowleys Road**, where a forestry camp was once active. Relics from the pioneering days including a steam traction engine and a horse drawn grader are located under the shade of a 1960s Californian redwood grove.

Two short walks begin at the rest area, meandering through rainforest to stands of old growth eucalyptus. Basic facilities are provided at the camping area, although there is no water, and boundary bollards restrict vehicle based campers.

Head south via **Dingo Tops Road** past the **Boot Hill Forest HQ** to **Rusty Road**, eight kilometres from the camping area. Turn hard right, signposted "**Potoroo Falls Picnic Area**", and wind back into **Tapin Tops NP** on a lesser used road. Turn right 3.3 kilometres later onto **Potoroo Road** for an eroded and slippery descent through macrozamia.

The final drop off arrives at a small carpark with basic facilities adjacent to the picnic area. A 700 metre walk upstream initially follows a defined path, before deteriorating to a slippery scramble and no chance of staying dry.

Retrace your steps to **Dingo Tops Road** and turn right for a sustained descent off the plateau. Broken views and a couple of creek crossings precede some character cottages and a serpentine run into **Wherrol Flat**.

Turn right onto sealed road signposted "**Wingham**" to cross **Dingo Creek** on the lofty **Ashlea Bridge**. Follow **Wherrol Flat Road** back to **#8 Tourist Drive**, and the final run into **Wingham**.

Barrington Tops

LOWER NORTH

Track Snapshot

TOUR ROUTE:
Gloucester to Scone via Copeland and Barrington Tops.

DURATION AND DISTANCE:
You could drive the 160 kilometre route in a day, but two would be better, to get a feel for the area.

TRACK DETAILS:
Routine driving across the Tops, with low range and good clearances neeeded if you choose to undertake the Barrington Trail side trip. Trailers OK.

WHEN TO GO:
The warmer months are best; rain and snow can close the route in winter.

CAMPING:
Basic facilities at Polblue (with other bush options across Barrington tops) and river side camps at Barrington, Cobark and Moonan Flat.

FUEL AND SUPPLIES:
Gloucester and Scone; limited supplies at Moonan Flat.

MAPS:
Natmap 1:100K Dungog, Camberwell, Upper Manning, Ellerston

OTHER INFORMATION:
Mountain bikers will appreciate the dedicated trails across the Tops, while bushwalkers and fisherfolk will find a range of possibilities to keep them happy.

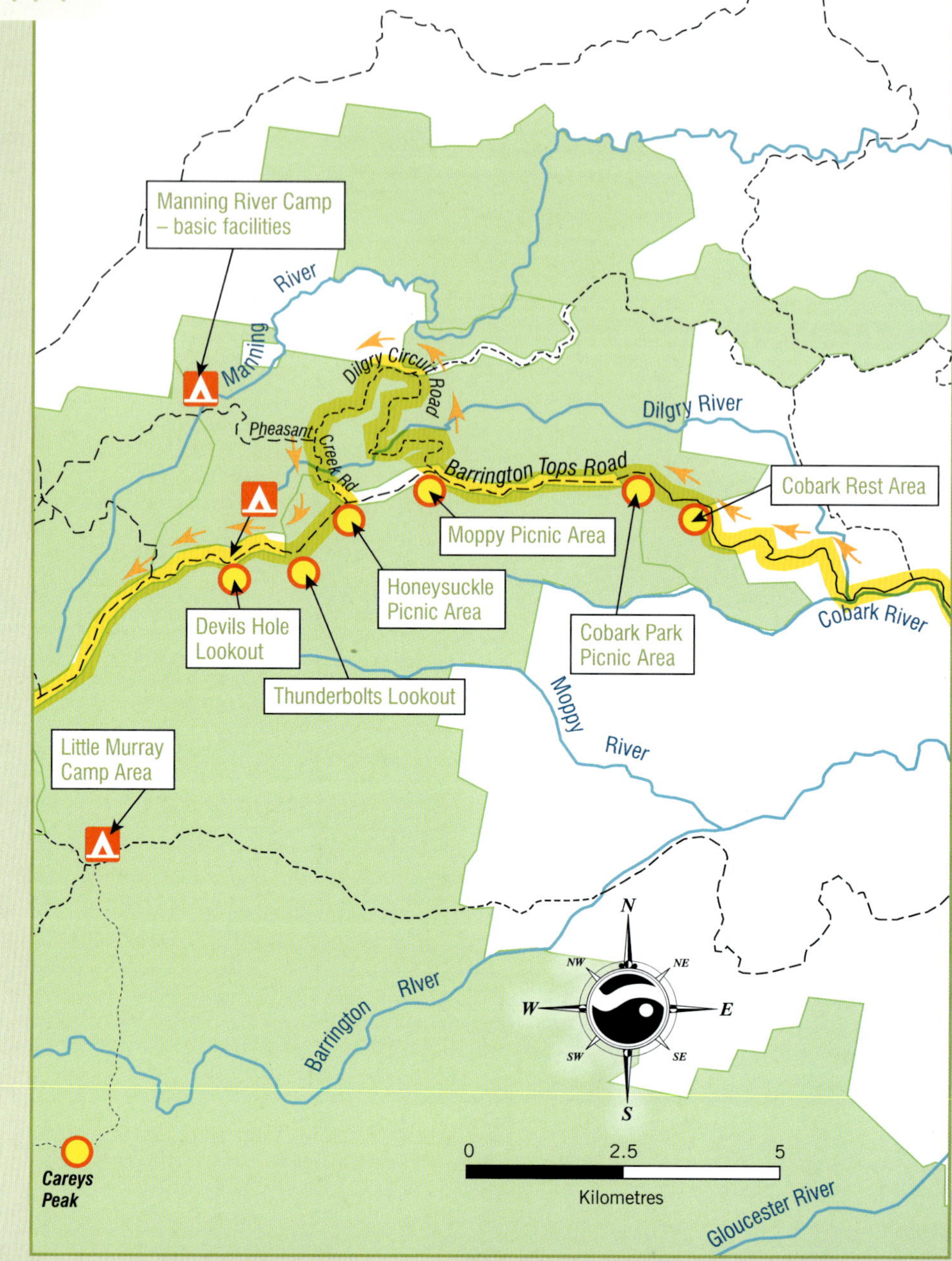

*This trek from **Gloucester** to **Scone** splits **Barrington Tops NP** from frontier cattle country and the northern state forest area. The drive into legendary bushranger territory climbs through heavily forested areas, to cross the almost mile high rocky plateau, before descending via a series of outlooks that take in some verdant pasture resembling that of the English countryside.*

Waterways are never far from view, and peat swamps release snow melt from the higher plains long into summer. Rain and snowfall are regular occurrences on the plateau even over the warmer months, making travel here an uncertain prospect for conventional vehicles. The main road together with other side tracks are occasionally closed to 4WDs following a serious weather event, but when open, offer excellent touring across The Tops.

We begin at **Gloucester** – a town established in 1899 on earlier station land at the foot of **Bucketts Range**. Head north east on **Park Street** to follow **Thunderbolts Way** toward signposted "**Scone**". (Captain Thunderbolt was a bushranger of the

Copeland Tops Forest

Left: *Dilgri Cascades area*

district during the 1860s. A string of thefts and hold ups committed over a 20 year period seem to be at odds with his reputation as a gentleman, and although he met his death by police gunshot, the outlaw never actually killed anybody.)

Cross the **Gloucester River** to follow bitumen through grassland to the locality of Barrington. A clutch of houses precede the **Barrington River** crossing with the **Barrington Reserve** and **Poleys Place** located on the right. (Camping with basic facilities is available at the riverside reserve – phone the **Barrington Store** on 02 6558 4249 for details. **Poleys Place** also offers camping possibilities and regular country music festivals – *www.poleysplace.com*).

Keep left at **Thunderbolts Way** some 7.7 kilometres from **Gloucester**, taking the **Scone Road** past an historic cemetery and into the **Copeland Reserve**. Creekside camping is permitted on the grassy banks here, with basic facilities provided.

Continue over **Copeland Creek** into the community of **Copeland**, where bellbirds ring out through the forest. Turn left toward signposted "**Copeland Tops SCA**" for a short run into an abandoned gold mining area. Houses and original cottages crowd the terraced valley, before you reach a parking area, and a couple of walking tracks.

A substantial mine operated here in the 1880s with relics strewn throughout the bush. Walkers can follow some or all of the tracks, taking extra care with children as some pits remain open. Unlike other gold towns of the day, **Copeland** lived on, retaining some of its pioneering character.

Return to the main road turning left to climb over the **Copeland Valley** and further into **State Conservation Area**. Grass trees and increasing jungle give way to taller forest, where grey box has been harvested for bridge building and other projects requiring a durable timber.

A sustained climb passes MVO tracks to either side with broken views over farmland. You will exit the state conservation area, and descend to the

BARRINGTON TOPS

Cobark River some 11.4 kilometres from **Copeland**. Cross a bridge over the rocky waterway, with pine trees flanking the eroded banks.

Rolling green hills and sweeping views open up on the winding run to a tee intersection, where you swing right to signposted **"Scone"**. Cross the **Cobark** again and follow the river past **Mud Hut Road** to a series of camping flats. (Private camping; phone 02 6558 5524 for details.)

Horseyards and a character cottage herald the drive into **Barrington Tops SF** with rock topping the unsealed road. Limited road maintenance is undertaken beyond the council limits, as tree ferns and lichen festooned trees usher the journey into **Cobark Rest Area** (table, seats, fireplace).

You will enter **Barrington Tops NP** about two kilometres later, passing **Cobark Park Picnic Area** and stands of messmate, to **Moppy Picnic Area**, some 26 kilometres from the **Cobark's** first crossing.

Veer right at **Moppy** onto signposted **"Dilgry Circuit Road"** following narrower track to the **Dilgry River** about four kilometres later. A minor track branches left prior to the bridge, to reach a small parking area 50 metres later.

Logging regrowth now nearly 40 years old, shades a lovely horseshoe bend in the river with a series of cascades bubbling past. Fireplaces are provided here making it an exceptional lunch stop or overnight camp for self sufficient travellers.

Soft Roaders	✓
Trailers	✓
Steep Climbs	
Water Crossing	
Good Clearance Needed	
Snorkel	
Road Tyres	✓
Avoid Wet Weather	✓
Navigation Skills	
Extra Fuel	

Above:
Thunderbolts Lookout

Continue beyond **Dilgry River**, keeping left at a junction 3.1 kilometres later. You will reach a signpost pointing to **"The Rock"** 3.5 kilometres beyond that, where a distinctive formation can be seen from the track.

Veer left onto **Pheasant Creek Road** 500 metres later (right turn leads to Antarctic beech forest and **Manning River Camp** with basic facilities) to cross the **Dilgri River** and reach a camping area on the left. Makeshift stone fireplaces are the only facilities here, although easy river access and a broad expanse of river flat will appeal to many people.

You will reach the **Barrington Tops Road** at **Honeysuckle Picnic Area**, about two kilometres beyond the camp. Turn right through a couple of potentially locked gates to climb through slender snow gums and snow grasses to **Barrington Tops NP**.

Thunderbolts Lookout comes into view shortly after, where an easy stroll through snowgum forest finishes at a boulder strewn escarpment. Views extend over a treefern understorey to distant ranges, with wildflowers colouring the walk in summer. **Devils Hole Lookout** offers similar views with a nearby camping area and secluded clearings.

The signposted **"Barrington Trail"** begins five kilometres west of **Devils Hole**, with the current track status prominently displayed. Closure is certain over the winter period (1/6 – 1/10), although wet weather can see it closed at any time of the year.

(If open, 4WDs with reasonable clearance can follow rock topped track over erosion control mounds to pass scenic wetlands and snowgrass meadows. A camp area at **Little Murray** is spread out over a grassy site, with a lengthy walking trail to **Careys Peak** via **Black Swamp**. **Barrington Trail** continues past **Junction Pools** to a picnic area at **Mount Barrington**, with an alternative – but still strenuous – walk to **Careys Peak**. You must return to **Barrington Tops Road** via the same track, as the trail reaches a dead end for vehicles.)

Continue west beyond the **Barrington Trail** turn off to climb the **Mount Royal Range**, and reach **Polblue Picnic Area**. The elevated plateau country here was used by sheep and cattle graziers from

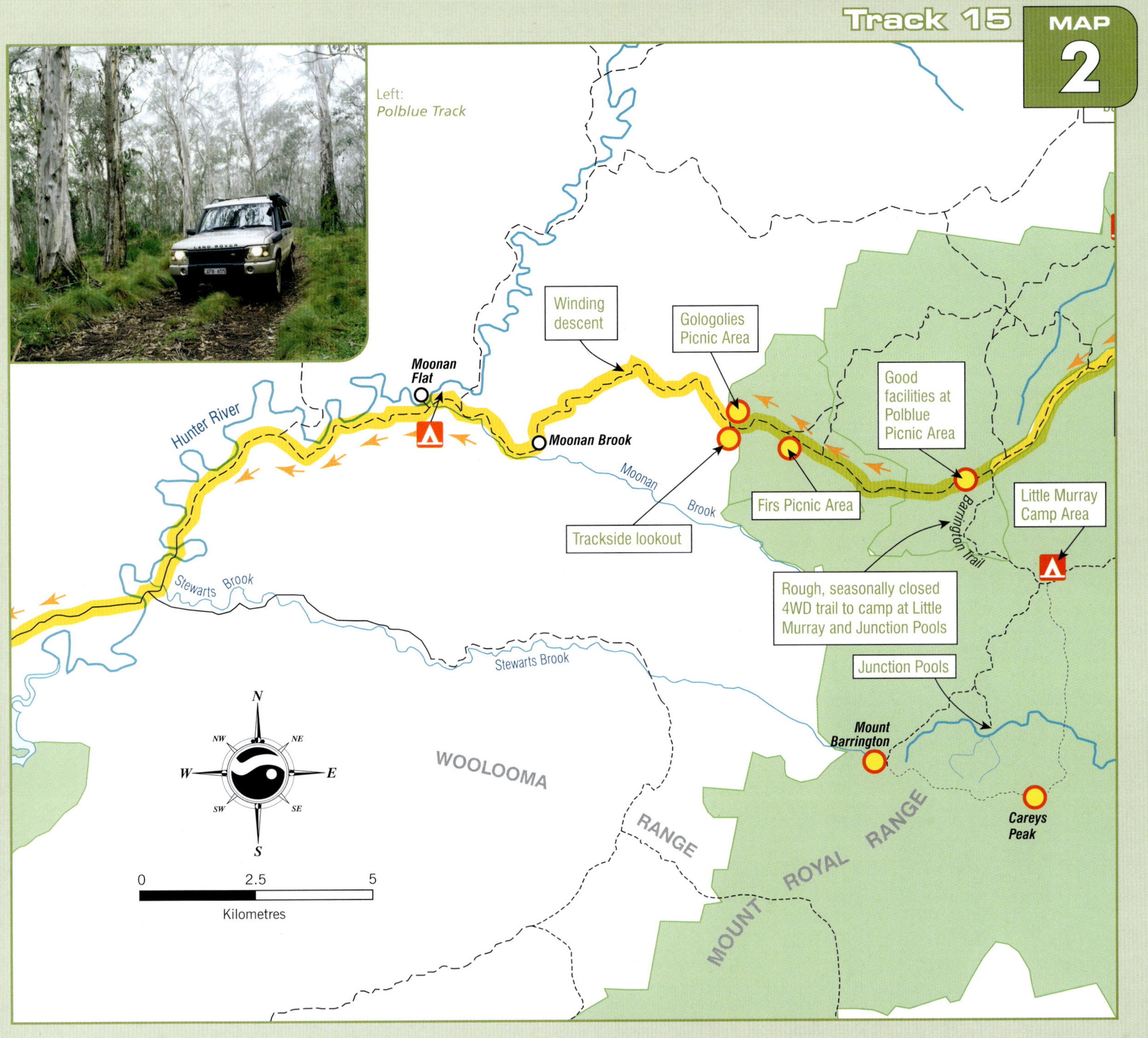

the mid 1800s. Stockyards were built, with **Tomalla Station** sited on the sheep droving route.

These days the highland swamps are home to wallabies and a variety of birdlife. Walkers can follow a one hour hike around **Polblue Swamp** with sections of boardwalk spanning multi coloured grasses and reeds.

Gas BBQ and toilets are located at the picnic area, with basic facilities also provided at the adjacent camping area. A large expanse of grass will appeal to many visitors, while mountain bikers will enjoy the dedicated tracks peeling off the main road.

Continue west from **Polblue** into **Stewarts Brook SF**, and leave NP as Mexican and Western Yellow pines dominate the landscape. You will reach The **Firs Picnic Area** about seven kilometres from **Polblue**, where a short track to the left enters a Douglas Fir plantation. Little light penetrates this eerie location, where the aroma of oregon timber lingers in the air.

Follow the main road past side tracks to reach a gate in the **Dingo Fence**, and the western limit of state forest. **Gologolies Picnic Area** is reached on the right, with camping possibilities, and a nearby lookout taking in one of the best views of **Moonan Brook** and its adjacent hills to be found.

The views continue as you descend on a winding run interspersed with crumpled mountainscape and a patchwork of bush and cleared land. A sequence of gullies and ridges point the way into **Moonan Brook**, where you turn right at a tee, signposted "**Scone**".

Follow the **Moonan Brook Valley** to another tee, swinging left over the bridge and into **Moonan Flat**. Weeping willows and old sheds flag a small hamlet with basic services, and camping at **Belmadar Park**.

Beyond **Moonan Flat** you will cross the **Hunter River** at a pair of bridges, and follow a sealed run into **Gundy**. Cultivated river flats and a proliferation of horse properties flag the major centre of **Scone**, as you reach this tour's end on the **New England Highway**.

Chapter 3

NORTHERN RIVERS

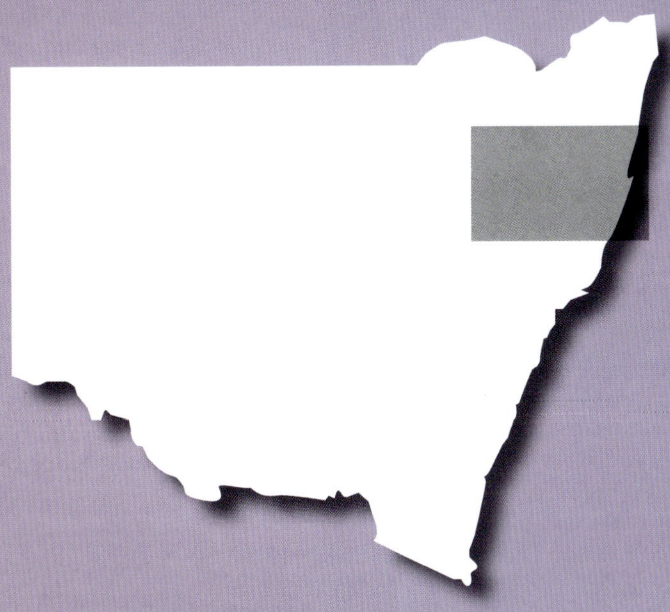

◀ *Red Cliff area*

TRACK 17

Old Grafton Road

LOWER NORTH

Historic rail siding
Deep crossing of river if taking Forbes Street
Deepwater
Old rail trestle bridge
Sugarloaf
Deepwater River
Bow Creek
Bezzants Road option avoids river crossing
Yoongan Creek
NEW ENGLAND HIGHWAY
Dundee
Severn River
0 5 10 Kilometres
to Glen Innes
to Glen Innes
GWYDIR

Above: *Mann River Valley from Tommys Rock*

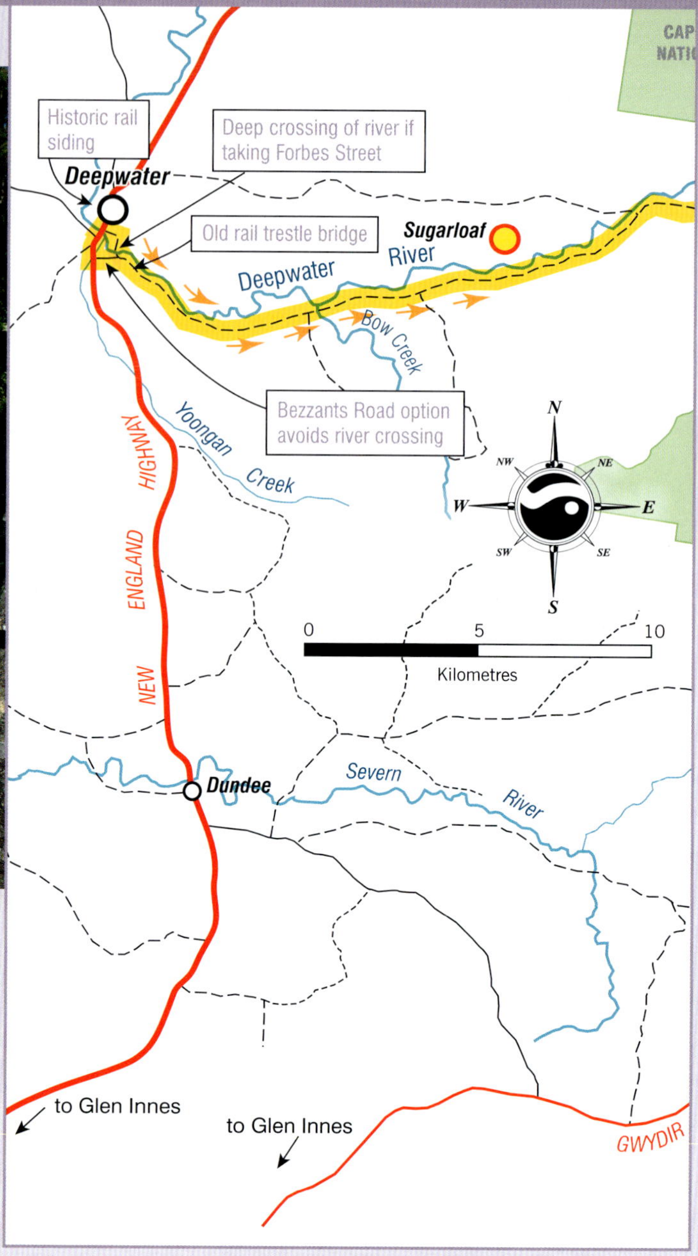

Track Snapshot

TOUR ROUTE:
Deepwater to Dalmorton via Mitchell and the Old Grafton Road.

DURATION AND DISTANCE:
Possible day trip, but more enjoyable over two with 150 kilometres of minor road and tracks.

TRACK DETAILS:
Easy driving for all vehicles over the main route, but low range equipped 4WDs needed for the Tommys Rock Lookout sidetrip. Trailers OK, except for Tommys Rock option.

WHEN TO GO:
Summer is a popular time to visit the Mann River, but this tour can be undertaken at any time in dry weather.

CAMPING:
There is good camping on the Mann River at the old gold mining centres of Mitchell and Dalmorton. Basic facilities are provided.

FUEL AND SUPPLIES:
Stock up on fuel and supplies at Glen Innes or Tenterfield (depending on your direction of travel into Deepwater) and note there are no supplies at Dalmorton.

MAPS:
Natmap 1:100K Glen Innes, Newton Boyd

OTHER INFORMATION:
Dalmorton at this tour's end offers a number of possibilities for further travel. Arrive with sufficient food and fuel for the exit journey.

*While the **New England** tablelands were establishing a reputation as the grazing lands of choice, the discovery of gold was attracting a new breed of settler. The **Mann** and **Boyd** rivers were especially productive, with a substantial reef deposit at **Dalmorton** supporting hundreds of miners in the early 1870s.*

*This easy tour traces **Deepwater River** to the ghost township of **Mitchell**, then picks up the **Old Grafton Road** to **Dalmorton**. Great scenery, good fishing and waterfront camping are features of this trek as you follow sections of an 1840s bullock dray track.*

Begin the tour in **Deepwater** some 40 kilometres north of **Glen Innes** on the **New England Highway**. An historic rail station marks the abandoned line, high on the **Dividing Range**. The building is now painted in fairly loud colours, but a cast iron water tank with the original pump system are still intact.

Vehicles will head south from town to cross **Deepwater River (Yoongan Creek** confluence) at a substantial bridge, then turn left onto **Bezzants Road**, about one kilometre from the town centre. Follow the gravel to a superb rail trestle bridge over **Deepwater Creek**.

(Dedicated 4WDers in a full sized 4WD with snorkel can reach this same point by following **Forbes Street** on the east side of town to a fording of **Deepwater**

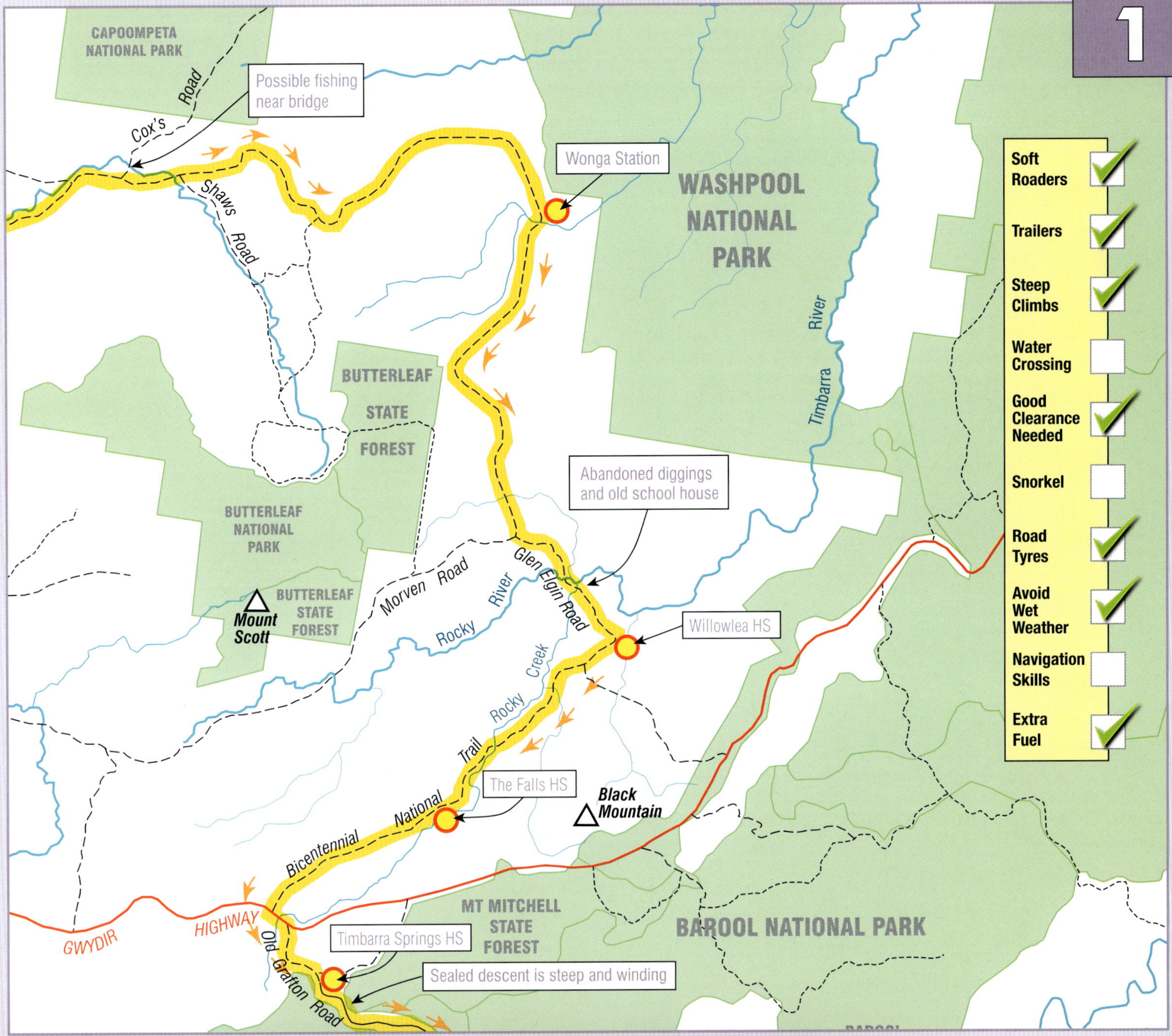

CAPOOMPETA NATIONAL PARK
Cox's Road
Possible fishing near bridge
Shaws Road
Wonga Station
WASHPOOL NATIONAL PARK
Timbarra River
BUTTERLEAF STATE FOREST
BUTTERLEAF NATIONAL PARK
BUTTERLEAF STATE FOREST
Mount Scott
Morven Road
Rocky River
Glen Elgin Road
Abandoned diggings and old school house
Willowlea HS
Rocky Creek
Bicentennial National Trail
The Falls HS
Black Mountain
GWYDIR HIGHWAY
Timbarra Springs HS
Old Grafton Road
Sealed descent is steep and winding
MT MITCHELL STATE FOREST
BAROOL NATIONAL PARK

Soft Roaders	✓
Trailers	✓
Steep Climbs	✓
Water Crossing	
Good Clearance Needed	✓
Snorkel	
Road Tyres	✓
Avoid Wet Weather	✓
Navigation Skills	
Extra Fuel	✓

OLD GRAFTON ROAD

Left: *Rocky River*

River. The crossing is wide and 600mm or more deep, so walk the river first, and avoid it altogether if it is flowing strongly.)

Either way you will drive under the trestle bridge to a scenic stretch of river, and cross into station country. Fishing and camping are not permitted on the private land, as you negotiate grids and some gates to the **Bow Creek** bridge.

Cross the reed fringed waterway to scenic country with shearing sheds and pasture dotted with exotic trees. The

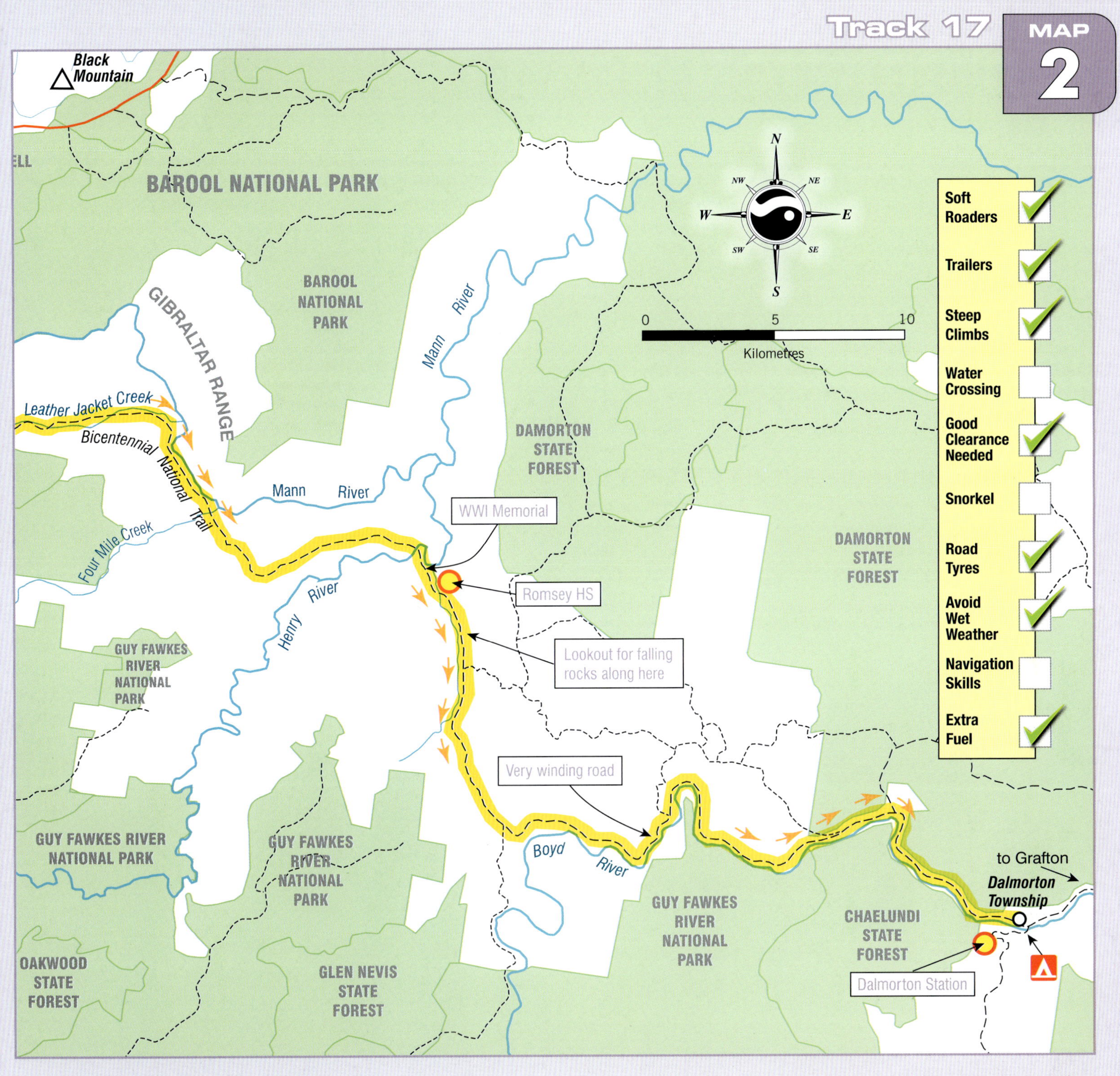

native bush cloaked hills of **Sugarloaf** flag some rocky outcrops, and the slow moving, almost glassy waters of **Deepwater River**.

You will reach a bridge on the left some 15 kilometres from **Deepwater** (nice reedy pools), where you keep straight, and continue past the next left turn at **Cox's Road**. Cross **Deepwater River** at **Shaws Road** and keep straight to begin a run into bush consisting of tree ferns, bracken and mossy boulders.

A gate and old yards at **Heatherglen** flag **Wonga Station**, some 30 kilometres from Deepwater. Continue through a gate to a creek and climb out on a lesser used part of the track to reach an open valley flanked by 1200 metre peaks.

Wildflowers colour the drive past turn offs to **Butterleaf SF**, before you reach better road at a tee intersection, 45 kilometres from **Deepwater**, where we will turn left on **Glen Elgin Road**. (A right turn on **Morven Road** takes you into the central hub of **Butterleaf SF**, where rocky outcrops mark the **Severn River** headwaters. A couple of lengthy walks lead visitors through logged areas of blackbutt and stringybark, to the commanding viewpoint of **Mount Scott**.)

Follow **Glen Elgin Road** to cross **Rocky Creek** at its twin bridges (and abandoned diggings), where an old school house remains. Keep right at **Willowlea HS** shortly after to follow the **Bicentennial National Trail** over **Rocky Creek** again and past **The Falls HS**. You will reach the **Gwydir Highway** six kilometres later, where you turn left toward signposted **Grafton**.

OLD GRAFTON ROAD

Cross the scenic **Timbarra River** headwaters then swing right almost immediately onto the **Old Grafton Road**. This mostly unsealed road began life as a bullock track in the 1840s, but evolved into an important supply route over the next 30 years as goods and produce were shipped in both directions. Back then a horse team took nearly a week to make the **Grafton** to **Glen Innes** run – these days you only need set aside a morning.

Head south on gravel past **Timbarra Springs HS** into the tree fern gullies of **Mount Mitchell SF**. Follow a sealed, but steep and winding descent over the **Great Divide**, to a picturesque causeway spanning a **Mann River** feeder creek (there is a small parking area on the south side).

You will reach the **Mann River Camping Area** some 10.4 kilometres beyond the **Gwydir Highway** turn off, although the right turn is sharp and vehicles towing camper trailers will have to swing wide. Grassy sites and river front sites are popular with campers and kangaroos alike, while basic facilities are provided.

This location was once known as **Robertson**, but renamed Mitchell in 1885 in anticipation of a prosperous village. Unfortunately the gold rush could not sustain the town's growth, and little remains today.

Further on you will cross the **Mann River** at a bridge (unserviced, but quieter camping just prior to the bridge) where river oaks reflect in the tannin tinged waterway. Continue to **Tommys Rock Lookout** turn off, about four kilometres from the bridge. If the potentially locked gate is open, low range equipped vehicles can drive the 4.7 kilometres to a lofty viewpoint.

Numerous erosion control mounds punctuate a steep and scrambling climb, as you keep right at **Tommys Trail walking track**, and arrive at a small carpark. Visitors have a 50 metre walk to a lumpy boulder summit with guarded rail lookout taking in the crumpled **Mann Valley**.

Return to the **Old Grafton Road** (using low range for the descent) and turn right to cross **Leather Jacket Creek**. A few cottages and bush retreats enjoy nice access to the waterway, but passing vehicles will have to make do

Below: *Boyd River*

Above: *Dalmorton Tunnel*

with an elevated view of the scree and rock shelves surrounding the sandy broadwater.

You will follow the **Bicentennial National Trail** past the **Gibraltar Range** into a cleared valley dotted with old farm houses. Drive over **4 Mile Creek** (**Mann River** tributary) into picturesque country, before crossing the **Henry River** at a cluster of cottages. A WW1 memorial stands just after the bridge, dedicated to the local men who never returned from the Great War of 1914 – 1919.

Pass **Romsey HS** to a bridge spanning one of the **Henry's** tributaries, with casuarinas fringing lush pasture. A steep escarpment forces the road to follow a tortuous path through deep cuttings where falling rock can be a hazard to drivers.

You will leave the northward flowing **Mann River** headwaters to meet the **Boyd River** in short order, as the latter meanders eastward. The ring of bellbirds echo from **Guy Fawkes River NP** to the south, as the never ending switchbacks keep you busy at the wheel.

Road engineer of the day, David Houison, designed the route to manage both gradients and waterway difficulties. A poorly paid workforce (some convict labour) undertook the back breaking task, which culminated in 1866 with a 20 metre tunnel chiseled through a rather troublesome rock cliff.

You will reach the tunnel some 52 kilometres from the **Mann River** camp (height limit in tunnel of 3.2 metres), and continue through onto **Dalmorton Station**. The old village of **Dalmorton** is a cluster of mostly private dwellings – left from the heady gold mining days, when thousands of people lived here, and up to 13 pubs dotted the district. Today only a derelict butcher's shop and countless mine shafts are all that remain of the boom days. There is good camping over the bridge on the **Boyd River**, with shady sites and basic facilities.

Visitors can stop here for a night or two, then continue to follow the **Old Grafton Road** – which is sealed beyond the **Nymboida Road** for the final 40 kilometres into **Grafton**. As a couple of options: our **Chaelundi** tour offers a link from **Dalmorton** back to the sealed **Armidale – Grafton Road**, while our **Nymboida River** trek heads north to the **Gwydir Highway**.

TRACK 18

Chaelundi

LOWER NORTH

Black Slate Range

Track Snapshot

TOUR ROUTE:
Dalmorton to Dundurrabin via Chaelundi Creek and Mount Hyland.

DURATION AND DISTANCE:
Although only requiring 100 kilometres of travel, most people will require two days to really enjoy the remote bushland and walks on offer.

TRACK DETAILS:
Easy in dry weather, and suitable for all vehicles. Those towing a trailer may have difficulty turning around at the Mount Hyland carpark.

WHEN TO GO:
Avoid wet weather, but open throughout the year.

CAMPING:
Basic facilities are provided at Dalmorton and Chaelundi.

FUEL AND SUPPLIES:
No fuel or services are available along this route. Stock up prior to reaching Dalmorton.

MAPS:
Natmap 1:100K Newton Boyd, Ebor

OTHER INFORMATION:
The World Heritage area of Mount Hyland is well worth visiting – undertake the well defined, but somewhat strenuous walk if you feel confident.

*The **Chaelundi** area of **New England** takes in sections of state forest and national park, together with a World Heritage block of forest at **Mount Hyland**. There are wild and unrestricted rivers and waterways etching this superb country, with flora and fauna aplenty.*

*This easy trek begins at **Dalmorton;** a former gold mining town on the old **Glen Innes – Grafton Road** (see our Old Grafton Road tour). We head into state forest and climb past **Guy Fawkes River NP**, to visit the old growth rainforest at **Mount Hyland,** and finish on the bitumen just out of **Dorrigo**.*

Head south from **Dalmorton**, crossing the **Boyd River** and passing its camping area on your right (basic facilities and river side sites). A sustained climb onto **Black Slate Range** enters state forest and some logged areas.

Most of the cedar was axed before 1880, then hoop pine followed until WW2, when the more difficult hardwoods became the trees of last resort. Timber harvesting has changed the face of this forest over the years, but there are many areas with dense regrowth, and **Chaelundi NP** even boasts of untouched pockets.

You will reach **Quarry Road** on the left about 8.5 kilometres from **Dalmorton** where you keep staight (left turn follows permit only track to **Doongoonge Camp** on **Chandlers Creek**, about seven kilometres away. Ph 02 6657 2309 for details). Follow the undulating ridge of **Black Slate Range** through clumps of macrozamia, with occasional broken views on either side.

Avoid the (usually signposted) side roads that fishbone into the plateau country. Old fencelines and some cattle are symbols of another chapter in this area's history, while sheltered gullies and pockets of dense jungle are equally apparent.

A grid, then climb through tree fern flags the boundary of **Guy Fawkes NP** some 28 kilometres from **Dalmorton**. Follow the boundary track on a rain shed divide, with the eastern block draining into **Chandlers Creek**, and the western catchment dropping in spectacular style to the **Guy Fawkes River** over half a kilometre below.

The dramatic landscape can be appreciated from a lookout near the

Chaelundi SF

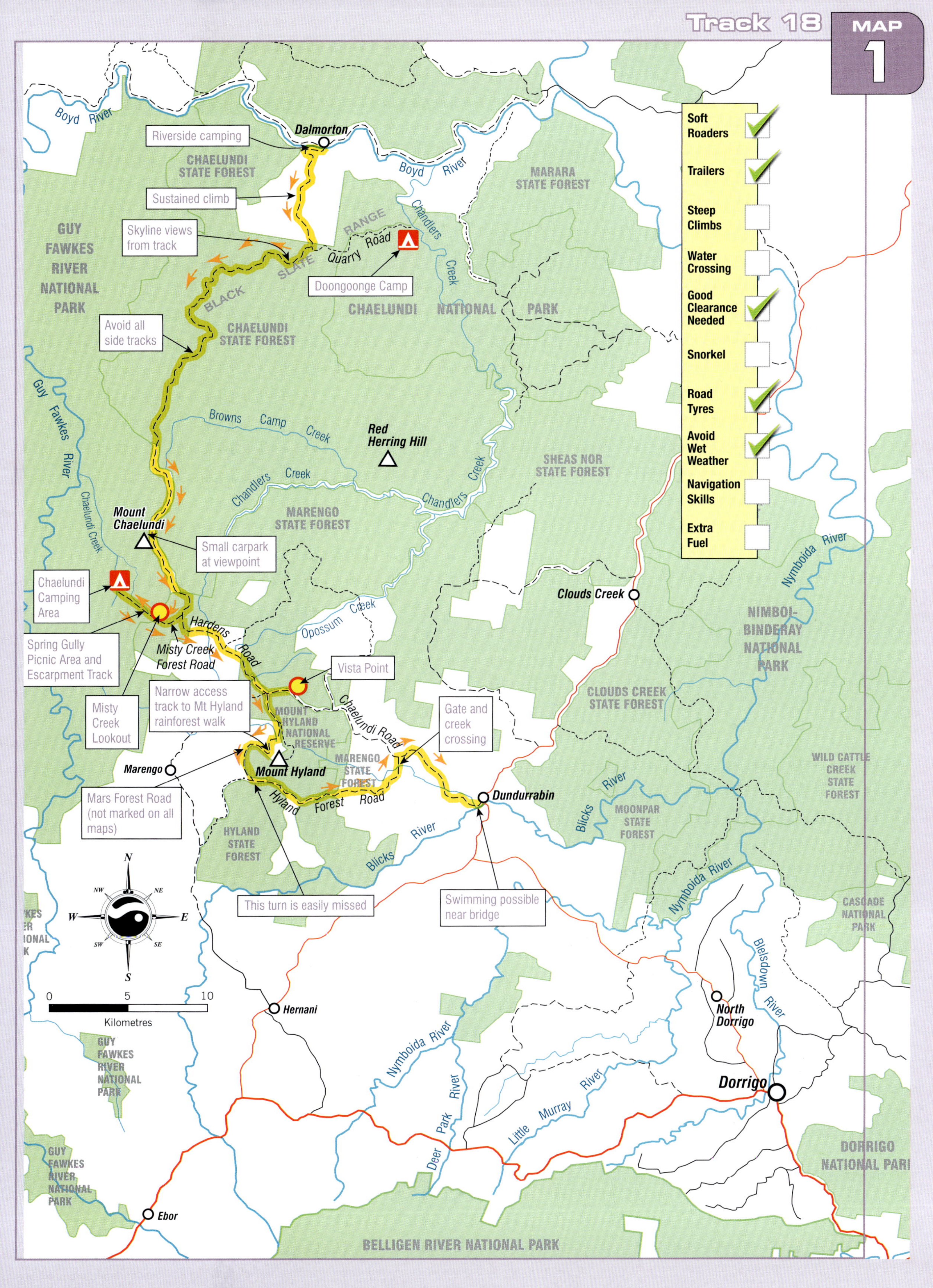
Soft Roaders
Trailers
Steep Climbs
Water Crossing
Good Clearance Needed
Snorkel
Road Tyres
Avoid Wet Weather
Navigation Skills
Extra Fuel
Riverside camping
Dalmorton
Sustained climb
Skyline views from track
Doongoonge Camp
Avoid all side tracks
Small carpark at viewpoint
Chaelundi Camping Area
Spring Gully Picnic Area and Escarpment Track
Misty Creek Lookout
Narrow access track to Mt Hyland rainforest walk
Vista Point
Gate and creek crossing
Mars Forest Road (not marked on all maps)
This turn is easily missed
Swimming possible near bridge
GUY FAWKES RIVER NATIONAL PARK
CHAELUNDI STATE FOREST
MARARA STATE FOREST
CHAELUNDI NATIONAL PARK
SHEAS NOR STATE FOREST
MARENGO STATE FOREST
NIMBOI-BINDERAY NATIONAL PARK
CLOUDS CREEK STATE FOREST
MOUNT HYLAND NATIONAL RESERVE
WILD CATTLE CREEK STATE FOREST
MOONPAR STATE FOREST
HYLAND STATE FOREST
CASCADE NATIONAL PARK
DORRIGO NATIONAL PARK
BELLIGEN RIVER NATIONAL PARK
Red Herring Hill
Mount Chaelundi
Mount Hyland
Clouds Creek
Marengo
Dundurrabin
Hernani
North Dorrigo
Dorrigo
Ebor
Kilometres

1380 metre peak of **Mount Chaelundi**. The 100 metre walking track to the rock viewing platform is difficult to see from this direction, but is located on the right, just as the track narrows a little through stands of grass tree, some 35 kilometres from **Dalmorton**.

A gradual descent in state forest meets a tee intersection about seven kilometres from the lookout. Turn right onto **Misty Creek Forest Road** for a 10 kilometre one way run into **Chaelundi Camping Area**.

This track is a realignment of that shown on earlier maps, but drops into **Guy Fawkes River NP** via a forest of tree fern and bluegum. **Misty Creek Lookout** is reached 3.8 kilometres into the drive, with a viewpoint just 100 metres from the carpark. Trigger plants colour an 800 metre circuit walk as you follow a tree shaded escarpment trail with views over the dissected landscape.

Spring Gully Picnic Area is 2.4 kilometres further on with walking track options that include the lengthy **Escarpment Track** – relatively flat for most of its length, with good views over **Guy Fawkes River** and the **Mann Range**. Less energetic visitors can enjoy the table, seats and fireplace provided.

Chaelundi Camping Area offers basic facilities and secluded camping on a short circuit drive. **Chaelundi Creek** trickles past the camp (nice bathing possibilities, but the water is not suitable for drinking) and a short walk leads to a viewing platform taking in a small falls.

Retrace your steps back to the last junction to turn right onto **Hardens Road**. Head south through **Marengo SF** to a block of cleared grazing land, keeping right at **Foaming Creek Road** 5.6 kilometres later.

Hardens Road veers right as we enter **Mount Hyland NR** and its World Heritage Area, about one kilometre beyond **Foaming Creek Road**. We will turn right here, but it is worthwhile continuing east for another kilometre to reach **Vista Point Lookout**. Visitors will find a shelter shed, table and seats, together with an open view taking in **Chaelundi Mountain** and the **Gibraltar Range**.

Return to **Hardens Road** and follow the western boundary of the nature reserve toward **Mount Hyland**. This road is not shown on all maps, and its chunky loose rock surface, and off camber sections demand caution. You will reach a turn off to the **Mount Hyland Walking Track**, about six kilometres from the lookout.

Follow a steep and narrow trail to a small carpark and picnic area within the World Heritage Area. **Mount Hyland** protects cool temperate rainforest flora and fauna (including many rare and threatened species), together with volcanic features of significance. The park achieved world heritage status in 1987.

Chaelundi Creek Falls

Mount Hyland track

A three kilometre circuit walk meanders through mountain walnut, sassafras and treeferns. This rainforest remains relatively undisturbed, with massive fallen trees encapsulated by moss and fungi, and wonga vines tangled across the dimly lit jungle. It will take a couple of hours to walk via the lowest of **Mount Hyland's** triple peaks, and there are some steep sections, but it is well worthwhile.

Return to **Hardens Road** and continue south for 700 metres, turning left at a tee intersection onto **Mars Forest Road**. You will hug the nature reserve boundary on your left, and veer left 2.5 kilometres from the tee, away from a lesser used track on the right. Follow the earthern track and turn left onto **Hyland Forest Road**, some four kilometres from the tee (this sign post is not visible until you get around the corner).

Mount Hyland summit

You will reach **Marengo SF**, veering left at an unmarked junction 1.8 kilometres later, then follow the roughish track through logged areas and the occasional tree fern gully. A rubble strewn descent brings you to a gate and creek crossing.

Drive for about a kilometre beyond the **Blicks River** tributary until you reach a tee intersection, where you swing right onto the main **Chaelundi Road**. Hardwood plantation and rural holdings flank the good gravel as you reach the **Blicks River** bridge and the community of **Dundurrabin** about six kilometres later. There is a nice section of river near the bridge where you can park the vehicle and have a swim.

The **Armidale – Grafton Road** runs through **Dundurrabin** with bitumen heading in both directions. Sealed road also heads to **Dorrigo**, via **Tyringham** and **Bostobrick**.

Above: *Driftwood at Broadwater*

Right: *Bundjalung Beach*

main arterial, allowing only walkers to explore the tea tree and heathland. Keep your speed down on this good road as coastal emus still dart about the bush, and their population has dropped below an estimated 80 birds.

You can turn right onto **Broadwater Beach Road** to a day use area with gas BBQ. Another parking area nearby gives walking access to Sandy Beach and its distinctive "coffee rocks" – a conglomerate of sand and dark organic material. Coffee rock features at other beaches in the area, including **Black Rocks** in **Bundjalung NP**.

Follow the **Broadwater Road** onto the **Richmond River**, where the township of **Broadwater** marks the **Pacific Highway**. You will pass a substantial sugar refinery then caravan park, to turn left and follow the blacktop past a koala reserve to **Woodburn**.

Five kilometres south of **Woodburn** you will turn left onto **The Gap Road**, signposted "**Bundjalung NP**". Swing right shortly after at a "No Through Road" sign, to cross **Sawpit Creek** and several single lane bridges.

Gravel paves the way into national park 5.4 kilometres from the **Gap Road** turn off as you follow its boundary south through dense jungle. Palm groves flag a road junction and lockable gate where you veer right (left track enters prohibited bombing range which is still used by the RAAF).

Continue through swampy country past a couple of MVO tracks to a bridge spanning **Jerusalem Creek**. This is nice flooded paperbark environment, and with a small parking area just prior to the bridge, visitors may spot kingfishers working the inky waterway.

An information board and fork in the road is reached 700 metres later at **Black Rocks Camp**, where a two kilometre vehicle loop track begins and ends. There are secluded camping opportunities amongst the paperbark and heathland coastal dune system, with a couple of old concrete bunkers found in the fenced off area (this section of coast was used for military training during WW2).

Walking tracks give easy river access (canoeing, swimming) and opportunities for surf fishing (whiting, flathead and tailor are the most common catches). Coffee rocks jut out from the fine white sands here, and mark beach access for 4WDs, via a rocky ramp.

Travel north of these rocks is not permitted, but the 12 kilometre run south along **Ten Mile Beach** is magic. Drop some air from your tyres prior to reaching the surf, and make sure that you are only a couple of hours either side of low tide – preferably on the outgoing tide – (driving above the high tide mark is not allowed; shorebirds may be nesting).

The beach run is relatively straight forward with a firm surface close to the water and some gravelly patches to negotiate. Water logged sections may need a dose of power from time to time, and as always use your indicators when passing oncoming traffic, and slow down for pedestrians.

The sand driving finishes at a clearly marked exit track on **Shark Bay**, where you should reinflate your tyres. You could turn left for 400 metres to the **Shark Bay Picnic Area** to do this (drive slowly on bagged tyres). The rest area has free gas BBQs, and basic facilities on a nice grassed apron, with the beach just 40 metres away.

Broadwater foreshore

Continue to follow the bitumen south to **Woody Head Camping Area**. Turn left through jungle canopy to a well serviced destination, with beach access and boating opportunities. Visitors have been coming here in numbers for over a century, and during the peak holiday period it is probably just too busy.

Four kilometres further south you will reach the township of **Iluka** looking over the **Clarence River**. Commercial (and amateur) fishing centres around the township, with various levels of accommodation available.

While you are in town, it is worthwhile visiting **Iluka NR** just north of the heads. World Heritage status has been bestowed upon this small parcel of littoral rainforest, and a three kilometre one way walk connects the town with the **Bluff Picnic Area** (it is an easier walk in the opposite downhill direction). Less energetic visitors can enjoy sweeping views of the **Clarence River** and **Yamba** beaches from the bluff.

Eroded sand bank

TRACK 21 YURAYGIR

LOWER NORTH

Sandon Bluff

Track Snapshot

TOUR ROUTE:
Maclean to Pebbly Beach via Yuraygir NP and the Coast Range Forest Road.

DURATION AND DISTANCE:
This 270 kilometre grand tour will require two days as a minimum, but preferably a couple more to enjoy the numerous beach camping possibilities.

TRACK DETAILS:
Mostly easy travel, but good clearances and low range needed on Coast Range Track. Beach travel is routine, although Pebbly Beach requires you to dip your pride and joy into a tidal river. Trailers OK.

WHEN TO GO:
All year round, but especially enjoyable over summer.

CAMPING:
Numerous possibilities throughout this tour. All offer basic facilities at least, and are indicated on the maps and in the text.

FUEL AND SUPPLIES:
Leave Maclean with all of the fuel, food and water needed for your stay at Yuraygir.

MAPS:
Natmap 1:100K Bare Point

OTHER INFORMATION:
Yuraygir offers one of Australia's best venues for coastal 4WD travel and camping opportunities. The lack of commercial developments is especially appealing.

***Yuraygir** is the king of coastal trips for 4WDers in NSW. More than 30,000 hectares of national park combine with hinterland state forest to protect beaches, rocky headlands, tidal rivers and countless lagoons. There is regular beach access for 4WDs, and a track network across the **Coast Range** that overlooks this superb piece of Australia.*

This trek takes in most of the magic coastal attractions, linked by a sometimes demanding drive on the beach or inland bush tracks. Dedicated 4WDers will revel in the destination, while discerning passengers will find great camping, fishing and hiking possibilities. Of course, there will be many opportunities just to kick back and absorb the flavour of this special place.

The **Clarence River** township of **Maclean** will mark this tour's beginning just off the **Pacific Highway**. A strong Scottish influence permeates the sugar cane and vegetable growing district, where fishing and prawning are staple industries.

Exit the **Pacific Highway** to follow **Jubilee Street** and signage for **Yuraygir NP**, onto **Brooms Head Road**. Brahman cattle indicate the quick transition to rural country, with the wetlands and canals of **Wooloweyah Lagoon** on your left.

You will reach the boundary of **Yuraygir NP** about 16 kilometres from **Maclean**, then take the **Lake Arragan** turn off three kilometres later. Keep left to reach a camping area on the picturesque lagoon system. It has basic facilities, with similar possibilities at adjacent **Red Cliff**.

Dedicated walkers can hike from here to **Angourie** (south of **Yamba**) via a 10 kilometre coastal trail. The four hour walk is rather strenuous, but rewards participants with great lookouts and the chance to spot dolphins, or even a whale over the cooler months. An overnight stop at **Shelley Headland** (carrying in all of your gear) is possible, and most people organise a vehicle to meet them at one end of the walk or the other.

Less energetic visitors will enjoy rock hopping at the foot of 20 metre high **Red Cliffs** – a kaleidescope of colourful sedimentary rocks that have helped with maritime navigation for many years. Other short walks include a nearby tidal lagoon just beyond the camp, that provides warm bathing waters, and the chance to see kangaroos drinking from a spring in the sand. Kangaroos are a regular visitor to the campground at **Red Cliffs**.

Return to the **Lake Arragan** turn off, and swing left toward **Brooms Head** to reach the **Sandon Road** turn off 3.2 kilometres later. We will turn right here, but

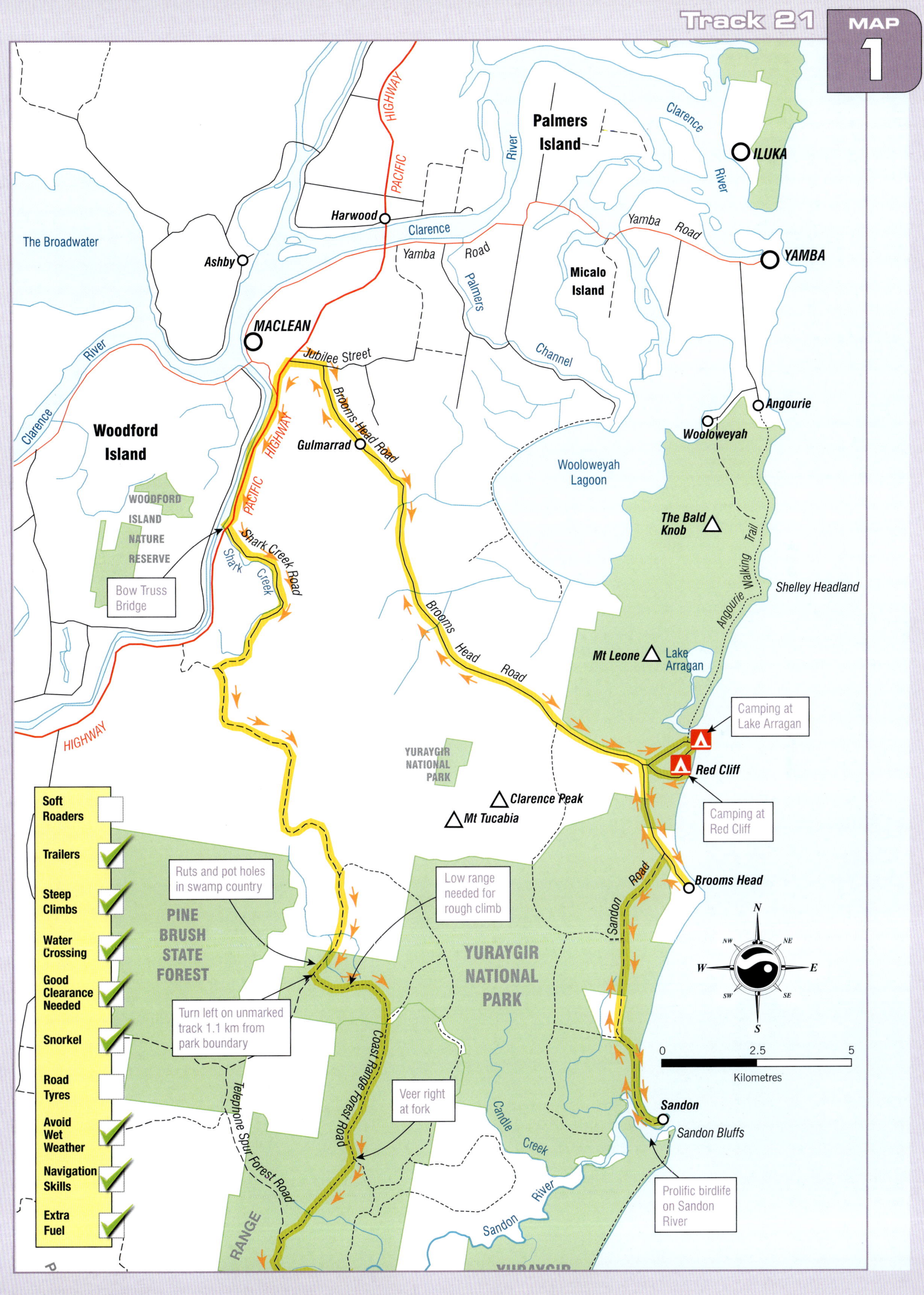
Palmers Island
Clarence River
ILUKA
PACIFIC HIGHWAY
Harwood
Clarence
Yamba Road
YAMBA
The Broadwater
Ashby
Palmers Channel
Micalo Island
MACLEAN
Clarence River
Jubilee Street
Brooms Head Road
Angourie
Wooloweyah
Woodford Island
Gulmarrad
Wooloweyah Lagoon
WOODFORD ISLAND NATURE RESERVE
The Bald Knob
Shark Creek Road
Shark Creek
Angourie Walking Trail
Shelley Headland
Bow Truss Bridge
Mt Leone
Lake Arragan
Camping at Lake Arragan
HIGHWAY
YURAYGIR NATIONAL PARK
Red Cliff
Clarence Peak
Mt Tucabia
Camping at Red Cliff
Soft Roaders
Trailers
Steep Climbs
Water Crossing
Good Clearance Needed
Snorkel
Road Tyres
Avoid Wet Weather
Navigation Skills
Extra Fuel
Ruts and pot holes in swamp country
Low range needed for rough climb
PINE BRUSH STATE FOREST
Brooms Head
Sandon Road
YURAYGIR NATIONAL PARK
N
NW
NE
W
E
SW
SE
S
Turn left on unmarked track 1.1 km from park boundary
Coast Range Forest Road
0
2.5
5
Kilometres
Telephone Spur Forest Road
Veer right at fork
Candle Creek
Sandon
Sandon Bluffs
Prolific birdlife on Sandon River
Sandon River
RANGE

Brooms Head lies directly ahead, where Norfolk Island Pines shelter a community of weekenders and fishing shacks. Visitors can undertake a short walk to appreciate sweeping headland views.

Follow the corrugated road south on **Sandon Road** through metre high grassland and coastal vegetation. Cattle ramps and stockyard mark an enclave of private land, before you trace a path along the sliver of land separating the **Sandon River** and **South Pacific Ocean**.

Sheoaks provide a little shade to the avenue of cottages lining the main street. Unsealed roads seem to keep the developers away, and although bustling in peak season, the camping area holds more charm than many other town based options nearby.

Shorebirds are prolific here over summer as they work the **Sandon River** margins for marine critters, while the larger Jabirus are occasionally spotted. Fishers and surfers are well rewarded and 4WDers are permitted to drive along **Sandon Beach**.

There is no access south of **Sandon Beach**, so retrace your steps to **Maclean**, and head south on the **Pacific Highway**. Turn left on **Shark Creek Road**, just prior to the old concrete bow truss bridge, about six kilometres from **Maclean**. Follow narrow bitumen through chocolate soil canefields to a roadside memorial on your left.

Gravel paves the way along the lily fringed water of **Shark Creek** to a junction seven kilometres from the highway turn off. Continue straight (right turn over bridge returns to highway) past tracks to either side and private residences.

Paperbark and swamp country herald a turn right away from a lesser used road, some eight kilometres from the last bridge. Turn right again 1.5 kilometres later to cross a creek into **Yuraygir NP**. The track quickly deteriorates into pot holes and ruts as you turn left onto an unsignposted track 1.1 kilometres into the national park.

Slip into low range for an eroded climb over steep gullies and rock shelves. Boulders and some loose sections mask increasingly deeper ruts and a need for accurate wheel placement, before you reach a tee intersection four kilometres later.

Turn right onto **Coast Range Forest Road** to follow a ridge through the 7950 hectare **Candole SF**, with regular ocean views. A steep drop off to the east permits travellers to see virtually every feature of the coast including **Sandon Bluffs** and **Brooms Head**. You may have to weave around some of the bigger fallen trees, as this track is not used regularly.

You will reach a fork 3.9 kilometres later where you veer right up a hill (not left through the gate), to follow a fenceline through a couple more old gates (this track may not be shown on some maps). Follow the climb onto **Summervale Range**, then to a tee intersection some 3.7 kilometres from the fork.

Turn left onto **Telephone Spur Forest Road** for a return to high range, but only a little improvement in the track surface. Four kilometres later you will reach a tee on **Candole Forest Road**, where you swing right over the upper **Sandon River**, and a series of feeder creeks. You will just clip national park before reaching bitumen at a tee intersection on the **Minnie Water Road**.

Swing left here, but note this junction as we will return this way, and the next leg of **Coast Range Road** is just a few kilometres to the west from here. Follow sealed road to a tee intersection on **Lake Hiawatha** and turn left toward **Minnie Water**. This small village has a store and popular surf beach (patrolled by lifesavers in summer, unlike the other **Yuraygir** beaches). Short walks take in pandanus and littoral rainforest, together with the town beach and its distinctive headland.

National park camping is available at **Illaroo Camp** nearby, with a number of sites sheltered by banksia, although the northern sites are a little busier than those in the south. Fires are permitted in suitable weather and basic facilities are provided, but swimming is not recommended.

4WDs can follow a narrow winding track to a corduroy beach access point with beach driving to **Sandon Village**. Fishing shacks at **Sandon Bluffs** mark the end of sand driving, but you will need return to **Illaroo**, as the **Sandon River** cannot be forded.

Sandon marks the northern boundary of the **Solitary Islands Marine Park** – a large expanse of **Coral Sea** that extends south to **Coffs Harbour**. A number of rocky outcrops provide habitat for marine life and the more obvious bird population, while soft corals grow on the ocean floor.

4WD wreck on beach

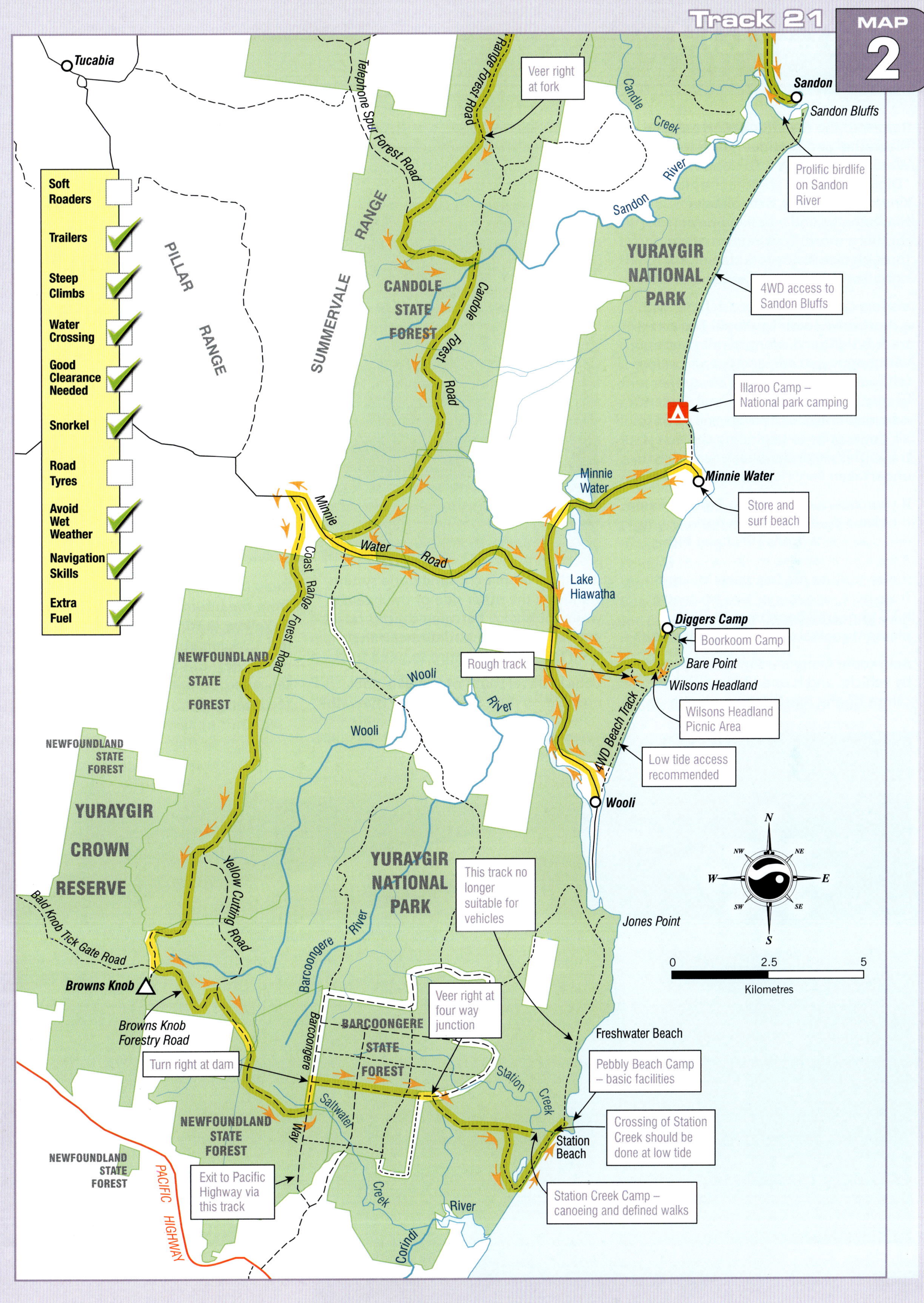

Tucabia
Sandon
Sandon Bluffs
Veer right at fork
Prolific birdlife on Sandon River
Soft Roaders
Trailers
Steep Climbs
Water Crossing
Good Clearance Needed
Snorkel
Road Tyres
Avoid Wet Weather
Navigation Skills
Extra Fuel
PILLAR RANGE
SUMMERVALE RANGE
Telephone Spur Forest Road
Coast Range Forest Road
Candle Creek
Sandon River
YURAYGIR NATIONAL PARK
4WD access to Sandon Bluffs
CANDOLE STATE FOREST
Candole Forest Road
Illaroo Camp – National park camping
Minnie Water
Store and surf beach
Minnie Water Road
Lake Hiawatha
Diggers Camp
Boorkoom Camp
Bare Point
Rough track
Wilsons Headland
Wilsons Headland Picnic Area
NEWFOUNDLAND STATE FOREST
Wooli River
Wooli
4WD Beach Track
Low tide access recommended
YURAYGIR CROWN RESERVE
Yellow Cutting Road
This track no longer suitable for vehicles
Jones Point
Bald Knob Tick Gate Road
Browns Knob
Browns Knob Forestry Road
Barcoongere River
Barcoongere Way
Veer right at four way junction
BARCOONGERE STATE FOREST
Freshwater Beach
Turn right at dam
Station Creek
Pebbly Beach Camp – basic facilities
Saltwater Creek
Crossing of Station Creek should be done at low tide
Station Beach
Exit to Pacific Highway via this track
Station Creek Camp – canoeing and defined walks
Corindi River
PACIFIC HIGHWAY
N NE E SE S SW W NW
0 2.5 5
Kilometres

Chapter 4

SOUTH EAST

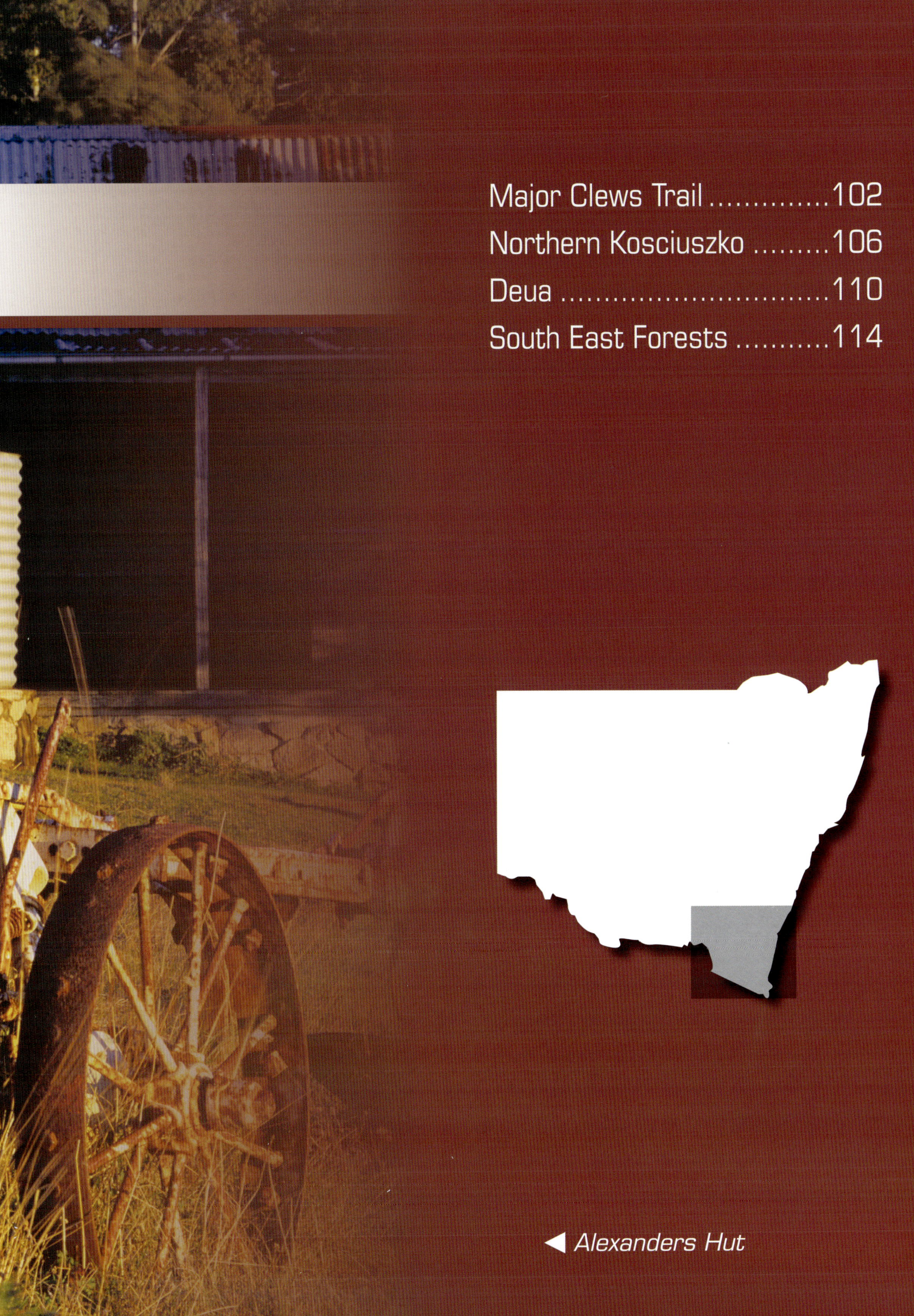

◀ *Alexanders Hut*

TRACK 24

NORTHERN KOSCIUSZKO

SOUTH EAST

Track Snapshot

TOUR ROUTE:
Rules Point to Providence Portal via the Northern Kosciuszko huts.

DURATION AND DISTANCE:
Allow at least two days for the 100 kilometre tour, with a one night stop at one of the character huts.

TRACK DETAILS:
Routine driving suitable for all vehicles and trailers.

WHEN TO GO:
Seasonally closed tracks limit travellers to late spring, summer and autumn.

CAMPING:
Basic facilities at Long Plain Hut, Cooinbil Hut, Cooleman Mountain, Magpie Flat, Ghost Gully Campground and Wares Yards. Serviced camping at Providence Portal.

FUEL AND SUPPLIES:
Nothing en route, Adaminaby is the best place to top up, with Tumut and Cooma offering a greater range of supplies.

MAPS:
Natmap 1:100K Tantangara

OTHER INFORMATION:
The historic huts provide emergency shelter all year round, but should not be used for routine overnight accommodation – always travel with a tent, swag or camper trailer.

Currango HS outbuilding

*The **Northern Kosciuszko** area was a magnet for pioneering graziers who drove stock across the high country from **Queanbeyan** to the upper **Murray**. Broad treeless plains and lush grasses combined with numerous reliable rivers, to offer good grazing over the summer months. A number of permanent homesteads sprang up across the region from the 1830s.*

This tour visits some of these vital refuges, and the alpine country that surrounds them. Some scenic attractions add to the mix, along an easy route that is suitable for all vehicles and drivers.

We begin at **Rules Point**, about 18 kilometres north of **Kiandra**, directly due east of **Yarrangobilly Caves**. You turn left onto **Long Plain Road**, through a seasonally closed gate, and follow gravel to cross a tributary of the **Murrumbidgee River**. The turn off to **Port Phillip Trail** is reached three kilometres beyond **Rules Point** on the right, and will be our eventual exit (providing the trail is open – this track crosses the upper neck of **Tantangara Reservoir** and can be closed for years, depending on water levels).

For now swing left to the **Long Plain Hut Campground**, driving through a treed area to a horse camp about one kilometre later. Snowgum and black sallee surround the early 1900s timber hut, with cypress pine lining boards. Vehicle based camping with basic facilities is pleasant here, under the shadow of **Yarrangobilly Mountain**.

Return to **Long Plain Road** and turn left to follow the **Murrumbidgee** past **Bryce Creek Trail** (MVO) and cross the infant river headwaters at a culvert nine kilometres later. Turn right to **Cooinbil Hut** 800 metres beyond that, following the kilometre long access trail to a weatherboard hut. The current cottage dates from 1905, although the original hut stood here 40 years prior to that. Camping with basic facilities is permitted nearby.

Return to **Long Plain Road** and continue north to **Blue Waterholes Trail** on the right 3.9 kilometres later. (The left option continues to follow **Long Plain Road**, then **Broken Cart Trail** on a slower run to **Boundary Road**, and past **Big Dubbo Hill**. You can veer left on **Bramina Road**, to reach **Barnetts Road**, then cross the **Goodradigbee River**, eventually reaching the locality of **Brindabella**).

We will however keep right to penetrate thicker woodland along an uneven road. **Cooleman Mountain Campground** is reached 2.5 kilometres later, with basic facilities and drive in grassy sites.

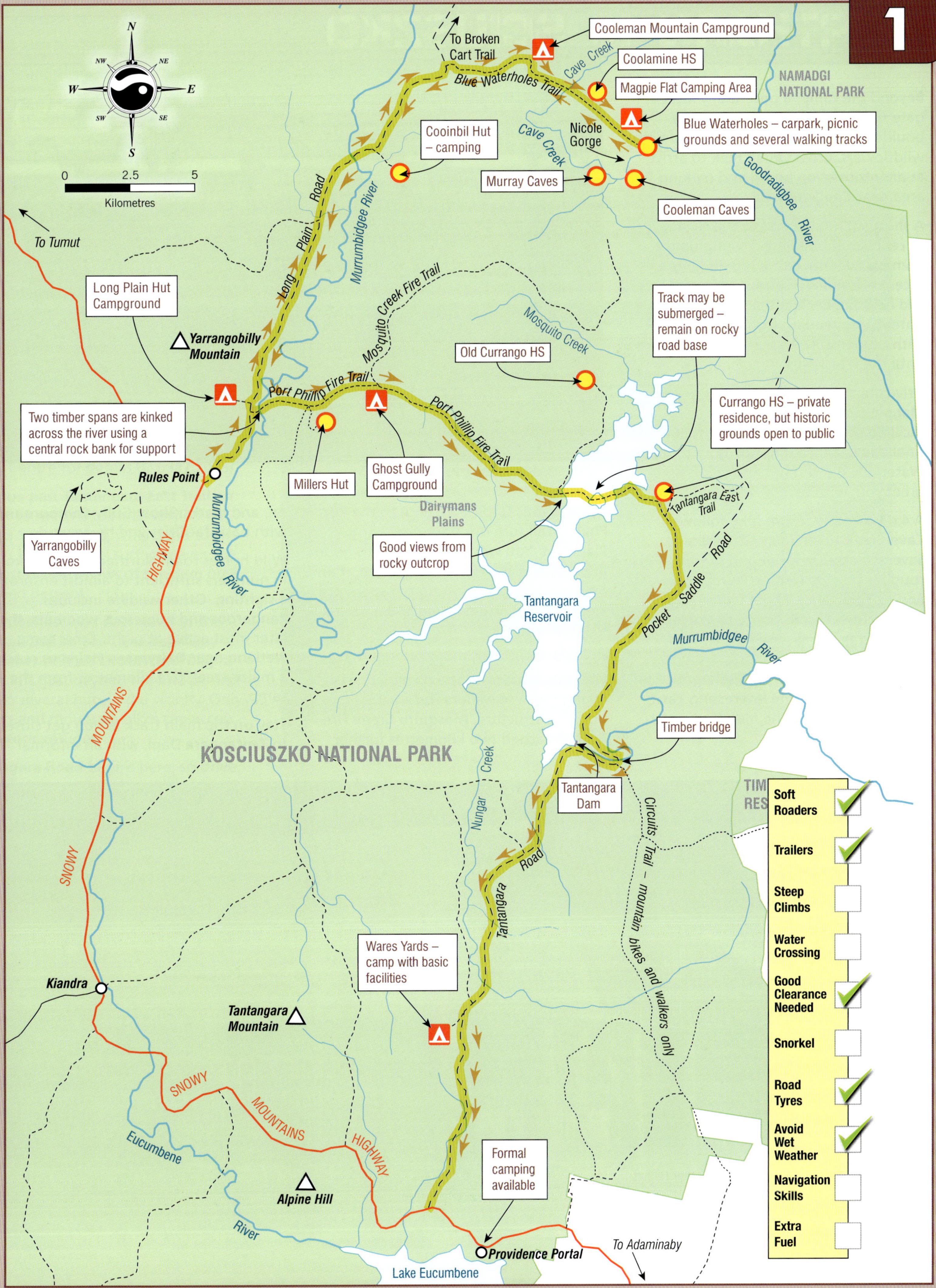

To Broken Cart Trail
Cooleman Mountain Campground
Coolamine HS
Magpie Flat Camping Area
Blue Waterholes – carpark, picnic grounds and several walking tracks
NAMADGI NATIONAL PARK
Blue Waterholes Trail
Cave Creek
Nicole Gorge
Cooinbil Hut – camping
Murray Caves
Cooleman Caves
Goodradigbee River
0 2.5 5
Kilometres
To Tumut
Long Plain Road
Murrumbidgee River
Mosquito Creek Fire Trail
Mosquito Creek
Long Plain Hut Campground
Yarrangobilly Mountain
Old Currango HS
Track may be submerged – remain on rocky road base
Port Phillip Fire Trail
Currango HS – private residence, but historic grounds open to public
Two timber spans are kinked across the river using a central rock bank for support
Rules Point
Millers Hut
Ghost Gully Campground
Dairymans Plains
Tantangara East Trail
Yarrangobilly Caves
Good views from rocky outcrop
HIGHWAY
Murrumbidgee River
Pocket Saddle Road
Tantangara Reservoir
MOUNTAINS
Timber bridge
KOSCIUSZKO NATIONAL PARK
Tantangara Dam
Nungar Creek
Circuits Trail – mountain bikes and walkers only
SNOWY
Tantangara Road
Wares Yards – camp with basic facilities
Kiandra
Tantangara Mountain
SNOWY MOUNTAINS HIGHWAY
Eucumbene River
Formal camping available
Alpine Hill
Providence Portal
To Adaminaby
Lake Eucumbene

Soft Roaders	✓
Trailers	✓
Steep Climbs	
Water Crossing	
Good Clearance Needed	✓
Snorkel	
Road Tyres	✓
Avoid Wet Weather	✓
Navigation Skills	
Extra Fuel	

You will reach **Woila Fire Trail** 400 metres from the boundary of national park, where you keep left on **Badja Fire Trail**, and pass banksia woodland, and a carpet of red heath. Cross a creek on a scenic wetland run with some slippery sections and erosion control mounds.

The **Badja Swamps** punctuate a drive past mossy boulders, as you continue through an old gate and follow a fenceline to a log bridge. Swing right at a swamp shortly after to begin a steady climb through superb eucalypt forest.

Follow the main fire trail past broken views to the right, as a sustained descent pulls you back into low range. Impressive fields of native flax lily colour the subsequent scrambling climb, some four kilometres beyond the bridge.

Pick your line carefully over the erosion mounds as a substantial drop off is ever present on the right track shoulder. A vague clearing prior to **Big Badja Hill** (about 6.2 kilometres from the log bridge) offers an informal lookout that is well worth a stop.

Walk back 100 metres to a prominent escarpment overlooking the **Woila Wilderness**. Lomandra colours the rocky understorey, while bottlebrush frames this superb piece of bushland – with excellent, unrestricted eastern views.

The signposted **Badja Trig Point** carpark is just 500 metres further on, and a 300 metre walk through low growing teatree finishes at a cairn. The eastern view is more restricted than the previous lookout, but sweeping views from here extend in an arc from **Gourock NP** in the north to the **Kybeyan Range** in the south and rural views to the west.

A sustained descent follows to the **Pikes Saddle** intersection two kilometres later. Turn left away from **Snowball Road**, keeping right on the **Braidwood Road** 100 metres later. Follow good road past **Gourock NP**, to pass **Jinden Ridge Road** on the left.

You will reach **Middle Mountain Road** some nine kilometres from **Pikes Saddle**, where you swing right to ford **Currambene Creek**. A bush camping area (no facilities) marks the rocky crossing, as you follow the fenceline of **Snowball Station**, keeping right 1.5 kilometres from the creek.

The track deteriorates into a rocky amble as a lush tree fern gully flags **Middle Mountain** on the left. You will skirt its 1160 metre peak, with wattles ushering the way to a junction 7.2 kilometres beyond the creek. Keep left away from **Snowball Road**, as wetlands mark your transition onto **Minuma Range Fire Trail**.

A steady climb over erosion mounds continues to **Dampier Trig Point** (1239 metres and no views). You will need to pick your line carefully over large rocks and rubble – a skill that will further develop on the tyre scuffed rock descent beyond the trig.

Woila Deua Wilderness from Big Badja Hill

Turn right onto **Dampier Mountain Fire Trail** 1.8 kilometres later, for a continuous descent into the **Deua Valley**. Lofty views and a couple of hairpin turns provide interest, as drivers hang on to their lowest gear, perhaps feathering the brake on the final drop off.

You will reach a tee intersection on the **Bendethera Fire Trail**, where you turn left to ford the **Deua River** at a wide pebbly crossing. A camping area is found on the other side, with basic facilities and a broad grassy area fringed with black wattles. Potential sites are spread out over the former station grounds, most with river access and fireplaces.

The old homestead no longer stands, but stock yards and the remains of a stone bakery oven can be seen in the homestead precinct. Water race remains etch the ground nearby, where river water was channeled to a commercial market garden. The area was settled in the 1860s, with one of the pioneering family's children stumbling upon a nearby caves network in 1875.

Visitors of today can enter the initial 200 metres of the caves (take a couple of good torches), by following **Conn Creek Walking Track** on an eight kilometre return hike. The main vehicle track crosses the **Deua** several times to follow a line of swamp oaks to the most distant camp, some five kilometres beyond the first crossing. Boggy sections and eroded river banks deserve caution especially toward the end of the drive.

Return to the **Dampier Mountain Fire Trail** and head east to cross the **Deua** yet again, veering left to begin a substantial climb onto **Bendethera Mountain**. A narrow and sometimes scrambling journey, it is well worth staying aware of potential pull over locations, in the event of oncoming vehicles causing you to reverse.

Veer right, 6.8 kilometres from the last river crossing, at **Bendethera Mountain** (no views) to pass a tree fern gully and some nice grass trees. Keep left at **Deua River Fire Trail** 5.6 kilometres later, to follow the better surface of **Little Sugarloaf Road**. You will pass **Messmate Road** and the **Plumwood Fire Tower** on a gradual descent to the

Above: Comans Mine stamper

Above left: Creek at Comans Mine

Top: Dampier Mountain Fire Trail

signposted **Hanging Mountain** turn off, 7.4 kilometres from the **Deua River Fire Trail**.

Veer left to a carpark 800 metres later, and a short walk to the lookout. **Donalds Creek** and **Wamban Mountain** dominate the foreground, with **Moruya SF** leading onto **Tuross Head** and the **South Pacific Ocean**.

Return to the lookout turn off and swing hard left to pass trackside glimpses of the ocean, and reach **German Creek Road** 2.1 kilometres later. Turn right here, keeping left 900 metres later, to follow a pocket of jungle with creeper running riot.

You exit **Deua NP** with skyline views on either side, reaching a tee on **Comerang Road**. Turn left through a logged area, then swing right onto **Comans Forest Road** 1.5 kilometres later. Pass by **Gulph Trig Forest Road** and skirt **Mount Coman** (445 metres) to descend to **Comans Mine Walking Track**, some 9.2 kilometres from the **Coman Road** junction.

An excellent 1.5 kilometre, one hour return walk descends from here to an old gold mine worked in the early 1900s. Mine shafts and the remains of the ore trolley tracks provide some clues as to the site's layout, but a substantial quartz battery is well preserved nearby. The remains of an old weir and a picturesque waterfall are found at the walk's end, but be careful of the slippery rocks.

Continue to descend over **Graveyard Creek** and the private residences of **Nerrigundah**. Cross a timber bridge, swinging left shortly after to reach the community hub at an historic gold escort monument.

Turn left here over **Gulph Creek**, keeping right at **Nerrigundah Ridge Road** 3.6 kilometres later, for broken ridgetop views. Exotic trees and dairying sheds mark the **Eurobodalla Valley**, as you reach the **Tyronne Bridge** spanning the **Tuross River**.

Cross the single lane bridge and turn left to follow river oaks and a series of attractive river flats. Plane trees provide autumn colour, with irrigators utilizing the now abundant water resource. You will pass the **Bodalla Cemetery** before reaching the **Princes Highway** shortly after.

There are formal accommodation options in **Bodalla**, but the camping is exceptional at **Belowra NP** near **Potato Point**. A private eco camp offers grassy beach side possibilities, with numerous kangaroos and emus wandering the sandy shoreline.

Chapter 5
OUTBACK NSW

◀ *Paroo River*

TRACK 27 MUTAWINTJI

OUTBACK NSW

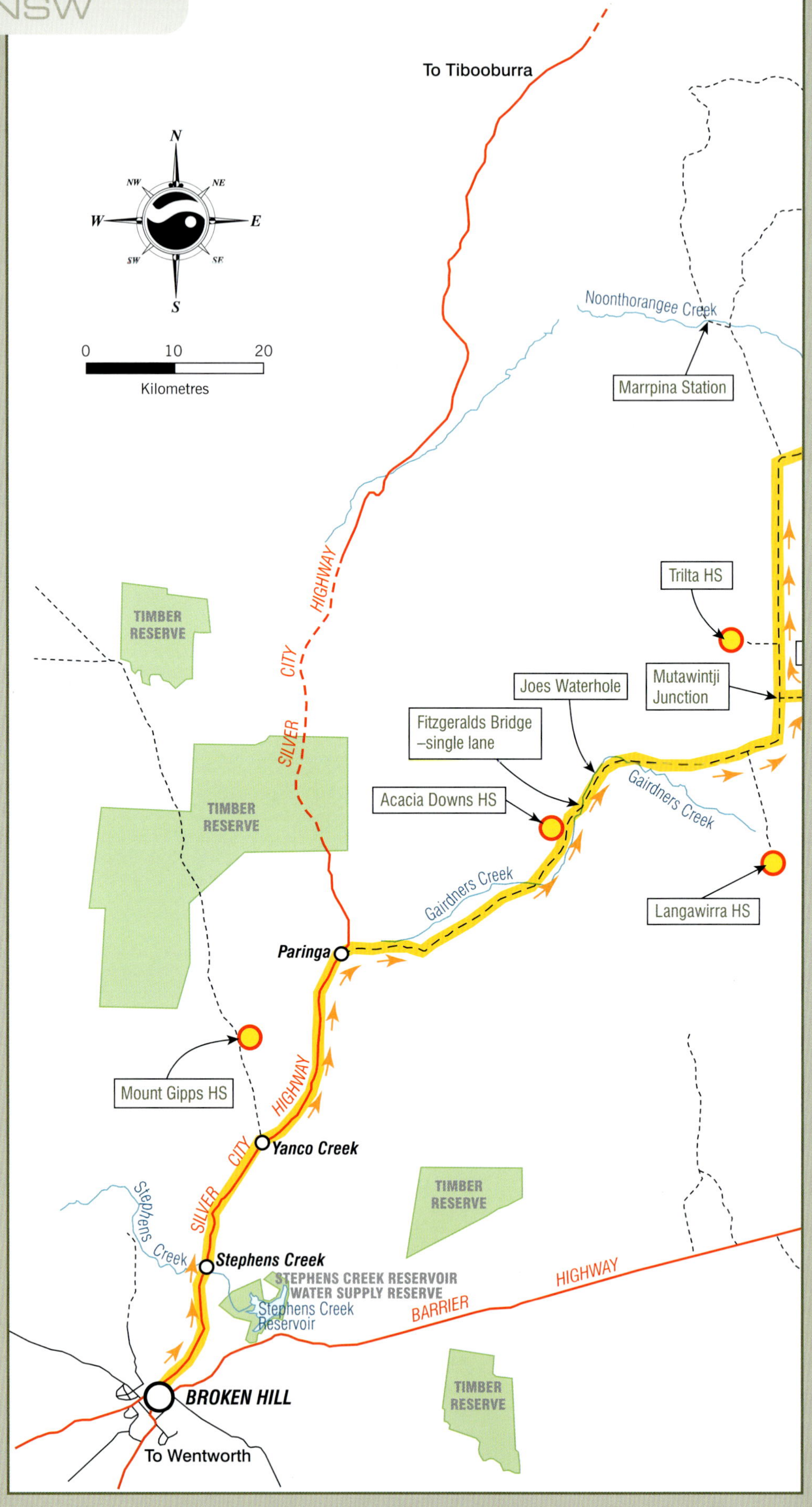

Track Snapshot

TOUR ROUTE:
Broken Hill to White Cliffs via Mutawintji NP.

DURATION AND DISTANCE:
You will need two days for the 300 kilometre trek, allowing for some walks within Mutawintji.

TRACK DETAILS:
Routine station tracks and some sealed sections, suitable for soft roaders and trailers.

WHEN TO GO:
Avoid the hot months and wet weather (April to October is the prefered period).

CAMPING:
Good facilities at Homestead Creek within Mutawintji.

FUEL AND SUPPLIES:
Broken Hill and White Cliffs – nothing en route.

MAPS:
Natmap 1:250K Broken Hill, Cobham Lake, White Cliffs

OTHER INFORMATION:
This tour is ideal for newcomers to outback travel, offering easy access and an authentic experience.

__Broken Hill__ marks the starting point for this trip through western NSW, where travellers will undertake an easy run through station country, see some stunning aboriginal artwork, and perhaps strike it rich on the __White Cliffs__ opal fields. Optimism a plenty still attracts hopefuls to this corner of the state, which was founded on mineral discovery almost 130 years ago.

Back then silver, lead and zinc were found in the district, with a substantial deposit located in present day __Broken Hill__. Boom years followed, with some 6500 workers chiseling away at the Line of Lode in the mid 1950s.

Unfortunately extraction costs blew out, making the mines less viable, and __Broken Hill's__ slow decline began. Fears of a ghost town proved unfounded though as tourism boomed and mining techniques improved. Today The Hill is a great place to spend a few days, sampling the outback flavour, and preparing to head further inland.

You will exit town on the **Silver City Highway**, taking **Buck Street** from the city centre, and veering right away from **Racecourse Road**. An art gallery

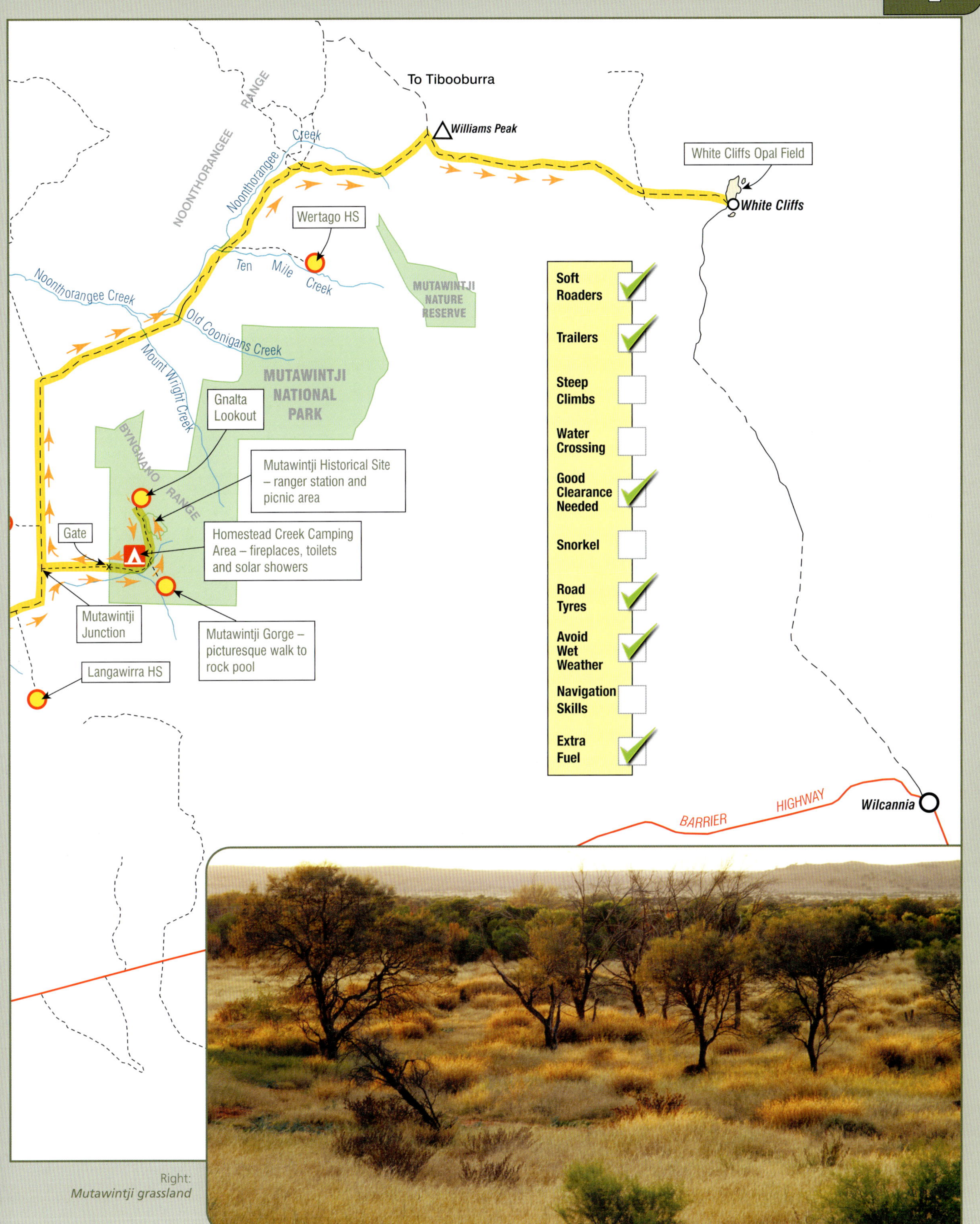

Right: *Mutawintji grassland*

and tearooms at **Stephens Creek** mark the end of commercial establishments for a time, as the sealed road heads northward.

Yanco Creek at about 33 kilometres marks a turn into the **Barrier Range** toward **Mount Gipps HS** and beyond. Keep right on the blacktop here, to cruise over a series of dips and floodways

Right:
Old building, White Cliffs

Below:
Old mill and tank near Mutawintji

for the next 24 kilometres, turning right at **Paringa** on the signposted "**White Cliffs**" turnoff.

The bitumen finishes after about 14 kilometres with **Acacia Downs HS** on the left, and the **Gairdners Creek** crossing some five kilometres after that. Slow down for the single lane bridge as it is not easily seen from the opposite direction. You will find a nice stand of redgums lining **Joes Hole Creek**, then swing left at the **Langawirra HS** access track (again a tight turn), before reaching the **Mutawintji** junction some 62 kilometres from the **Silver City Highway** turnoff.

Turn right at the signposted junction for a one way return visit into national park. It is a nine kilometre run into the boundary of **Mutawintji**, before a gate and 40 kph zone indicate your arrival. You will drive six kilometres to a visitor centre, then veer left along what was the old **Broken Hill – White Cliffs** coach road.

Visitors can drive a 10 kilometre section of this track passing features of historic and scenic interest. Aboriginal artwork is protected within the park and includes examples near a day use area, together with an important site, accessible only in the company of a guide (ring 08 8080 7000 for details).

Other features of the drive include the remains of the **Rockholes Hotel**, and several walks and lookouts featuring the **Byngano Range**. The camping area at **Homestead Creek** has fireplaces (bring your own wood in), toilets and solar showers. There is an excellent walk along **Mutawintji Gorge** that passes prominent red cliffs to a picturesque rock pool.

It is well worth stopping for a day or two in the park as a couple of the walks are lengthy and quite demanding, but on leaving, retrace your steps to the main **Mutawintji** turn off. Swing north here following the main road past the **Trilta HS** turnoff, before swinging right at the **Marrpina Station** junction some 26 kilometres later.

You will cross **Mount Wright Creek** and reach a sealed section of road through **Old Coonigans Creek**. The road passes an opening between the **Noonthorangee Range** on your north, and the **Byngano Range** to the south, before **Wertago HS** is passed on the right.

A four way intersection is met on top of a crest, with signposted "**White Cliffs**" pointing the way eastward. Turn right here, then cross the wide gravelly base of **Noonthorangee Creek** about 11 kilometres later, before reaching a tee intersection on the main **Tibooburra – White Cliffs Road**.

White Cliffs cemetery

Swing right at the intersection past the prominent landmark of **William Peak** on your left. The road improves some 10 kilometres later as you enter the **Central Darling Shire** (and away from Unincorporated Area where little road maintenance is done). Flatter country with extensive gibber plains paves the way toward the now visible **White Cliffs** on the horizon. You will reach a tee intersection, then turn right for the last couple of kilometres into town.

Compared with **Broken Hill**, **White Cliffs** is just a dot on the map, although aerial photographs show at least 50 000 dots where hopeful miners have penetrated the earth's skin looking for opal. The frenzy began in the 1880s and continues to this day.

A seven kilometre loop drive from the town centre passes old and working claims, with some areas open to the public. Services within the town are basic, but cover most needs, with food, fuel and camping available. An underground motel offers some luxury and respite from the summer heat, while art galleries and opal sales help the town's economy.

Options for travel out of town include a 95 kilometre run south to **Wilcannia** (links up with our **Darling River** trek), or a 139 kilometre drive north to the **Silver City Highway** (see our **Corner Country** trek). You may also use **White Cliffs** as the staging point for our **Paroo River** run.

Left:
Opal fields, White Cliffs

TRACK 28 Paroo River

OUTBACK NSW

*It's not often that the **Paroo River** overflows toward the **Darling**, but when it does a string of lakes brim over, creating an inland sea. Tens of thousands of birds are attracted to the massive wetland, which can hold water for several years. Some species of waterbirds take the opportunity to breed, on a river system that is not obstructed with man made weirs and lakes.*

*The trek from **White Cliffs** to **Hungerford** takes in a section of the relatively new **Paroo – Darling National Park**, closely following the **Paroo** to the Queensland border. Our starting point is White Cliffs and having exited to the east with the pioneer cemetery on your left (well worth a look to get a feel for this area's heritage) you reach a series of grids and **Polpah Station**. Watch out for stock on these station roads, especially near water points where they often congregate.*

Some 21 kilometres from **White Cliffs** you cross a grid into **Arrowbar Station** (now part of the national park). **Mirriappa Creek** is reached four kilometres later with a second channel another kilometre further on. A track branches right here to a waterhole, where there is talk of establishing a camping area within the national park (ph 08 8083 7900 for current advice before camping, and be aware that open fires are not permitted anywhere within the NP).

You will reach the **Wilcannia – Wanaaring Road** at a tee junction about 35 kilometres from **White Cliffs**. Turn left onto better road, reaching a rough crossing of **Pine Creek**, then keep right at the **Peery HS** turnoff. A series of creek crossings mark the drive to the signposted **Peery Lake** turnoff, some 21 kilometres along the **Wanaaring Road**.

Track Snapshot

TOUR ROUTE:
White Cliffs to Hungerford via the Paroo River

DURATION AND DISTANCE:
The 340 kilometre trek will take two days (or more as it is easy to take a liking to this country).

TRACK DETAILS:
Rough station tracks pave the entire tour, but soft roaders and trailers are suitable if driven with care. Floodways are a particular hazard for lower slung vehicles.

WHEN TO GO:
Avoid the hot Summer months; April – October is the best time.

CAMPING:
White Cliffs, Hungerford and Wanaaring offer good camping possibilities. A bush camp near the Paroo is a possiblity – ring 08 8083 7900 for current advice.

FUEL AND SUPPLIES:
White Cliffs, Wanaaring and Hungerford.

MAPS:
Hema Outback NSW

OTHER INFORMATION:
Like all outback treks (with the possible exception of some sandy deserts) avoid wet weather. It is illegal to drive on water affected tracks and potentially dangerous to boot.

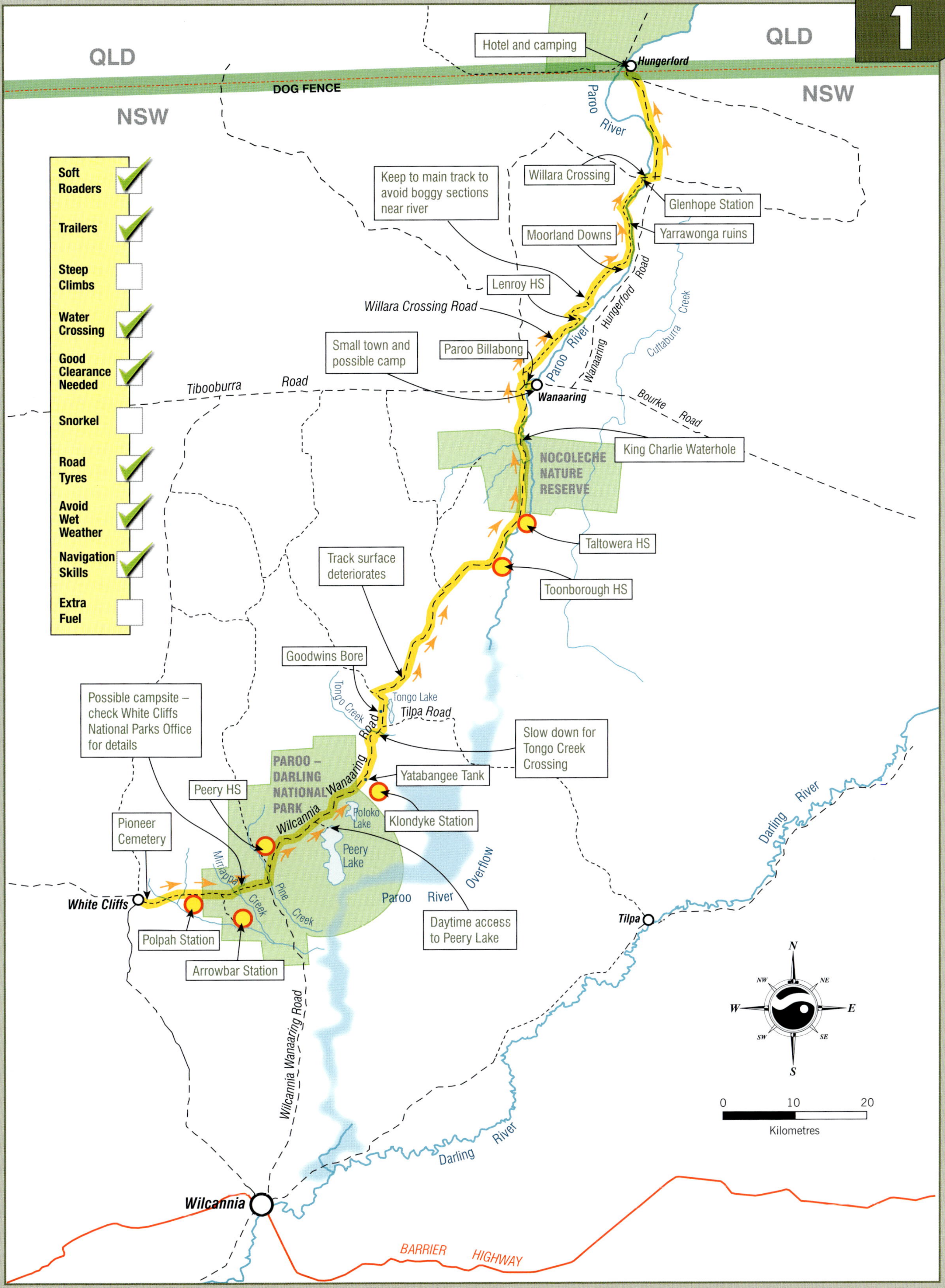
QLD
NSW
DOG FENCE
Hungerford
Hotel and camping
Paroo River
Willara Crossing
Glenhope Station
Keep to main track to avoid boggy sections near river
Moorland Downs
Yarrawonga ruins
Lenroy HS
Willara Crossing Road
Hungerford Road
Wanaaring Road
Cuttaburra Creek
Small town and possible camp
Paroo Billabong
Tibooburra Road
Wanaaring
Bourke Road
King Charlie Waterhole
NOCOLECHE NATURE RESERVE
Taltowera HS
Toonborough HS
Track surface deteriorates
Goodwins Bore
Tongo Creek
Tongo Lake
Tilpa Road
Wanaaring Road
Slow down for Tongo Creek Crossing
Yatabangee Tank
Klondyke Station
Poloko Lake
Peery Lake
PAROO – DARLING NATIONAL PARK
Wilcannia
Possible campsite – check White Cliffs National Parks Office for details
Peery HS
Pioneer Cemetery
Mirrapa Creek
Pine Creek
Paroo River Overflow
Daytime access to Peery Lake
White Cliffs
Polpah Station
Arrowbar Station
Tilpa
Darling River
Wilcannia Wanaaring Road
Wilcannia
BARRIER HIGHWAY
Soft Roaders
Trailers
Steep Climbs
Water Crossing
Good Clearance Needed
Snorkel
Road Tyres
Avoid Wet Weather
Navigation Skills
Extra Fuel
N
NE
E
SE
S
SW
W
NW
0
10
20
Kilometres

PAROO RIVER

This is your only opportunity to visit the lake system, and it is well worth making the three kilometre run into a day use parking area. If the lake holds water, birds will be plentiful, although the greater numbers congregate on **Peery's** southern shores which is inaccessible to the general public. Mound springs are also a feature of **Peery**, again these are off limits, as are a number of significant Aboriginal sites.

Continuing northward, braided creek lines dissect the open gibber plains, as **Poloko Lake** emerges just into view. **Klondyke Station** is passed on the right as we exit national park at a grid, with **Yantabangee Tank** on the right.

Cattle and sheep are now part of the picture as you enter noticeably more treed station country and a couple of creek crossings. Watch out for **Tongo Creek** – it has a tight turn on entry and exit. Keep to the left two kilometres later, away from the **Tilpa Road** on your right.

Goodwins Bore features an unusual rendered brick tank, together with a windmill just off the road. You will catch a glimpse of **Lake Tongo** on the right near here, then cross a string of floodways. The road deteriorates to track status as you reach unincorporated area (land not within a shire boundary, and requiring locals or government assistance with road maintenance).

Keep right at the **Tibooburra** turn off, some 43 kilometres beyond **Goodwins Bore**, and watch out for a hard right turn at **One Mile Bore**, nine kilometres later. **Toonborough** and **Taltowera Homesteads** mark the journey into **Nocoleche Nature Reserve** where camping, shooting and dogs are prohibited.

This nature reserve was first purchased by the NSW government to study the impact of feral pigs. It later became clear that the former station was in itself an important wetland with permanent waterholes along the **Paroo** and **Cuttaburra Creek**. You will pass several MVO tracks to arrive at the **King Charlie Waterhole** turn off some 21 kilometres from the park boundary.

Turn right to make the 500 metre detour to this day use waterhole, where birds and native fish species thrive. Pioneering pastoralists recognised the value of the permanent water source here, establishing a sheep run sometime in the 1880s. Times proved variable though, and the property changed ownership eight times within the century.

Return to the main road and turn right to leave the nature reserve shortly after, before reaching a tee intersection and turning right to **Wanaaring**. You will pass a road to the left (this is the **Paroo's** west bank alternative run to **Hungerford**, and our prefered route beyond **Wanaaring**), then cross the **Paroo Billabong** into **Wanaaring**.

A clutch of 20 or so houses, together with school, police, store and fuel outlet make up the outback community. A pub and campground may entice you to stay the night, just as it did more than a century ago, when the town provided support for surrounding sheep properties, including a wool scouring plant on the banks of the **Paroo**.

Hungerford is our next destination, just over 100 kilometres to the north. The main gravel road is located to the east, about 12 kilometres from town, on the **Bourke Road**. It is the quickest run to the Queensland border, but we prefer to take the **Willara Crossing Road** which more closely follows the river, albeit with nearly a dozen gates to open and close.

Head west out of town, back over the **Paroo Billabong**, then turn immediately right after the bridge to signposted "**Hamilton Gate**". You will veer right again six kilometres from town onto a signposted turn "**Willara Crossing**", although the signage is hard to see at the turn.

Riverine trees are visible on the right as you pass **Lenroy HS** on the left, and reach a number of station track options over the next 10 kilometres. Keep to the more clearly defined through road, and avoid lesser used tracks, which can be boggy due to the river floodplain proximity.

Numerous gates mark the next 40 kilometres as **Moorland Downs** and the ruins of **Yarrawonga** are passed, before an old timber stockyard heralds **Glenhope Station**. Keep to the right away from the homestead, and swing east to yet another gate, for a crossing of the **Paroo**. It is a rocky base, and the multiple water paths through this undulating area make it a scenic location. A side track to the gauging station would make a nice lunch stop or informal camp.

Two kilometres further east from **Willara Crossing** you will reach the main **Wanaaring – Hungerford Road**. Turn left here to travel a routine 30

Willara Crossing road

kilometres to reach a gate in the **Dog Fence** (Qld border), and the township of **Hungerford**.

A clutch of houses form the backbone of this community with the **Royal Mail Hotel** being the obvious centrepiece. Originally a Cobb and Co staging post, the 1873 structure still provides food and refreshment for visitors, together with gravity fed diesel fuel and accommodation. A caravan park is also available in town with good facilities.

Options beyond **Hungerford** include continuing to follow the **Paroo** to its source, or taking the **Dowling Track** to **Thargomindah** (see our MAKE TRAX QUEENSLAND guidebook for details of both).

Right: *Dog Fence gate*

Below: *Hungerford Hotel*

TRACK 29 CORNER COUNTRY

OUTBACK NSW

Silver City Highway

Track Snapshot

TOUR ROUTE:
Tibooburra to Cameron Corner via Sturt NP.

DURATION AND DISTANCE:
The 240 kilometre run can be done in a day, with many options to extend the time frame.

TRACK DETAILS:
Old station country tracks provide routine travel conditions, but low range and reasonable clearances may be required to negotiate low sand hills on the Middle Road leg

WHEN TO GO:
Avoid the hotter months and sustained wet weather (April to October is best).

CAMPING:
National Park camping with basic facilities at Dead Horse Gully, Olive Downs, Mount Wood and Fort Grey. No campfires are permitted within the national park, but gas BBQs are provided. Commercial opportunities are available at Tibooburra and Cameron Corner.

FUEL AND SUPPLIES:
Tibooburra and Cameron Corner.

MAPS:
Natmap 1:250K Milparinka

OTHER INFORMATION:
Nearby Milparinka is well worth a visit. The restored sandstone courthouse stands prominent in the old gold mining town, and there are significant reminders of Sturt's expedition through this area in 1845.

*Charles Sturt and his intrepid party of explorers dragged a 27 foot whaleboat into the harsh interior of this country, arriving in modern day **Tibooburra** to temperatures of 40 degrees and dust storms. Their hopes of finding a vast inland sea evaporated in the extreme weather and desolate country. In reality they were millions of years late; the sea level had long since retreated, leaving only desert and the occasional fossil to mark its passing.*

*Sturt was a determined leader however, and continued his push northward during the winter of 1845 to establish **Fort Grey** as a forward camp. The depot was to become a vital staging point for later forays toward this country's centre.*

*These days with all of the hard work now done by Sturt (and others), travel into **Corner Country** is both safe and accessible. **Sturt National Park** encompasses a large section of north west NSW, with **Cameron Corner** marking this state's junction with **Queensland** and **South Australia**.*

*The most direct route from **Tibooburra** to **Cameron Corner** can be undertaken by almost any conventional vehicle in the dry, but wet weather will quickly transform these roads. Summer rainfall is usually more of a nuisance for travellers, as it can cut unsealed roads for a short time. However the more troublesome winter rains can see vehicles stranded for days at a time – good enough reason to always travel this part of the country with up to date weather information.*

This tour takes in much of the national park by avoiding the usual routes, and following old station roads in addition to some dedicated 4WD sections.

You will begin at **Tibooburra** on the **Silver City Highway**. This small township survives on a struggling pastoral industry and tourism in the main, although basic services are available. The town's two pubs look at each other from across the main road, and can each offer accommodation, meals and friendly outback hospitality.

Both establishments date from the late 1880s when gold mining and grazing were competing as the district's main focus. The transition from prospecting to sheep put enormous pressure on the limited resources across **Corner Country**, with water and timber being items of great demand.

The gold mining industry expanded slowly as techniques such as dry blowing took over from puddling and other water intensive wet sieving methods. A display of mining apparatus can be found at **Golden Gully**; a couple of kilometres north of town.

While this site is a reconstruction of the earlier days, it has been well assembled, with relics and camps spread across a rather forlorn looking patch of dirt. Nearby **Dead Horse Gully Campground** is the closest bush camp to **Tibooburra**, but with toilets, tables and gas BBQs, it makes an excellent stop over.

You can explore this area on foot via **The Granites Nature Trail** as it weaves through a maze of jumbled boulders. Bloodwoods and red gums line usually dry creek beds, where wildflowers may emerge following rain. Sturts desert pea

Soft Roaders	
Trailers	✓
Steep Climbs	
Water Crossing	
Good Clearance Needed	✓
Snorkel	
Road Tyres	✓
Avoid Wet Weather	✓
Navigation Skills	
Extra Fuel	

The Granites

is commonly seen and you may be lucky enough to spot a euro hopping about the rocky terrain, as it looks for shade during the heat of the day, or grazes on native grasses late in the afternoon.

Visitors preparing to leave **Tibooburra** should fill up with fuel and water before setting out along the **Wanaaring Road**, to the east of town. You will pass an airstrip on your left as good gravel paves a way for 25 kilometres to signposted **Gorge Loop Road**. Turn left here to find the historic remains of an ambitious wool scouring operation, at the end of an access track on your right.

Because clean wool was lighter than raw fleece, the freight costs were lower after scouring; an outcome of considerable value in this remote region of NSW. Also vital for the graziers operation was a reliable supply of water. This site displays a reconstructed horse drawn whim and a "walking beam" – each of which was employed to lift water from wells dotted across the spread.

Nearby **Mount Wood HS** dates from 1886, when 500 000 acres of land was set aside for sheep grazing. Some of this land and the private homestead complex have now become part of **Sturt National Park**. A campground at **Mount Wood** is located north of **Thompsons Creek**, with birdlife and other animals attracted to its dam.

Continue north along **Gorge Loop Road** through open gibber plains and mitchell grasses. The flat landscape extends for many kilometres as you follow a slightly undulating trail over potential floodways and silcrete pebbles. Lines of thicker vegetation trace the dry creek beds, while gidgee groves mark an opening in the **Mount Wood Hills**.

Swing to the west as you follow **Twelve Mile Creek** past a gorge lookout. Walkers can climb a rocky outcrop here that takes in the **Bulloo River Overflow** to the east, and **Caryapundy Swamp** to the north, both of which spill across the Queensland – NSW border.

The **Gorge Loop Road** continues westward past a number of artesian bores, with the **South Torrens Bore** now assisted by a huge windmill. Back in its heyday, this bore alone accounted for nearly 500 000 litres of water per day that gushed to the surface – an unsustainable drain on the artesian basin that was to continue for ten years.

Horton HS ruins are situated further up **Twelve Mile Creek** on the edge of gibber plain. While the external concrete slab and galvanised iron residence looks sound, the interior is slowly deteriorating under the harsh conditions.

Follow the **Gorge Loop Road** to its conclusion on the **Silver City Highway** (a journey of 52 kilometres from **Mount**

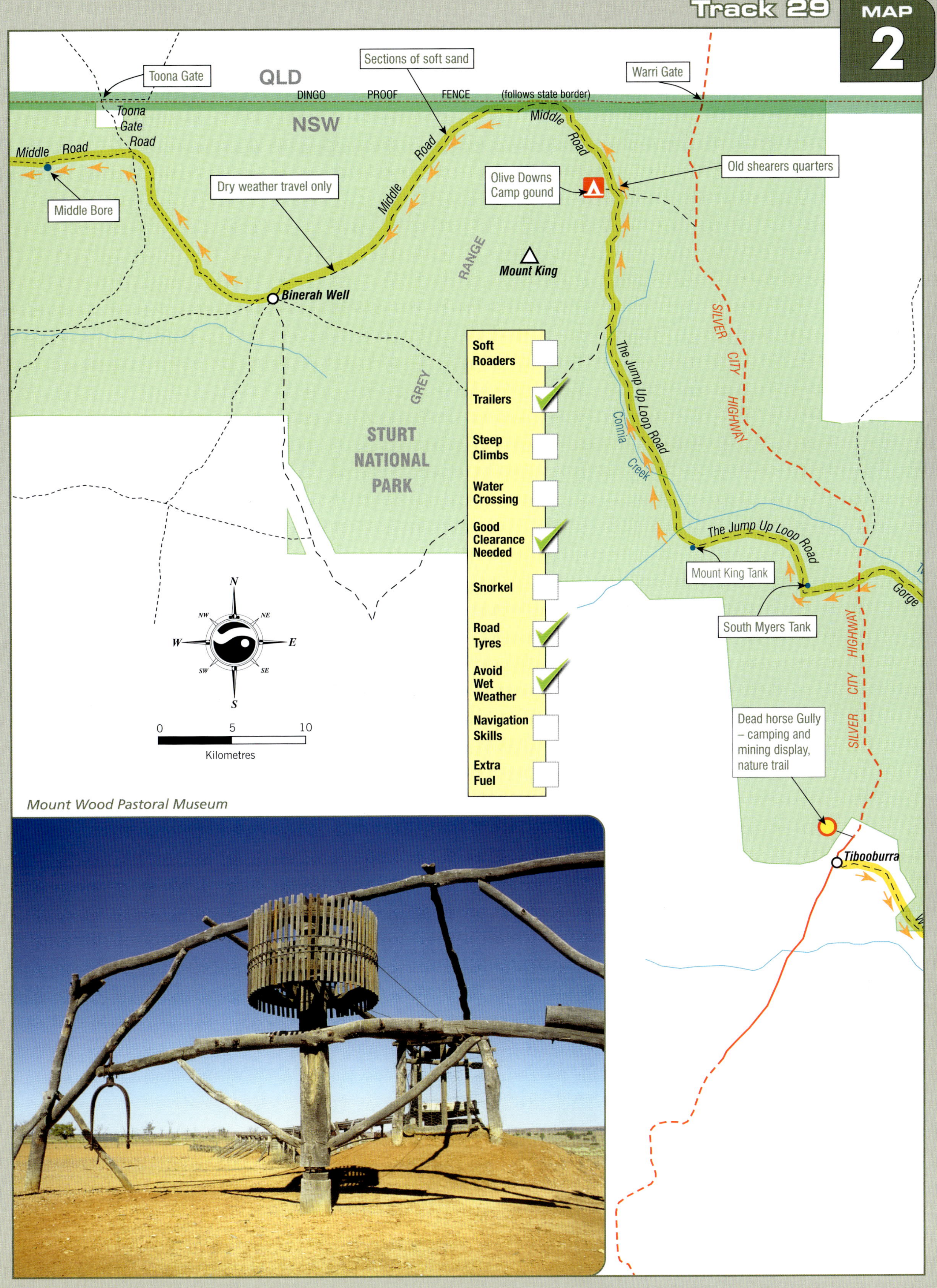

Mount Wood Pastoral Museum

Fort Grey

Wood HS), and continue along **Jump Up Loop Road**, beginning on the west side of the highway. This road follows **Twelve Mile Creek**, before branching along **Connia Creek** to head northwards, reaching **Olive Downs Campground**, some 38 kilometres from the highway.

Along the way you will pass **South Myers** and **Mount King Tanks** – both waterholes were originally part of **Mount King Station**, and eventually merged, together with a parcel of land into **Sturt National Park**. Birdlife is especially noticeable at these two waterpoints, with parrots, budgerigars and galahs regularly spotted. Other wildlife to be found in **Corner Country** includes emus, wedge tailed eagles, and a sizable population of red kangaroos.

Follow coolibah lined **Connia Creek** on a journey toward the impressive jump ups of the **Grey Range**. These gleaming white and autumn toned mesas stand distinctly above the horizon, with flat tops and steep sides. Layers of dissimilar conglomerates have formed the ranges, with erosion undercutting the tough upper cap, leaving a series of tabletop mountains 150 metres above the plains.

You will reach **Olive Downs Campground** at the foot of **Mount King** and find the usual facilities – toilets, tables and gas BBQs. Campfires are not permitted across the park, and while water tanks are provided, it is best to carry plenty of your own.

Continue north from the campground turn off to reach a century old shearer's quarters, now roofless on the right side. Turn left here and follow an access road toward **Olive Downs HS**, but swing right onto **Middle Road**, just before you reach the private homestead complex.

Signposted 4WD only, **Middle Road** will be closed in wet weather, but when open offers relatively easy passage across the state's northern most reaches. Old yards and derelict fences mark the journey to the **Dingo Proof Fence**, delineating the state's border. Sections of soft sand will have you in and out of 4WD as you head west, back away from the netting fence and along **Fromes Creek**.

You will follow some rutted country to disused **Binerah Well**, which marks the completion of **Middle Road's** first leg, some 31 kilometres beyond **Olive Downs**. Turn right onto the **Toona Gate Road**, with range country emerging from the east, and follow the good gravel for 14 kilometres.

The second leg of **Middle Road** begins at this junction, where you swing left into increasingly desolate country. Redder sand dunes mark the transition into the eastern **Strzelecki Desert**, with some sand hills reaching 15 metres above the lower lying claypans.

Middle Road weaves a path over the lower dunes, but some corrugated climbs may pull you back to low range, or even require a tyre pressure reduction

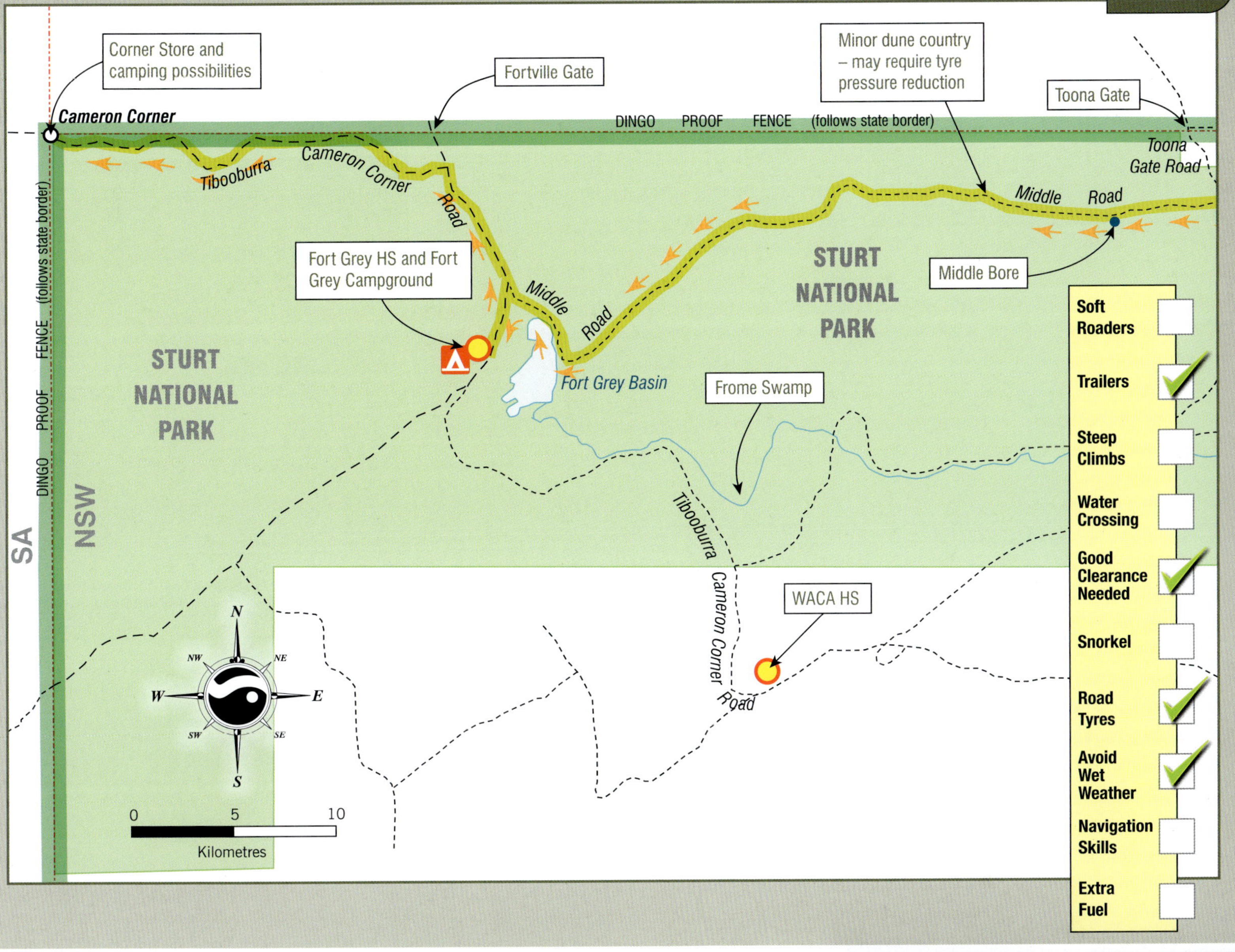

Corner Store and camping possibilities
Cameron Corner
Fortville Gate
Minor dune country – may require tyre pressure reduction
Toona Gate
DINGO PROOF FENCE (follows state border)
Toona Gate Road
Tibooburra Cameron Corner Road
Middle Road
Middle Bore
STURT NATIONAL PARK
Fort Grey HS and Fort Grey Campground
Fort Grey Basin
Frome Swamp
SA
NSW
Tibooburra Cameron Corner Road
WACA HS
N NE E SE S SW W NW
0 5 10
Kilometres

Soft Roaders	
Trailers	✓
Steep Climbs	
Water Crossing	
Good Clearance Needed	✓
Snorkel	
Road Tyres	✓
Avoid Wet Weather	✓
Navigation Skills	
Extra Fuel	

for successful progress. Gibbers and canegrass swampland heralds your approach into the **Fort Grey Basin**, and the possibility of sighting some buzzards.

The main **Tibooburra – Cameron Corner Road** is met 39 kilometres beyond the **Toona Gate Road**, where you can turn left toward **Fort Grey**. The old **Fort Grey HS** marks a left turn to **Fort Grey Campground** and the usual facilities.

You have now reached Sturt's most northerly base camp, and the site of a stockade where protection was found from local aboriginal groups. Sturt's men planted pumpkins and melons, and were sustained by a significant waterhole. The outpost confined horses and numerous bullocks, while ensuring the safety of some 200 sheep.

Today it is possible to walk to the **Sturt Tree** – a blazed coolibah on the **Fort Grey Basin**, or simply take in this remote mulga and hakea country now recovering from the ravages of unsustainable grazing.

Return northward from **Fort Grey** to the **Middle Road** junction, and continue beyond that intersection for nine kilometres to the **Fortville Gate** turn off. Keep left at this junction, and continue along the main road for 22 kilometres.

The **Corner Store** marks **Cameron Corner** and the three states' junction. Food, fuel and camping opportunities are available to travellers, who must first drive through a gate on the **Dog Fence**. You will have some fun jumping from state to state, and taking the obligatory photos around the corner post.

Old meathouse near Camerons Corner

TRACK 30

DARLING RIVER

OUTBACK NSW

Track Snapshot

TOUR ROUTE:
Wentworth to Bourke tracing the Darling River upstream.

DURATION AND DISTANCE:
Three days would be the minimum time frame to take in the highlights of this 800 kilometre drive.

TRACK DETAILS:
Unsealed station tracks in the main, suitable for all vehicles and trailers.

WHEN TO GO:
The cooler months (April – October) are best, but avoid wet weather, which will quickly prevent vehicle travel.

CAMPING:
There is river side camping at all of the towns detailed, together with station stay opportunities. Check maps and text for details.

FUEL AND SUPPLIES:
Regularly available at the towns en route, but keep topped up, as wet weather could strand you for days at a time.

MAPS:
Hema Outback NSW

OTHER INFORMATION:
An iconic road trip oozing with history and character towns.

Tandure Lake

There was a time when the quickest way to travel through the parched outback of NSW was by boat. Steamers plied the ***Darling*** *on a tortuous route past sheep stations and fledgling towns. These days the fluctuating river levels preclude reliable boat travel, but 4WDers can follow the* ***Darling's*** *serpentine path via station tracks and the communities marking a handful of bridge crossings along its length.*

The track and road system offers a choice of travel on either side of the river, but these notes follow the lesser used of the two options in the main, crossing the river as required. Camping opportunities are plentiful, together with station accommodation and the usual formal offerings from the main towns en route.

This trek follows an 800 kilometre run from the ***Darling's*** *confluence with the* ***Murray*** *to its origins near* ***Bourke****, where several upstream rivers coalesce. In dry weather this is an easy run, but even a hint of rain will raise the bar in short order.*

We begin the journey at **Wentworth** – an historic town on the **Murray / Darling junction**. A lock and weir at the downstream end of town (Lock #10 on the Murray) keeps the water level high at **Wentworth**, and in fact the back up from the weir usually creates a body of water extending for about 60 river kilometres upstream on the **Darling**.

The Darling was opened up for river trade in the 1850s and by the late 1880s **Wentworth** was Australia's busiest inland port. In 1895, 485 vessels were recorded as having been processed by the Customs House. Originally known as **Hawdon's Ford**, the town was renamed **Wentworth** after the explorer William Charles Wentworth. Its population continued to grow, and the town centre features many colonial buildings dating from the river boat days. If you prefer to see the town and its surrounds from the river, there are tourist cruises operating most days of the year.

Visitors will find a wide range of accommodation possibilities available in the town. At **Willow Bend Caravan Park,** just upstream of the **Darling** confluence, the tree where Charles Sturt anchored for the night may still be seen, along with its commemorative plaque. The

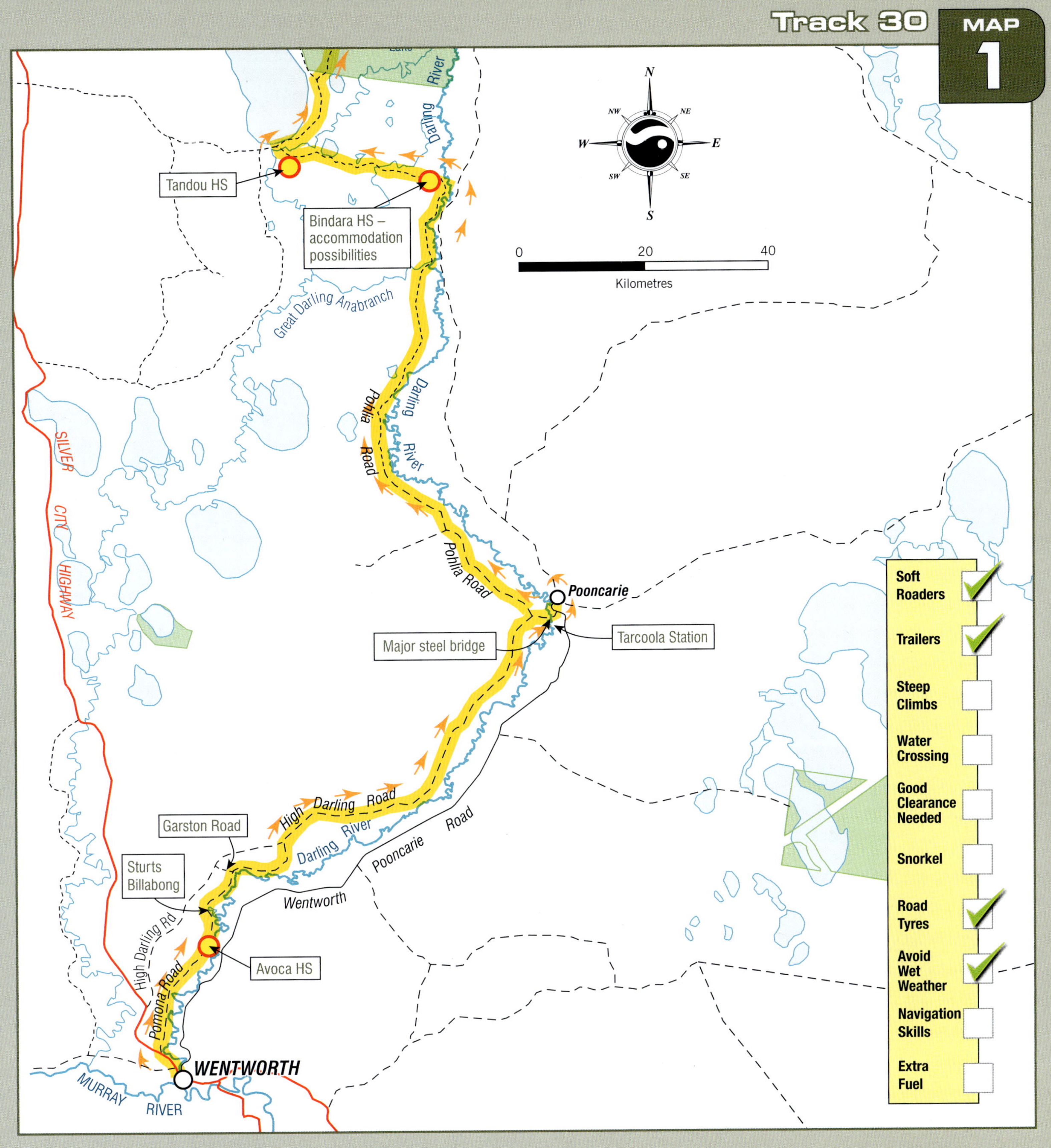

town has two supermarkets, a couple of cafes, a bakery and some great places to get a meal.

Head west out of town on the **Silver City Highway**, turning right six kilometres later on the **Pomona Road**. Vineyards and a clutch of houses flag unsealed road shortly after as you pass **Pomona** and **Avoca Homesteads**.

Avoca marks the extent of back up water from **Lock 10** and its weir on the **Murray**. It offers terrific overnight accommodation, as well as day visitor morning and afternoon teas. Accommodation options include the homestead itself, cottages and the Jackaroos Quarters, and river side camping.

More details at *www.users.bigpond.com/lawsavoca*

Continue past **Sturts Billabong** and **Garston Road** to reach the **High Darling Road** junction some 34 kilometres from **Avoca HS**. Turn right at the intersection signposted **"Pooncarie"** to head away from the river through a graveyard of skeletal trees.

DARLING RIVER

Sandy soil and well marked grids offer easy travel, as you return to irrigated land closer to **Pooncarie**. Veer right away from **Pohlia Road** to reach a major steel bridge (built 1963) spanning the **Darling River**, and a short run into **Pooncarrie**.

Originally gazetted as **"Pooncaira"** in 1863, the area was settled by Europeans from the 1840s. Explorers Burke and Wills reached the **Darling River** at nearby **Tarcoola Station** and made camp at what is now **Bilbarka Park** in September 1860 – the initial push into their ill-fated expedition. The town gradually developed into a service centre for surrounding pastoral properties and a port for river trade on the **Darling**.

Modern day **Pooncarie** has a general store and fuel outlet, together with the old pub and abandoned iron buildings. The original wharf no longer stands, but visitors can appreciate its significance from the information board adjacent. Check with the **Telegraph Hotel** if you want to use the river side camping area.

Cross back over the **Darling** and follow **Pohlia Road** for some 93 kilometres on a deteriorating track to **Bindara HS**. This is a great place to stay, with a river side camping area, cabin accommodation and roaring log fire to boot. **Bindara** is part of what used to be **Netley Station**; one of the biggest stock runs on the **Darling** with its own wharf in the river boat days. More details at *www.outbackbeds.com.au*

Many maps of this area still show a track heading north from **Bindara**, however this has been closed to the public for 32 years. Instead you will swing to the west and head for **Tandou Station** on the southern edge of **Kinchega NP**. You will reach a tee intersection about 30 kilometres west of **Bindara**, where you swing right to enter the national park and head toward **Menindee**.

There are many things to see and do within **Kinchega**; for example, the **Emu Lake Drive** leads past **Emu Lake** to **Kinchega Woolshed** and onwards to some great river side camping. **Lake Drive** heads west, passing **Lake Cawndilla**, **Cawndilla Camping Area** and **Lake Menindee**. **River Drive** is a continuation of **Emu Lake Drive** and follows the western river bank, offering more great camping. Information on the park and these drives can be found at **Kinchega Woolshed**.

As an alternative to camping in the national park, there are commercial camping grounds in **Menindee** (poulation 400). Good camping areas include **Copi Hollow Caravan Park** (15 kilometres north of Menindee, on the shores of **Lake Pamamaroo)** and **Menindee Lake Park** (closer to town, on **Lakes Shore Road**, adjoining **Lake Menindee**). Other accommodation options include **Maidens Hotel**, a renowned hostelry, where Burke and Wills spent a few nights on their expedition of 1860 (it was called **Paines Hotel** at that time).

Beyond **Menindee**, it is worthwhile taking a look at the **Main Weir** of the **Menindee Lakes system**. This imposing structure controls the flow of water in the lower reaches of the **Darling**. The weir is signposted off the eastern **Wilcannia Road** about 12 kilometres from the edge of town and is only a short detour. There are a couple of camping areas near the weir (including the one used by Burke and Wills) which are quite popular with canoeists and anglers. These are easily accessible from this side of the river unless water levels are unusually high.

Return to the east bank road and follow the dirt nothward veering right some 16.5 kilometres from **Menindee** to cross a substantial bridge over **3 Mile Creek**. You will reach a game reserve about 34 kilometres out of **Menindee**, which provides hunting opportunities in season.

Informal camping is also possible here, with pelicans, sea eagles and other birds abundant. You will follow a levee bank on your left (vehicle track on top of levee parallels main road) to reach a wildlife refuge area a few kilometres later.

Continue past sheep grazing on **Viewmont Station** to reach **Barraroo Station**, then the impressive grounds of **Tintinallogy HS**. Corrugated iron sheds and old telegraph posts dot the harsh country, as increasing sand drifts colour the run to **Talyawalka Creek**. You will reach the **Barrier Highway** about 155 kilometres from **Menindee**, where you turn left for an 18 kilometre sealed run into **Wilcannia**.

Kinchega wool press

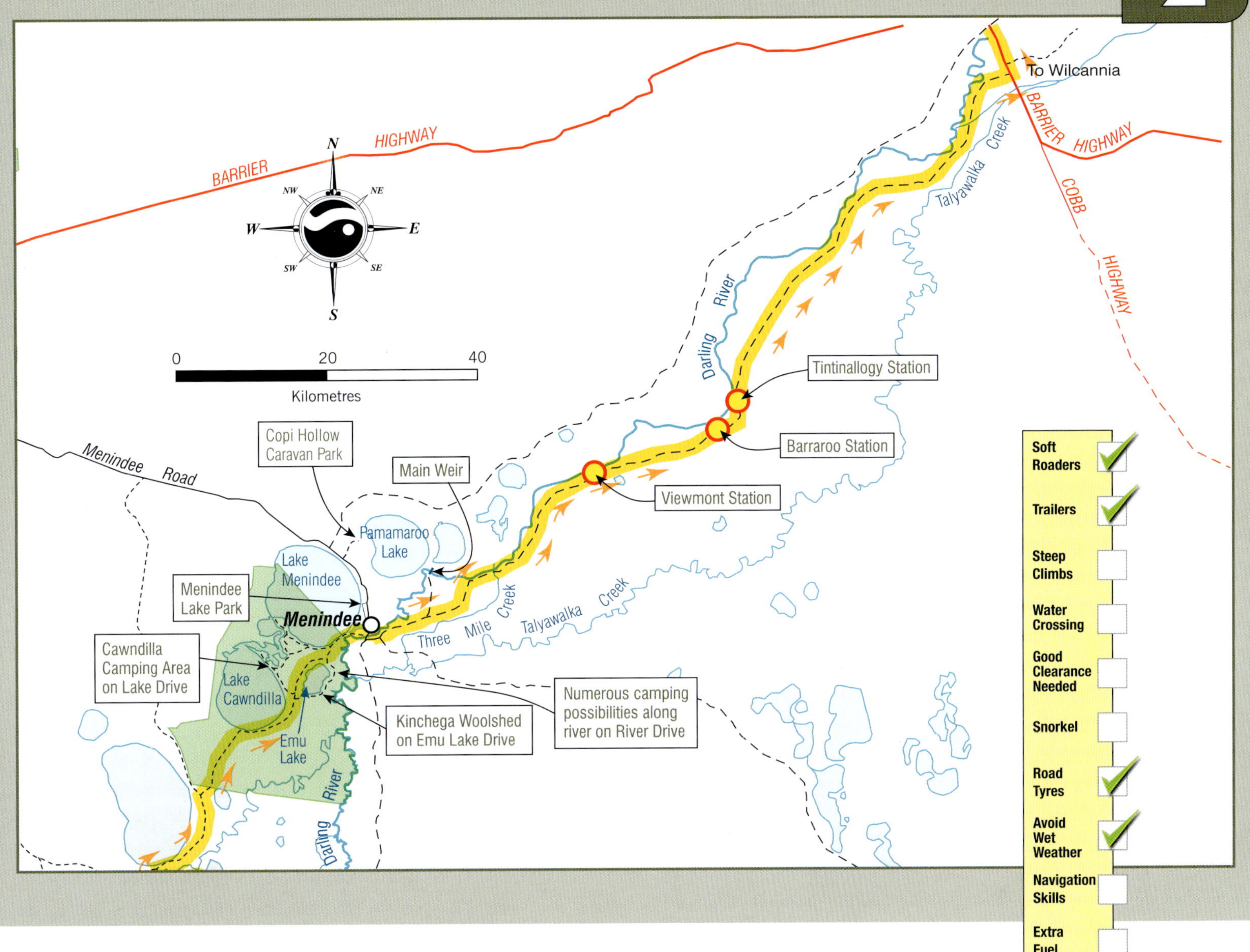

Wilcannia has a population of about 700 and is an old riverboat town with many buildings dating from the late 1800s (the shire offices have a heritage trail brochure and map that describes all of the notable buildings in town). The camping area is on the east bank, alongside the new **Darling Bridge**, and is only a short walk into the town centre. Only a few shops and services operate within the town, and accommodation options include two motels.

Remain on the **Darling's** west bank to head north from **Wilcannia** on the **Hamilton Road**. Cross **Kalyyanka Creek**, then the more substantial **Paroo River Bridge**, with obvious floodplain flanking the usually dry waterway. Numerous grids punctuate the journey through **Mount Murchison** – slow down for most as they feature a rather sharp entry and exit. Old yards and fences precede the boundary of **Paroo Darling NP**, some 17.6 kilometres from the **Paroo** crossing.

Continue past **Bonview Station** and **Rosedale HS** to reach a tee intersection on the **Wanaaring Road** at **Tilpa**. We will continue upriver by turning left here, but the corrugated iron pub is well worth a stop. Informal camping is available at the **Tilpa Weir**, some six kilometres north of the whistle stop town on the east bank. Easy water access is possible upstream of the weir, with plenty of shade on offer.

Head north from **Tilpa** on the west bank to pass **Kallara Station** (accommodation possible, *www.kallarastation.com.au*) to a major junction 27 kilometres from **Tilpa**. Keep right to cross **Talyawalka Creek** and reach **Idalia HS** 20 kilometres later. **Idalia** also offers camping and other accommodation on a nice river bend (*www.idaliastationstay.com.au*).

You cross **Talyawalka Creek** yet again to pass **Trilby Station** (*www.trilbystation.com.au* for accommodation details). Turn right at a tee intersection 21 kilometres beyond **Trilby HS** to cross a bridge over the **Darling** and arrive at **Louth**.

With a nominal population of about 50, the town has a limited range of services, including hotel, general store and fuel outlet. There is also a B&B (in the old Post Office), and an informal camping area alongside the bridge. The town cemetery is regularly visited for a headstone that was positioned to reflect the evening sun onto the bereaved's front door once a year upon her birthday.

We leave the brightly painted town via the more commonly used east bank, taking wider road (though still potentially rutted) over sealed grids – luxury! Pass by **Rose Isle Station** with its neat river side camping and shearers quarters accommodation to reach the **Gundabooka NP** turn off a couple of kilometres later.

(The **Gundabooka** detour offers an alternative route to **Bourke** via the **Kidman Way**. Campers will find basic facilities at **Dry Tank**, with a couple of short walks on offer. **Bennet Gorge** has basic facilities and other walking possibilities, but no camping. Aboriginal rock art is also represented in the park, with an impressive site located at **Mulareenya Creek**.)

Continue north from **Toorale East** to cross **Hume Creek** on an elevated bridge, with a memorial plaque to the Sturt Expedition of 1829. There is nice river side camping here, via an unsignposted track directly ahead that leads for about a kilometre to the **Darling**.

The **Fort Bourke Stockade** is reached on the left some 87 kilometres from **Louth**. Visitors who take the short detour will pass a wildlife refuge, before reaching a replica stockade, similar to the one built by Major Thomas Mitchell and party in 1835.

Return to the main road and head north to reach the **Kidman Way**, and a left turn toward **Bourke**. With a population of about 2600, this town is a major centre for the district, and most services are available.

There is a variety of accommodation on offer in and around town, including a caravan park. Eight kilometres north of the town centre, **Kidman's Camp Tourist Park** has good amenties and is conveniently situated adjacent to the **Back o' Bourke Hotel**. **Kidman's Camp** is also home to the **Jandra paddle steamer** which runs a popular tourist cruise.

Lake Pamamaroo

Tilpa Hotel

There is self sufficient camping at **Mays Bend**, just north of **Kidman's Camp**. Access is found by continuing north (on the **Cunnamulla Road**) beyond **North Bourke**, and turning east at the old signpost for **Bullamunta Caravan Park** (the park is long closed). This turn off is about 5.5 kilometres from the **Back o' Bourke Hotel**. Follow a pot holed track through to the river and the day visitor area. Better camps will be found further upstream, as you swing to the left on narrower track.

On the opposite side of the river, and at about the same distance from **Bourke**, there is additional bush camping. In this case take the **Brewarrina Road** east from town and look out for the track going off to the left, just before a cattle grid.

Bourke Weir and **Lock** are downstream of the town centre, and may be reached via **Anson Street**. The weir was originally just a lock (part of the scheme that made

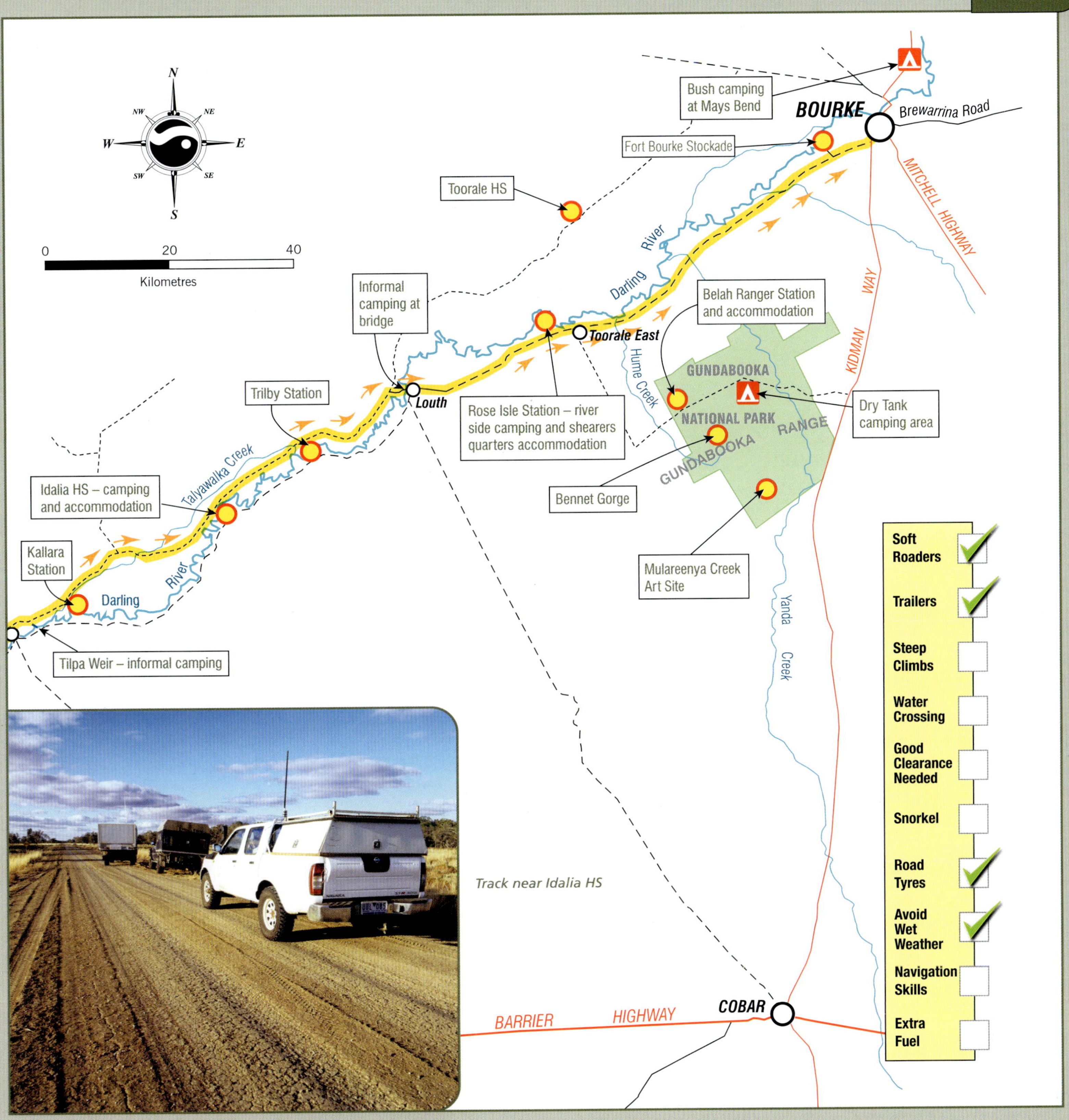

Track near Idalia HS

the **Murray – Darling System** navigable at low water levels) and was converted into a typical Murray River style Lock and Weir in 1941. Closer to the town centre, **Bourke Wharf** is a lofty reminder of the river boat days and is a popular place for a picnic.

Options for travel beyond **Bourke** include the 100 kilometre bitumen run to **Brewarrina** (population 1500, on the banks of the **Barwon River**), or 200 kilometres of gravel west to **Wanaaring** (nice camping on the **Paroo River**). You could also head north west for 70 kilometres to **Fords Bridge** (a small settlement on the **Warrego River** with camping opportunities and the well known **Warrego Hotel**), or continue to **Hungerford** on the Queensland border (home to the **Royal Mail Hotel** – a Cobb and Co hostelry from yesteryear.

TRACK 31 LACHLAN RIVER

OUTBACK NSW

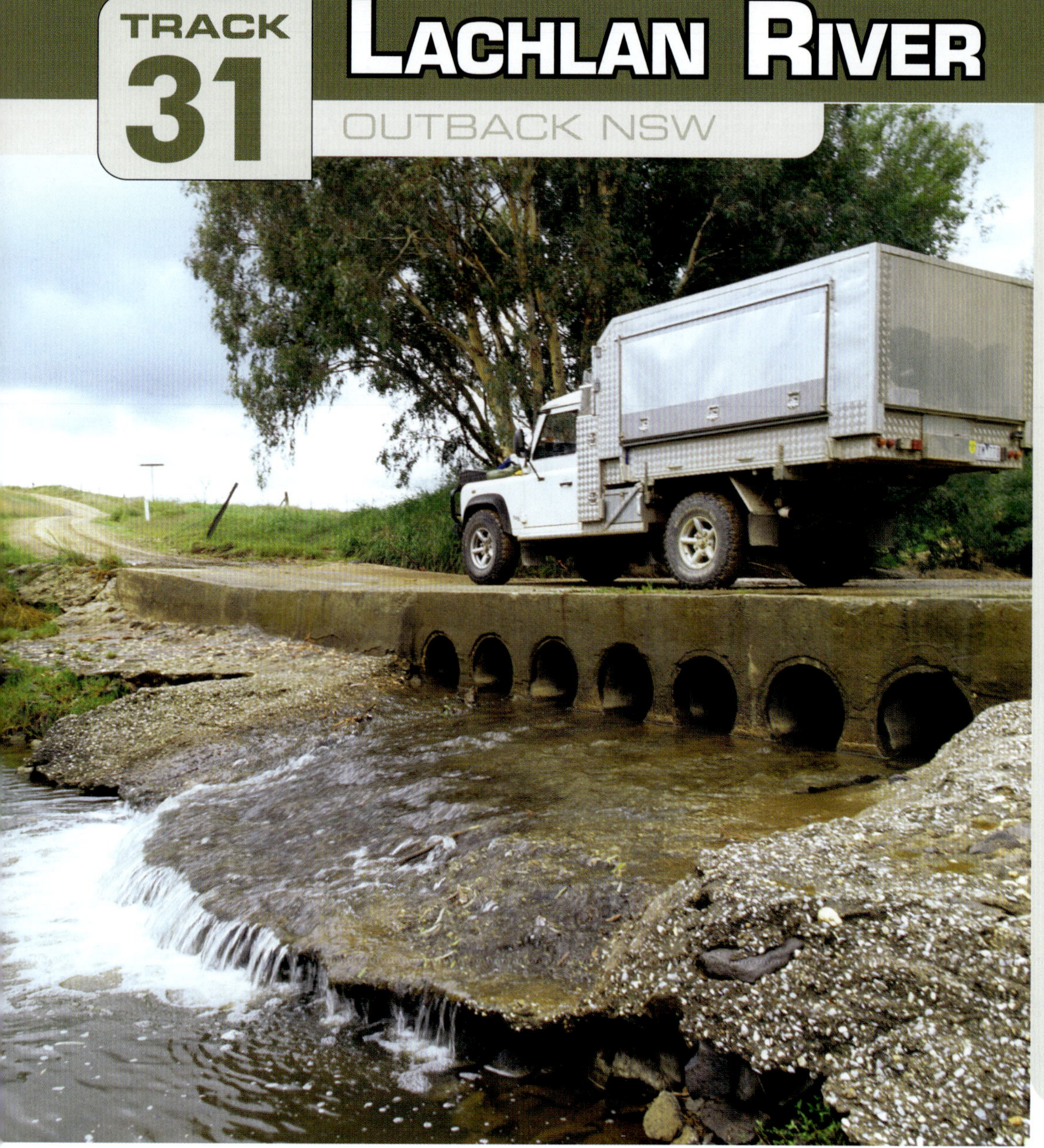

Road to Reids Flat

Track Snapshot

TOUR ROUTE:
Gunning to Oxley following the Lachlan River.

DURATION AND DISTANCE:
Three or four days will be required to complete the 980 kilometre trek, allowing for regular stops.

TRACK DETAILS:
A combination of forestry roads, station tracks, and some bitumen offers easy travel; suitable for all vehicles and trailers.

WHEN TO GO:
All year round, avoiding sustained wet weather.

CAMPING:
Commercial campgrounds at every town, and some bush possibilities along the route.

FUEL AND SUPPLIES:
Available at every town except Oxley at the conclusion of the tour. Carry enough fuel for an additional 100 kilometres beyond Oxley.

MAPS:
Natmap 1:250K Goulburn, Bathurst, Forbes, Cargelligo, Booligal

OTHER INFORMATION:
This is a great journey following one of NSW's almost mythical waterways. The transition from mountains and productive river flats to the drier western reaches of the state brings home the diversity of landscape across its length.

*When John Oxley travelled the length of the **Lachlan River** in 1817 he was less than enthusiastic about its prospects for development. He concluded that it is "impossible to fancy a worse country than the one we are travelling over now". Oxley had followed much of the **Lachlan's** contorted 1500 kilometre route, to be confronted with marsh area and desolate scrub away from the river flats.*

These days 4WDers can undertake a similar journey through thirsty inland country, albeit from the comfort of a vehicle, and appreciate the influence of pastoralists who have extracted a viable fruit, vegetable, and grazing industry from the vital river water. Seasonal variation plays its role too – in times of plentiful rain the river brings life to inland NSW, while drought will see it contract to a series of waterholes.

This trip begins at **Gunning**, just a few kilometres off the **Hume Highway** between **Yass** and **Goulburn**. An 1870s pub together with cafe and character buildings line the main street. Free short term camping is permitted on **Meadow Creek**, where ducks cruise the willow lined weir. Toilets and showers are provided, and the **Telegraph Hotel** is just a short stroll away.

You will head out of town on the **Dalton Road**, winding up and over the rail line to pass an historic siding. Grazing dominates the undulating terrain, with both sheep and cattle being run. **Dalton** is reached 12 kilometres later, where fossilized rock can be seen on **Oolong Creek**. Some rustic steel sculptures adorn the local pub, where you turn right to head out of town.

You will cross a few gullies in the old gold mining area, before reaching a scenic stretch of **Kildare Creek**. Its cast iron bridge first carried traffic in 1935, and remains viable to this day. Keep left at **Bulleys Crossing Road** to follow the **Lachlan's** sandy river bed on your right.

A bridge spans **Blakney Creek** as you pass some pine plantation, on your way to a junction 38 kilometres from **Gunning**. Turn right toward signposted "**Crookwell**", to cross the **Lachlan** at a causeway. Continue on the **Mullengrove Road**, then turn left, five kilometres from the river.

You will pass a homestead and church on the left, before swinging left again at the locality of **Mullengrove**, and continuing to a tee intersection on the **Crookwell – Boorowa Road**. Turn left on the blacktop past a church marking the locality of **Narrawah**, to make a scenic run westward – especially colourful in autumn. Another isolated church and cemetery flashes by as superb range views mark the approaching **Lachlan River**.

A substantial bridge spans the now gathering waters, as you continue

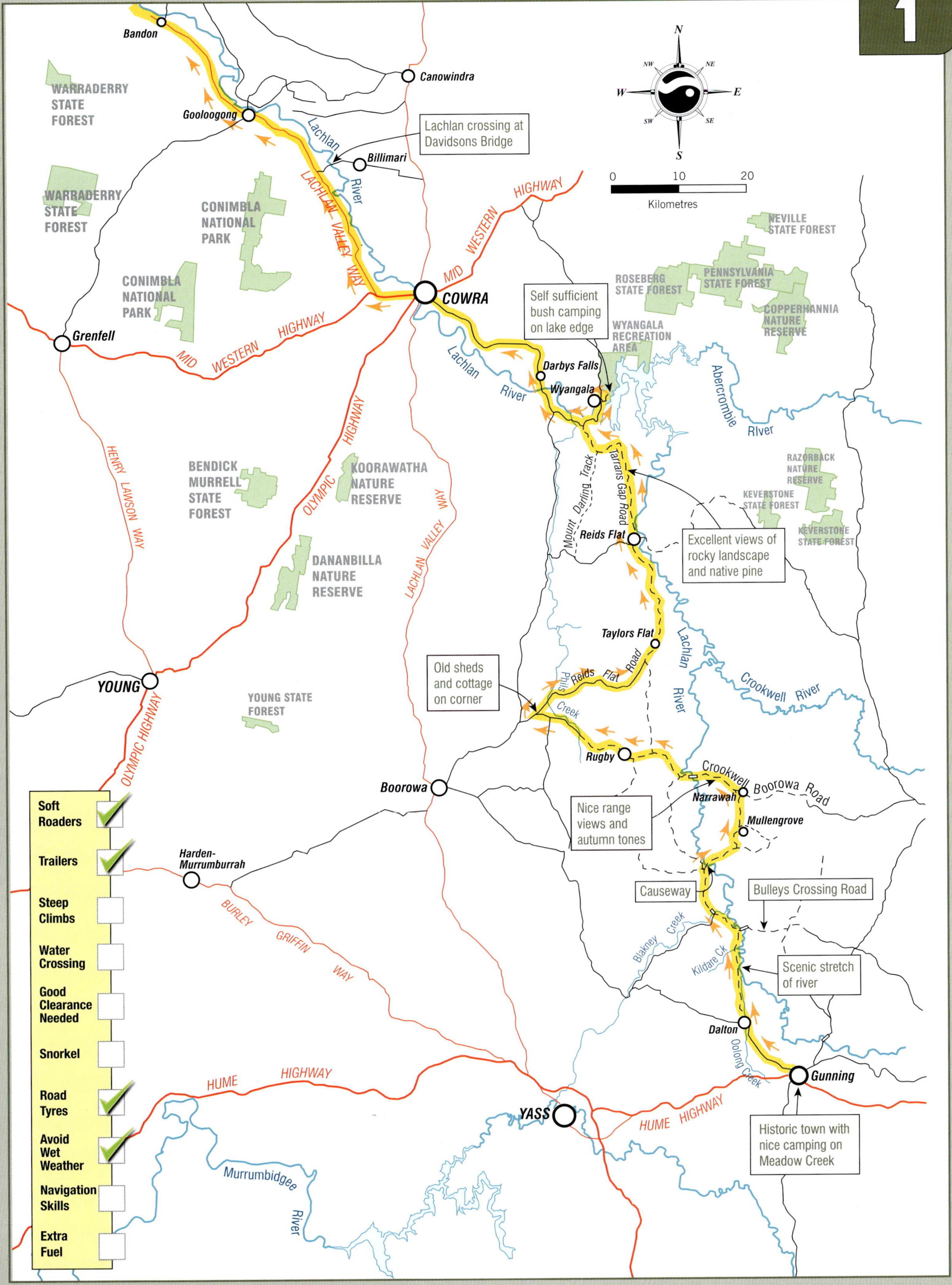

Bandon
Canowindra
WARRADERRY STATE FOREST
Gooloogong
Lachlan River
Lachlan crossing at Davidsons Bridge
Billimari
LACHLAN VALLEY WAY
WARRADERRY STATE FOREST
CONIMBLA NATIONAL PARK
CONIMBLA NATIONAL PARK
N
NW
NE
W
E
SW
SE
S
0 10 20
Kilometres
MID WESTERN HIGHWAY
NEVILLE STATE FOREST
COWRA
Grenfell
Self sufficient bush camping on lake edge
ROSEBERG STATE FOREST
PENNSYLVANIA STATE FOREST
COPPERHANNIA NATURE RESERVE
WYANGALA RECREATION AREA
Darbys Falls
Wyangala
Lachlan River
Abercrombie River
HENRY LAWSON WAY
OLYMPIC HIGHWAY
BENDICK MURRELL STATE FOREST
KOORAWATHA NATURE RESERVE
Mount Darling Track
Tarrans Gap Road
RAZORBACK NATURE RESERVE
KEVERSTONE STATE FOREST
KEVERSTONE STATE FOREST
Reids Flat
Excellent views of rocky landscape and native pine
DANANBILLA NATURE RESERVE
LACHLAN VALLEY WAY
Taylors Flat
Reids Flat Road
Lachlan River
Crookwell River
YOUNG
YOUNG STATE FOREST
Old sheds and cottage on corner
Phils Creek
Rugby
Crookwell Boorowa Road
Boorowa
Narrawa
Mullengrove
Nice range views and autumn tones
Harden-Murrumburrah
Causeway
Bulleys Crossing Road
BURLEY GRIFFIN WAY
Blakney Creek
Kildare Ck
Scenic stretch of river
Dalton
Oolong Creek
Gunning
HUME HIGHWAY
YASS
HUME HIGHWAY
Historic town with nice camping on Meadow Creek
Murrumbidgee River

Soft Roaders	✓
Trailers	✓
Steep Climbs	
Water Crossing	
Good Clearance Needed	
Snorkel	
Road Tyres	✓
Avoid Wet Weather	✓
Navigation Skills	
Extra Fuel	

LACHLAN RIVER

toward **Boorowa**, past **Rugby** and **Phils Creek**, on a winding road. Veer right onto **Reids Flat Road**, some 23 kilometres from the **Lachlan**, at a corner marked by an iron clad cottage and a couple of timber slab sheds.

Continue straight over some causeways past **Taylors Flat**, to the larger **Reids Flat** community on the **Lachlan**. First settled in 1872, the town now consists of a primary school, ripple iron clad hall, and a clutch of older houses.

Drive north beyond **Reids Flat** via **Tarrans Gap Road**, where monolithic rocks are strewn across valley after valley. It is a scenic run where willows line the water course, and elevated stops offer some superb views through patches of native pine. Keep right at the **Mount Darling Track** junction, to reach a tee intersection and a right turn toward **Lake Wyangala.**

A weir at **Wyangala** holds back water from the **Lachlan** and **Abercrombie Rivers** to a maximum depth of 72 metres. Its intricate network of arms

Lake Wyangala

spread like tentacles over an area 2.5 times the size of Sydney harbour, making the destination popular with anglers and boaters.

A couple of private caravan parks are located lakeside, but self contained 4WDers can venture to an unserviced area in state park to bush camp. (Follow the **Reg Hailstone Way** past **Mt McDonald Rural Fire Brigade** shed, to turn right three kilometres later. A steep descent makes its way to the lake edge and numerous camping possibilities.)

Leave **Wyangala** via **Darbys Falls**, crossing the **Lachlan River**, and arriving in **Cowra** on the bitumen. This sizable town is well worth a stop, to appreciate the award winning **Japanese Gardens**,

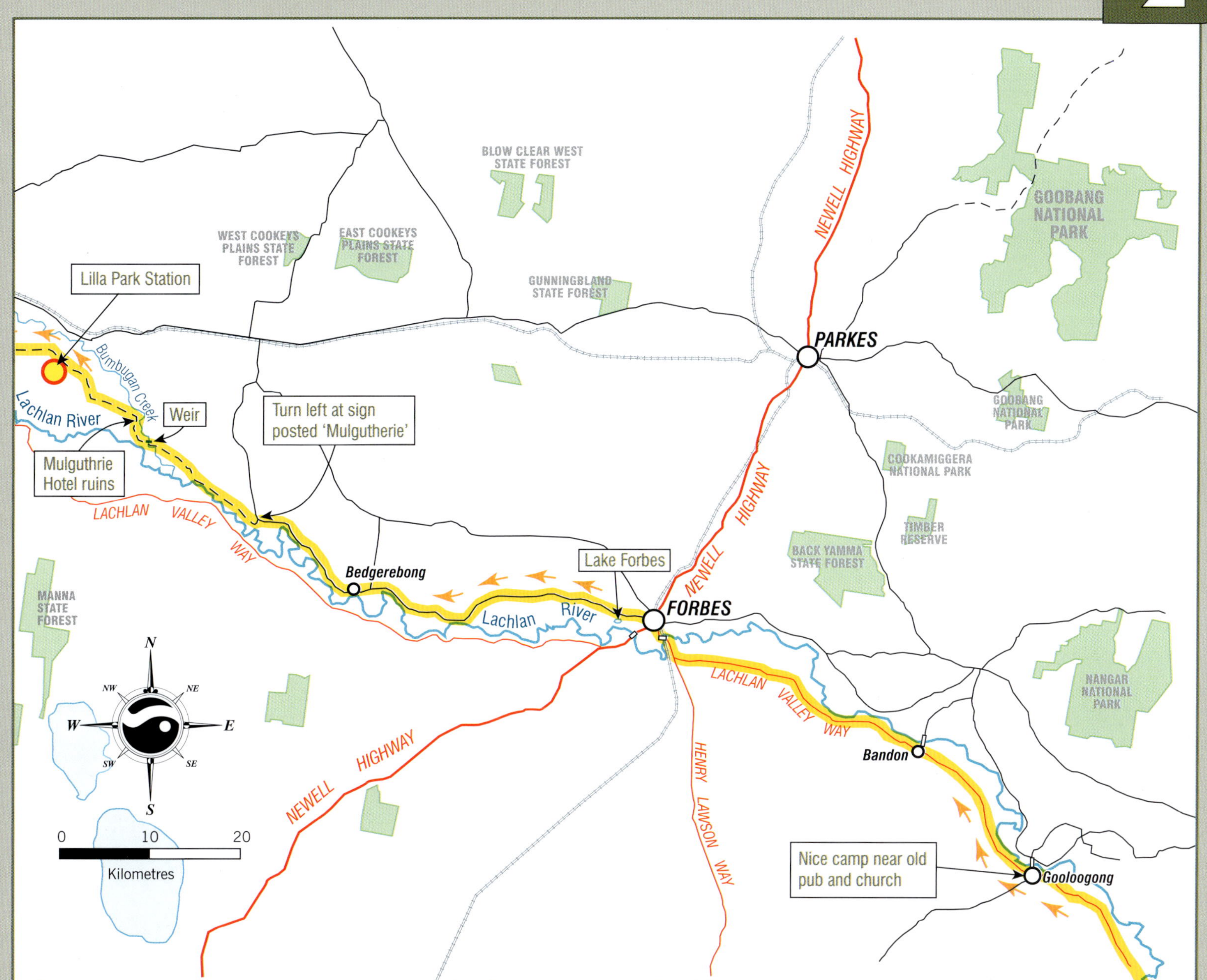

and sample some of the local foods and wines on offer. **Cowra** was also the site of a mass POW breakout during World War 2, and monuments to the event hold interest for many.

Sealed road paves the way from **Cowra** to **Forbes** for an easy 90 kilometre run along the **Lachlan Valley Way**. Rich soils sustain pumpkin and watermelon crops, with cattle and sheep grazing filling in the gaps. The **Lachlan** can be crossed at **Billimari** (**Davidsons Bridge** – lockable in flood), **Bandon** and **Gooloogong**. The latter crossing offers a nice camping area near an old pub and church.

You cross the **Lachlan** at **Forbes** on a substantial steel bridge. **Forbes** is a reasonable sized town on the **Newell Highway**, and offers most services to travellers. The towns to come west of **Forbes** also cater for most needs, but when heading inland it is a good policy to keep things topped up where possible.

Blacktop continues west of **Forbes** via the **Lachlan Valley Way** with a northern option following station country tracks. Both possibilities hug the river fringe and were regularly used by Cobb and Co from the late 1860s. A series of 10 plaques have been erected along the route, where change stations and hotels once stood between here and **Hillston**. They are prominently marked and offer an insight into the pioneering days on the lower **Lachlan**.

The **Lachlan Valley Way** is well signposted to **Booligal**, but these notes take you through via the river's northern side to pick up some of the lesser visited attractions – via unsealed road.

Leave town via **Brownes Lane** (north side of river) passing **Lake Forbes** with its recreation area on the left. A clutch of houses mark the floodplain township of **Bedgerebong** 33 kilometres later, before turning left at signposted "**Mulgutherie**" 16 kilometres after that.

The river is followed closely now, as you pass a weir on **Bumbugan Creek**, then the site of the **Mulgutherie Hotel**, first opened in 1876. The establishment was closed by the 1895 floods, when coaches were diverted via the southern road, and

LACHLAN RIVER

Left: *River scene*

little remains today, except for a few bricks and broken bottles lying at the foot of a rocky rise.

Travellers enter **Lilla Park Station** 13 kilometres from the hotel site to find stocks of Santa Gertrudes cattle – a breed indicative of the drier, harder country we are heading into.

You reach the river again at **Condobolin** where food, fuel and water can be replenished and accommodation found. Campers may prefer the basic facilities of **Gum Bend Lake**, and all visitors will get a great view of the district from **Mount Tilga** – some eight kilometres north of the town on the **Cobar Road**.

We will continue the **Lachlan** run via the **Cobar Road**, but turn west just after the rail crossing on the signposted "**Kiacatoo**" road. Drive past grain silos and sheds, keeping left away from the **Eubalong West** turn off. There is an excellent rest stop at the river crossing here, some 44 kilometres from **Condobolin**. A public hall and tennis court mark a horse shoe bend in the river where an old pump station sits in disrepair.

Follow the narrow bitumen west to the old **Culgong Hotel** site 10 kilometres later, where peppercorn trees mark the endeavours of 1886. Veer left onto gravel, closely following the **Lachlan**

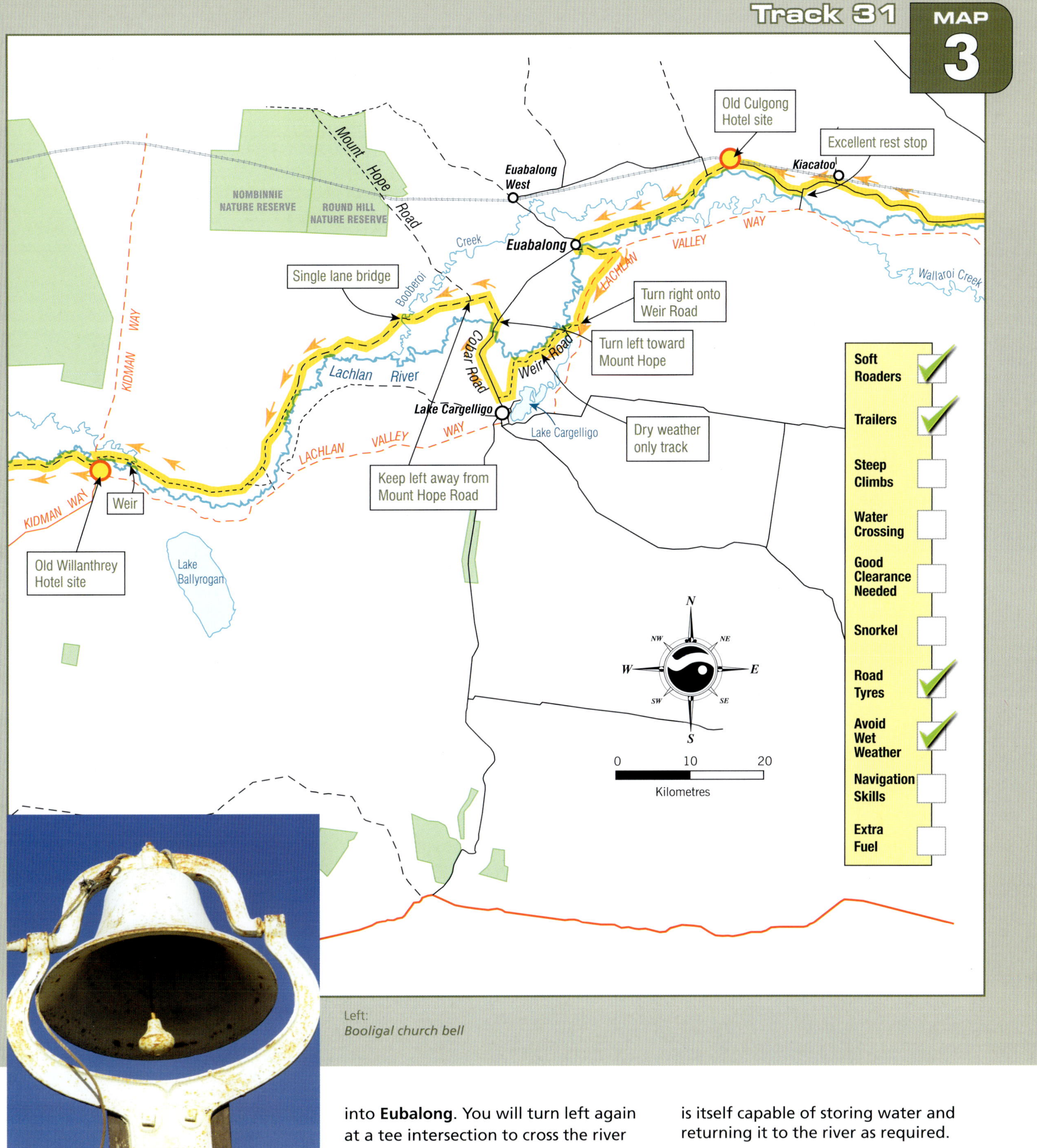

Left:
Booligal church bell

into **Eubalong**. You will turn left again at a tee intersection to cross the river almost immediately. Turn right on the **Lachlan Valley Way**, and head south for 10 kilometres to **Weir Road**.

Swing right here to reach a weir on the **Lachlan**, together with its regulator system, that banks the river's flow, allowing it to spill over into a series of lakes and canals. The largest lake (**Cargelligo**) covers 1620 hectares, and is itself capable of storing water and returning it to the river as required.

A dry weather track network zigzags along the **Lachlan** allowing visitors to see the various waterways. Follow the main track through a gate and grid, past stands of native pine and coolibah, into the northern end of **Lake Cargelligo** township. If the track is closed follow the main road south past broad acres of cropping land to a tee, then turn right into the town.

LACHLAN RIVER

River scene at Redbank Weir

TIMBER RESERVE
TIMBER RESERVE
Bush camping on Redbank Weir
Character pub and accommodation
Oxley Road
Penarie
MURRUMBIDGEE RIVER
BALRANALD
YANGA NATURE RESERVE

The township is your last place to consume fresh fruit and vegetables before heading toward **Hillston**, as you will pass into the fruit fly exclusion zone, roughly mid journey. Replace supplies at **Hillston** for the remainder of this trip.

Leave town via the **Cobar Road**, crossing the **Lachlan** 13 kilometres out, then swing left toward **Mount Hope**. Turn left again four kilometres later, before keeping left on gravel, away from the **Mount Hope Road**. You will pass an old steam engine mailbox at **North Whooly Station**, where salt bush is being commercially cultivated.

A single lane bridge over **Booberoi Creek** precedes an especially winding section of river, as a series of stations, grids and channels are passed. You will reach **Willandra Creek** (and a nearby weir), before reaching a tee intersection on the **Kidman Way**.

Turn left to cross the **Lachlan**, then swing right 200 metres later at the old **Willanthrey Hotel** site. A recently renovated slab hut sits near where the original hotel was built in 1862. A store also traded from here until 1963.

Stay on the gravel heading west past a huge shade cloth area, with citrus fruits and packing sheds dominating the river flats. Lengthy boom irrigators work the fertile soils, with potatoes, corn and beans being staple produce.

You will cross the **Lachlan** at **Hillston** taking the **Mossgiel Road** out of town, turning left toward signposted **"Willandra NP"**, then left again at signposted "**Merungle**" road. This clay based road is unsuitable if wet – and even the gravel topped **Lachlan Valley Way** may be impassable in wet weather (check at **Hillston** before leaving).

Keep straight past some almond groves where massive irrigators work, to an open channel system distributing the vital river water. You will cross a couple of intersections on this route, reaching the **Cobb Highway**, some 77 kilometres from **Hillston**.

Turn left for the run south over several creeks and floodways to arrive in **Booligal** about 19 kilometres later. A one teacher primary school, old church and pub dominate the small community, where camping is permitted at the **Lachlan** crossing. Visitors can see the old weir propped up with redgum posts, near a windmill on the south side of town.

We leave **Booligal** on the north side of the bridge, taking **Boxyard Road** to the junction of **Alma Road**. Keep left here following lowlands through a channel system to the naturally formed **Lake Bullogal**, some 60 kilometres from **Booligal**. You will reach a tee intersection where a left turn takes you over the **Lachlan** at **Corrong Bridge**. The waterway has narrowed here, hemmed in by widespread reeds.

If you turn left again (east) on the south side of the river you will reach **One Tree**

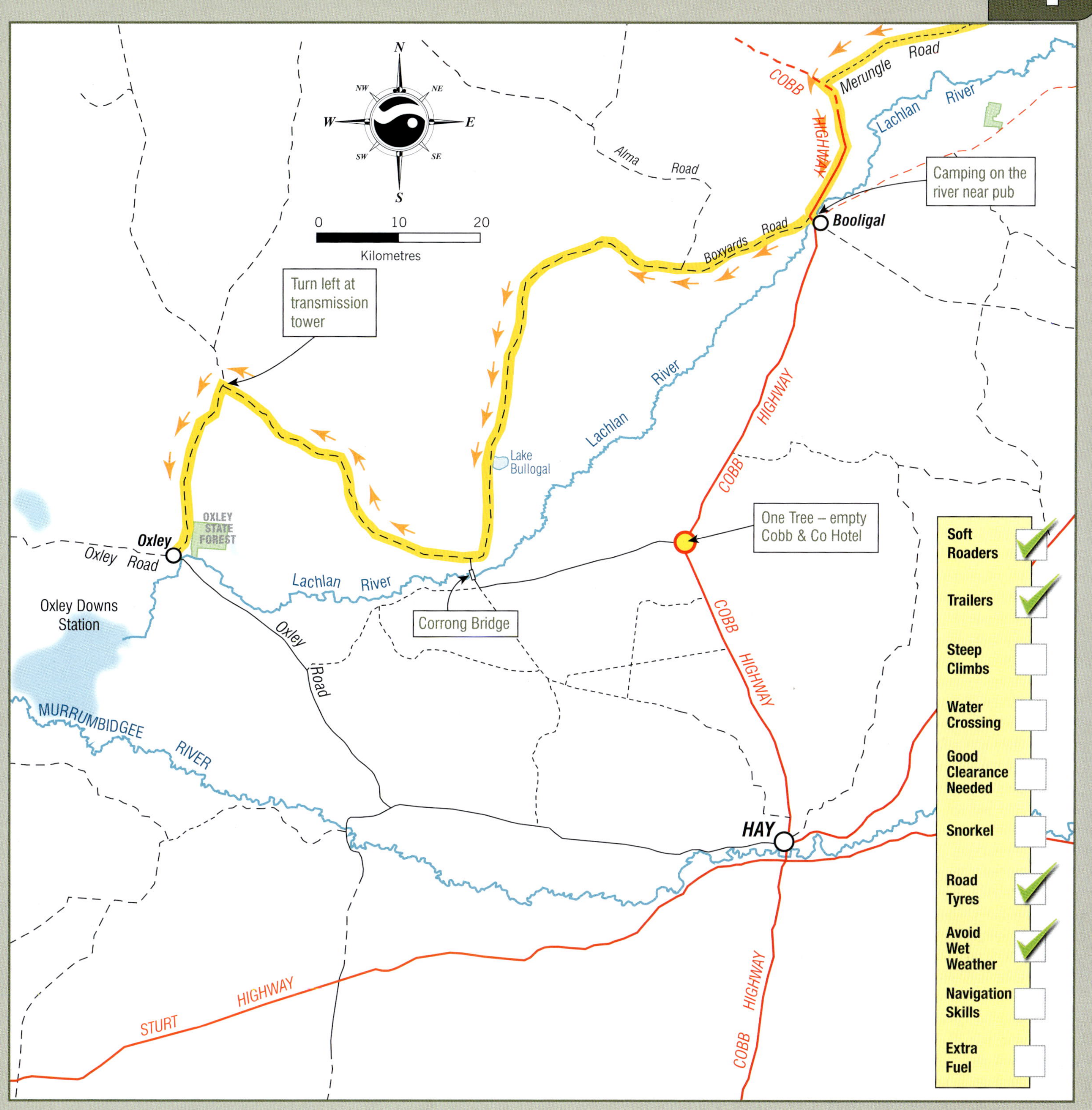

24 kilometres later. The empty Cobb and Co hotel sits on the **Cobb Highway**, looking rather lonely with just plains extending in every direction. We will however return to the **Lachlan's** north bank, and continue on westward for a further 38 kilometres.

Turn left at a radio transmission tower to arrive in **Oxley** 23 kilometres later. These days only a handful of houses comprise the small community, with a bridge over the now trickling river marking its final journey.

The **Lachlan** disappears into swamp country on **Oxley Downs**, just short of reaching the **Murrumbidgee River**. Options beyond **Oxley** include heading east to **Hay** via the blacktop, or an unsealed westward run into **Penarie** and its character filled pub. Accommodation is available here, or head cross country to **Redbank Weir** on the **Murrumbidgee** for bush camping possibilities.

TRACK 32 MACQUARIE MARSHES

OUTBACK NSW

Track Snapshot

TOUR ROUTE:
Carinda to Warren via Quambone and the Macquarie Marshes.

DURATION AND DISTANCE:
The 190 kilometre tour is easily done as a day trip.

TRACK DETAILS:
Station tracks and some bitumen make for easy travel by all vehicles, including those towing.

WHEN TO GO:
Wet weather will close the unsealed roads, but travellers can visit at any other time.

CAMPING:
Private camping at Willie Retreat.

FUEL AND SUPPLIES:
Carinda and Warren.

MAPS:
Natmap 1:100K Carinda, Quambone

OTHER INFORMATION:
Access into the marshes is only permitted in the company of a guide (ph 02 6842 1311 for details).

*To early European explorers the **Macquarie Marshes** spelt the end of the **Macquarie River**. This natural depression almost 50 kilometres long and eight kilometres wide appeared to soak up all that the river could deliver. It was not until 1846 that Thomas Mitchell found that water did indeed leave the marshes, making its way into the **Barwon**, **Darling** and **Murray Rivers**, and eventually the ocean.*

Unfortunately the sustained drought of recent years and increased demand for the valuable water upstream has seen the flows steadily diminish. A lack of flooding is responsible for shrinking red gum forests and a reduced birdlife population. On the positive side however the marshes are still a significant breeding ground for many bird species, and drier roads allow reasonable access into the area.

This trek begins at **Carinda** – a small town 67 kilometres south west of **Walgett**. A pub and store together with a couple of dozen houses mark the sheep grazing area, as you head south via the unsealed **Quambone Road**.

Conneelibah HS flags a turn off to **Sandy Camp**, 16 kilometres later, (although it is a homestead rather than a camp, and not open to the travelling public in any case). This is a shorter run into the marshes, but it is much rougher, and it bypasses the hamlet of **Quambone**. So keep left at the junction, to pass station country, where sheep, cattle and cropping seem viable in equal measure.

You will reach **Sandy Camp Road** on the right, some 59 kilometres from **Carinda** where we will turn west, however **Quambone** lies just a few kilometres further south. Visitors with time to spare can venture into the hamlet where the consequences of drought and population drift are all too obvious.

Return to **Sandy Camp Road**, and follow it over **Merri Merri Creek**, then the more

Below:
Birdlife viewing area

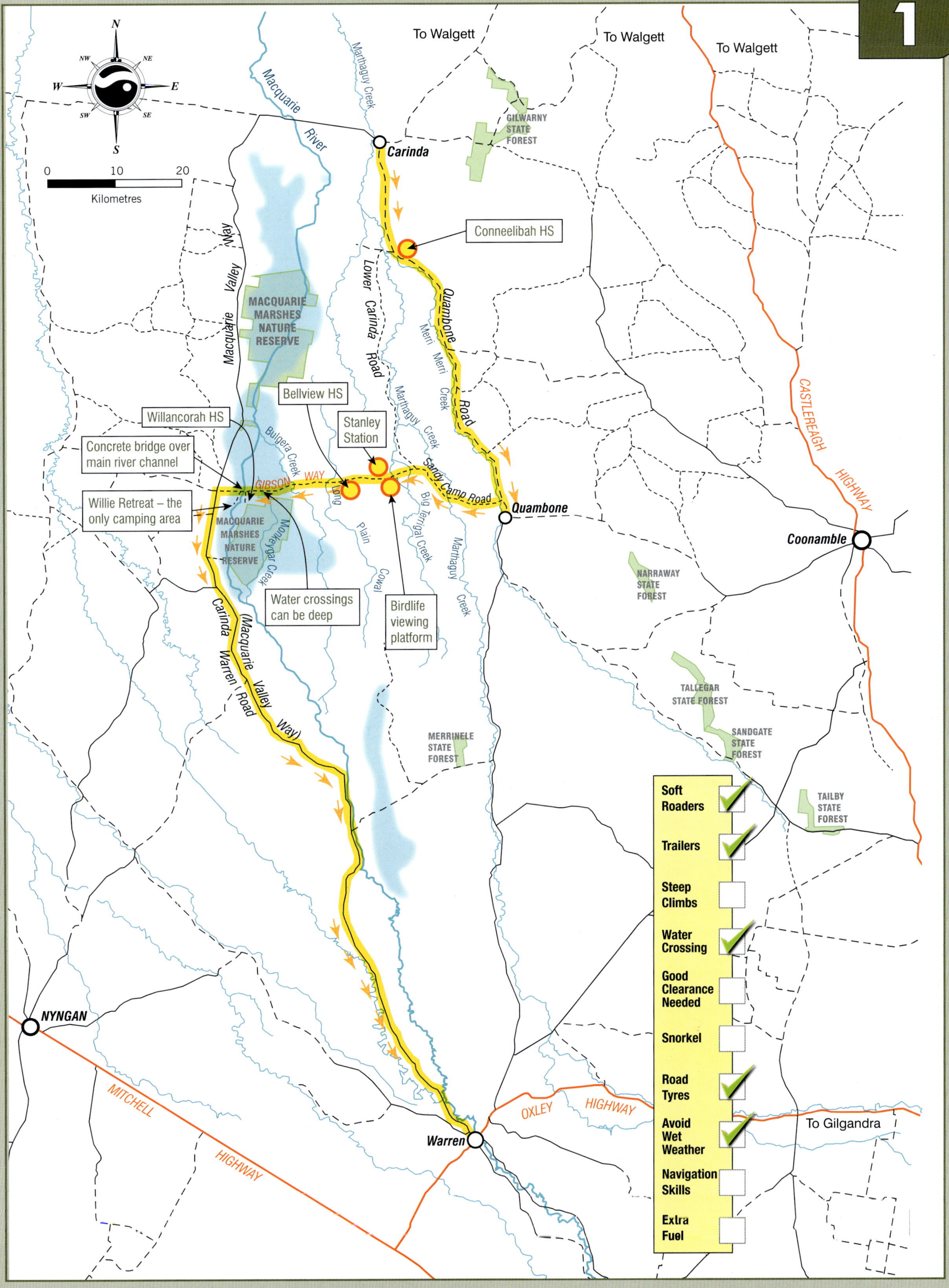

N
NW NE
W E
SW SE
S
0 10 20
Kilometres

To Walgett
To Walgett
To Walgett
Marthaguy Creek
Macquarie River
Carinda
GILWARNY STATE FOREST
Conneelibah HS
Macquarie Valley Way
MACQUARIE MARSHES NATURE RESERVE
Lower Carinda Road
Quambone Road
Merri Merri Creek
Marthaguy Creek
Bellview HS
Willancorah HS
Stanley Station
Concrete bridge over main river channel
Bulgera Creek
GIBSON WAY
Sandy Camp Road
Long Plain
Big Terrigal Creek
Quambone
Willie Retreat – the only camping area
MACQUARIE MARSHES NATURE RESERVE
Monkeygar Creek
Cowal
Marthaguy Creek
CASTLEREAGH HIGHWAY
Coonamble
NARRAWAY STATE FOREST
Water crossings can be deep
Birdlife viewing platform
Carinda Warren Road
(Macquarie Valley Way)
TALLEGAR STATE FOREST
SANDGATE STATE FOREST
MERRINELE STATE FOREST
TAILBY STATE FOREST
NYNGAN
MITCHELL HIGHWAY
OXLEY HIGHWAY
Warren
To Gilgandra

Soft Roaders	✓
Trailers	✓
Steep Climbs	
Water Crossing	✓
Good Clearance Needed	
Snorkel	
Road Tyres	✓
Avoid Wet Weather	✓
Navigation Skills	
Extra Fuel	

substantial **Marthaguy Creek** shortly after that. **Stanley Station** is reached 14 kilometres from the turn off (where the lower **Carinda Road** intersects. Keep left as you begin the wetland journey over **Little** then **Big Terrigal Creeks**.

A wildlife viewing platform is located at the latter crossing, elevated above the swamp land. Although feral pigs are still a problem in the area, it is **Macquarie's** birdlife that is most abundant. Swamphens, spoonbills, and ducks are routinely seen, with hawks and sea eagles occasionally spotted. The emu population is also significant across the floodplains.

Continue the drive west on the **Gibson Way** past **Bellview HS** with its sprawling cluster of old buildings and farm structures. A bridge spans **Long Plain Cowal**, before **Bulgera** and **Monkeygar Creeks** are crossed. In wet years the water here can be deep and wide, as you make your way past roof high reed beds.

The turn off to **Willancorah HS** precedes a concrete bridge over the **Macquarie River's** major channel. A turn off on the left to **Willie Retreat** is reached

Left: *Emu eggs*

Below: *Water crossing near Willie Retreat*

Above: *Macquarie Marsh birdlife*

Right: *Macquarie River*

following the crossing, where travellers will find their only opportunity to camp in the area. Accommodation is also available in the historic shearers quarters; part of a much larger property that included a Cobb and Co change station.

Two kilometres further on you reach a cross roads on the main **Carinda – Warren Road**. Turn left to follow the southern nature reserve block some 107 kilometres into the larger town of **Warren** on the **Oxley Highway**. You will pass a turn off to the marshes area about 12 kilometres from **Willie Retreat**, where a network a tracks follow the main river route. Access to the Ramsar protected sections are only permitted in the company of a guide (ph 02 6842 1311 for details). It is a routine drive following sealed road into **Warren** where most services are available.

TRACK 33 Mount Kaputar

OUTBACK NSW

*Travellers using the **Newell Highway** for a quick run across NSW into Queensland or Victoria, may like to drop into **Mount Kaputar** for a day or overnight visit. The surprisingly lofty peaks of the **Nandewar Range** are an interesting diversion from the lowland cropping and stock country that flashes by the windscreen for hours at a time.*

*It is an easy run on good gravel, though 4WD offers some reassurance should heavy rain or snow fall unexpectedly, and the run to **Upper Bullawa** is mostly dirt. Commanding viewpoints and pleasant camping opportunities combine with numerous walking trails and abundant wildlife, to offer a broad range of activities for visitors.*

Australia's cotton capital, **Narrabri,** marks the **Namoi River's** crossing on the **Newell** and the beginning of this tour. Follow **Maitland Street** east on the **Old Gunnedah Road**, turning left onto the sign posted **Kaputar Road,** and passing the airport on your left.

Old ruins dot the rural drive as you follow in the footsteps of Oxley and Mitchell, who opened up this country for pioneering pastoralists in the 1830s. Stockyards and a series of windmills trace the run up **Bullawa Creek** past farmlets to a bridge over the pebbly waterway.

Follow the valley through rocky country to a larger station at the foot of the range, then reach gravel at a distinct fork some 29 kilometres from **Narrabri**. The climb to **Mount Kaputar** branches to the right, but we will turn left onto **Upper Bullawa Creek Road** for a short detour to a day use area within **Kaputar NP**.

Track Snapshot

TOUR ROUTE:
Narrabri to Mount Kaputar via Upper Bullawa and return.

DURATION AND DISTANCE:
Day trip of 70 kilometres (125 kilometres return).

TRACK DETAILS:
Easy travel, suitable for all vehicles, but caravans not permitted.

WHEN TO GO:
All year round, but beware of regular snow falls over winter and the possibility of rain at any time. Wildflowers in spring.

CAMPING:
Bush camping with excellent facilities at Bark Hut and Dawsons Spring.

FUEL AND SUPPLIES:
Narrabri offers all supplies and services..

MAPS:
Natmap 1:100K Horton

OTHER INFORMATION:
Nearby Sawn Rocks and WAA Gorge are well worth a visit, and there are numerous walking tracks throughout the national park.

Upper Bullawa Track

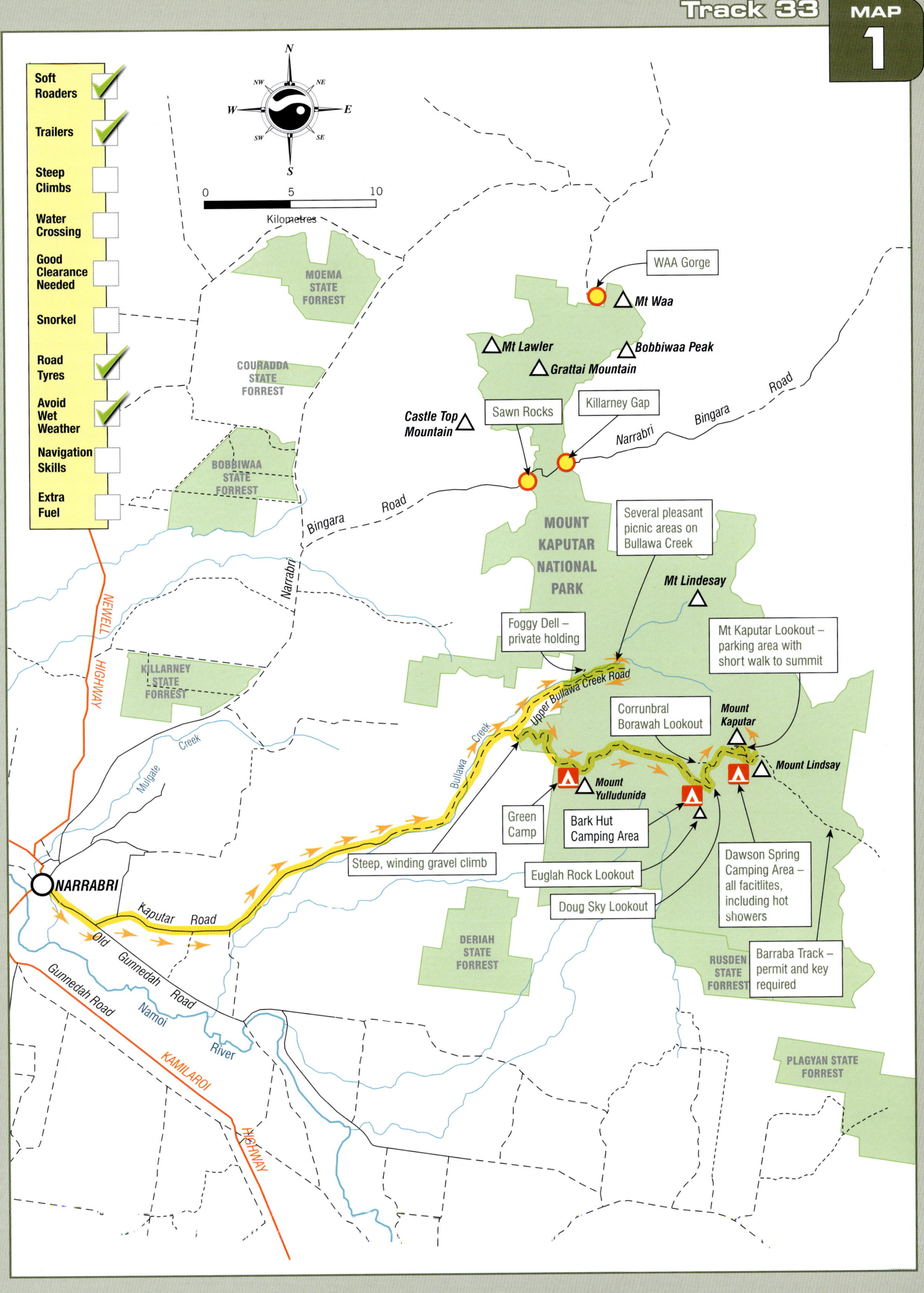

Soft Roaders
Trailers
Steep Climbs
Water Crossing
Good Clearance Needed
Snorkel
Road Tyres
Avoid Wet Weather
Navigation Skills
Extra Fuel
N
S
E
W
NW
NE
SW
SE
0
5
10
Kilometres
MOEMA STATE FORREST
COURADDA STATE FORREST
BOBBIWAA STATE FORREST
KILLARNEY STATE FORREST
WAA Gorge
Mt Waa
Mt Lawler
Bobbiwaa Peak
Grattai Mountain
Castle Top Mountain
Sawn Rocks
Killarney Gap
Narrabri
Bingara
Road
MOUNT KAPUTAR NATIONAL PARK
Several pleasant picnic areas on Bullawa Creek
Mt Lindesay
Foggy Dell – private holding
Mt Kaputar Lookout – parking area with short walk to summit
Upper Bullawa Creek Road
Corrunbral Borawah Lookout
Mount Kaputar
Mount Lindsay
Mount Yulludunida
Green Camp
Bark Hut Camping Area
Euglah Rock Lookout
Doug Sky Lookout
Dawson Spring Camping Area – all facitlites, including hot showers
Barraba Track – permit and key required
Steep, winding gravel climb
Bullawa Creek
Mulgate
Creek
NEWELL HIGHWAY
NARRABRI
Kaputar Road
Old Gunnedah Road
Gunnedah Road
Namoi River
KAMILAROI HIGHWAY
DERIAH STATE FORREST
RUSDEN STATE FORREST
PLAGYAN STATE FORREST

Falls near Bark Hut Camp

A couple of grids and roughish creek crossings precede entry into the national park, and a lovely grassland colored with wildflowers. Rocky bluffs dominate the view now as you pass an old abandoned header, and other relics from an earlier time.

Keep right at **Foggy Dell** (private holding) about 5.4 kilometres from the previous fork to reach several secluded picnic areas, sheltered by river oaks. Tables, seats and wood BBQs are provided at each clearing, with **Bullawa Creek** trickling at your feet.

The track deteriorates to wheel furrows from here, and finishes at "**Camp Palmer**" - a block of private property established in the early 1970s. Visitors can park their vehicles at the last (much larger) picnic area, and walk to the creek with birdlife sounds gradually drowned out by the roar of cicadas.

Retrace your steps to the **Mount Kaputar Road** fork and swing hard left onto narrow winding road signposted "No Caravans". Good gravel paves the sustained climb back into national park, passing monolithic features streaked with lichen.

Elevated lookouts take in a kaleidescope of color with eucalypts, native pines and at least 20 species of acacia glowing in various shades of green. Ironbarks cling to the drier slopes, while snow gums dominate the 1500 metre high peaks.

Green Camp is reached seven kilometres from the fork and offers dedicated walkers the staging point for a strenuous climb to **Yulludunida Crater** – part of the volcanic foundations to this area, with nearby **Mount Lindsay** thought to have been a volcano.

Patchy bitumen paves the way further up past grasstree stands to the **Bark Hut Camping Area** about eight kilometres later. This site grew from a forestry hut established in the 1940s to coordinate logging in the area. Timber was harvested into the 1950s, but little remains of the endeavour except for some of the larger stumps.

Good camping with all facilities is a feature of **Bark Hut** now, with terraced sites and a short walk to **Euglah Rock Lookout**.

Old header, Upper Bullawa

Doug Sky Lookout

Switchbacks continue the sustained climb past **Doug Sky Lookout** (one of the best views toward the south) and the **Kaputar Plateau Walk** (6km, 4 hour return walk into range country with generous lookouts) Less energetic visitors will appreciate a turn off to **Corrunbral Borawah Lookout** ("**The Governor**") just a couple of kilometres further on by vehicle.

You will reach a tee intersection some 21 kilometres from the national park entrance fork, and return to gravel for a left turn toward **Mount Kaputar's** summit. Follow a short roughish track to a parking area and make the final ascent on foot via timber stairs. At 1510 metres, the viewing platform takes in a broad swathe of northern country, with views extending up to 150 kilometres.

Return by vehicle back to the tee and continue southward past **Barraba Track** on the left. (This demanding 4WD trail can only be undertaken in one direction

Mount Kaputar summit

from the eastern **Barraba** side, and requires permission at **Barraba**, a key for the locked gate, and effectively no rain in the preceding days.)

The turn off to **Dawson Spring Camping Area** is reached shortly after the **Barraba Track** junction, and is a lovely camp amid snowgum and taller timber, with all facilites including hot showers, BBQs and fireplaces (bring your own wood). A network of walking tracks radiate from this location with lookouts taking in much of the south's crumpled landscape and **Mount Lindsay** to the east.

Vehicles must return from **Eckfords Carpark** (at the base of a transmission tower complex) and retrace their path to **Narrabri**. Visitors impressed with this country could follow bitumen from **Narrabri** to **Sawn Rocks**, or more gravel (dry weather only) to **WAA Gorge**. Both destinations are within the national park, and feature short walks to their respective features (**Sawn Rocks** are geometrically shaped columns of basalt on a lovely creek, while the twin waterholes of **WAA Gorge** are highly significant to the local Gamilaraay People.

Notes...

No matter where you are, ARB has you covered.

VICTORIA

ARB STORES

Head Office
ARB Kilsyth
42-44 Garden Street
Kilsyth VIC 3137
Tel: (03) 9761 6622

ARB Ballarat
891 Latrobe Street
Delacombe VIC 3356
Tel: (03) 5336 4605

ARB Brighton
793 Nepean Highway
Bentleigh VIC 3204
Tel: (03) 9557 1888

ARB Dandenong
6/4A Lonsdale Street
Dandenong VIC 3175
Tel: (03) 9793 0002

ARB Geelong
304 Thompson Road
North Geelong VIC 3215
Tel: (03) 5272 2611

ARB Bairnsdale
623 Princes Highway
Bairnsdale VIC 3875
Tel: (03) 5152 1226

ARB Bendigo
17-21 Phillips Drive
Kangaroo Flat VIC 3555
Tel: (03) 5445 7100

ARB Echuca
89A Ogilvie Avenue
Echuca VIC 3564
Tel: (03) 5840 2600

ARB Hoppers Crossing
73-79 Old Geelong Road
Hoppers Crossing
VIC 3029
Tel: (03) 9749 5905

ARB Keilor Park
34 Commercial Place
Keilor East VIC 3033
Tel: (03) 9331 7333

ARB Pakenham
20 Commercial Drive
Pakenham VIC 3810
Tel: (03) 5940 5500

ARB Shepparton
180 Benalla Road
Shepparton VIC 3630
Tel: (03) 5822 1877

ARB Somerton
798 Cooper Street
Somerton VIC 3074
Tel: (03) 9460 9988

ARB Traralgon
351 Princes Highway
Traralgon East VIC 3844
Tel: (03) 5174 9190

ARB Warragul
10 Howitt Street
Warragul VIC 3820
Tel: (03) 5623 5599

ARB STOCKISTS

G-Wiz Automotive & 4WD Centre
21-23 Union Street
Sale VIC 3850
Tel: (03) 5144 7990

Gippsland 4WD Centre
Lot 7 Princes Highway
Traralgon VIC 3844
Tel: (03) 5174 1560

Highcountry Parts & 4×4
201 Mt Buller Road
Mansfield VIC 3722
Tel: (03) 5779 1900

Horsham Off Road
72 McPherson Road
Horsham VIC 3400
Tel: (03) 5381 1766

Mildura 4WD Accessories
55 Seventh Street
East Mildura VIC 3500
Tel: (03) 5021 3213

Myrtleford Tyre & Battery
73 Myrtle Street
Myrtleford VIC 3737
Tel: (03) 5752 1175

Outback 4WD
174 Canterbury Road
Bayswater VIC 3153
Tel: (03) 9720 6226

Oz Auto 4WD Centre
Factory 1, 34
Stephenson St
Seaford VIC 3198
Tel: (03) 9775 0378

SG Offroad Wonthaggi
136 McKenzie Street
Wonthaggi VIC 3995
Tel: (03) 5672 5899

South Eastern 4WD Centre
182 Centre Road
Narre Warren VIC 3805
Tel: (03) 8786 5090

SG Offroad Leongatha
2 Tilson Court
Leongatha VIC 3953
Tel: (03) 5662 5554

Swan Hill Off Road
1 Nyah Road
Swan Hill VIC 3585
Tel: (03) 5032 2700

Wangaratta 4WD Centre
205 Tone Road
Wangaratta VIC 3677
Tel: (03) 5722 2979

Warrnambool Offroad
1117 Raglan Parade
Warrnambool VIC 3280
Tel: (03) 5561 4354

Yarra Valley 4WD
35 Maroondah Highway
Healesville VIC 3777
Tel: (03) 5962 3124

WESTERN AUSTRALIA

ARB STORES

ARB Bunbury
2/12 George Street
Bunbury WA 6230
Tel: (08) 9721 2099

ARB Canning Vale
77 Banister Road
Canning Vale WA 6155
Tel: (08) 9455 4366

ARB Geraldton
78 North West
Coastal Hwy
Geraldton WA 6530
Tel: (08) 9921 8077

ARB Mandurah
69 Gordon Road
Mandurah WA 6210
Tel: (08) 9583 3200

ARB Osborne Park
66 Collingwood Street
Osborne Park WA 6017
Tel: (08) 9244 3553

ARB South Hedland
2 Hamilton Road
South Hedland WA 6722
Tel: (08) 9160 4900

ARB Wangara
11 Buckingham Drive
Wangara WA 6065
Tel: (08) 9409 5764

ARB Welshpool
143 Welshpool Road
Welshpool WA 6106
Tel: (08) 9358 3688

ARB STOCKISTS

Action 4WD
19 Gillam Drive
Kelmscott WA 6111
Tel: (08) 9390 3011

Adventure 4×4
3 Crocker St
Rockingham WA 6168
Tel: (08) 9529 2229

Albany 4WD & Camping Centre
6 Minna Street
Albany WA 6331
Tel: (08) 6819 7777

All 4×4 Services
63 Strelly Street
Busselton WA 6280
Tel: (08) 9754 8588

Avon 4 Wheel Drive Centre
20 Peel Terrace
Northam WA 6401
Tel: (08) 9622 5818

Derby 4×4 and Marine
Lot 920 Wells Street
Derby WA 6728
Tel: (08) 9193 1919

Falcon Auto Parts & Accessories
Unit 17 651-669
Old Coast Rd
Falcon WA 6210
Tel: (08) 9534 6722

Goldfields Off Road
2 Federal Road
Kalgoorlie WA 6430
Tel: (08) 9091 4797

Kununurra 4WD Spares
21 Konkerberry Dr
Kununurra WA 6743
Tel: (08) 9169 1150

Make Tracks
44 Elgee Road
Midland WA 6056
Tel: (08) 9374 0777

Minshull Mechanical Repairs
96 Guy Street
Broome WA 6725
Tel: (08) 9192 5326

Off Road Equipment Myaree
61 McCoy Street
Myaree WA 6154
Tel: (08) 9317 4900

Pilbara Motor Group
7 Crane Circle
Karratha WA 6714
Tel: (08) 9144 6500

Pilbara Auto & 4×4
42 Bonderoo Road
Tom Price WA 6751
Tel: (08) 9188 1700

Pilbara Motor Group - Newman
18 Pardoo Street
Newman WA 6753
Tel: (08) 9154 3600

Southern Suspension & 4WD Centre
53 Norseman Road
Esperance WA 6450
Tel: (08) 9072 0917

West Coast 4WD Centre
U2 /10 Pensacola Tce
Clarkson WA 6030
Tel: (08) 9408 6448

QUEENSLAND

ARB STORES

ARB Biggera Waters
23 Gateway Drive
Biggera Waters QLD 4216
Tel: (07) 5537 8800

ARB Bundaberg
9/106 Takalvan Street
Bundaberg QLD 4670
Tel: (07) 4153 2929

ARB Burleigh Heads
48 Kortum Drive
Burleigh Heads QLD 4220
Tel: (07) 5535 9223

ARB Caboolture
129 Morayfield Road
Caboolture QLD 4510
Tel: (07) 5499 1955

ARB Cairns
59 Aumuller Street
Portsmith QLD 4870
Tel: (07) 4035 3350

ARB Caloundra
47B Caloundra Road
Caloundra QLD 4551
Tel: (07) 5491 4500

ARB Capalaba
1/168 Redland Bay Road
Capalaba QLD 4157
Tel: (07) 3823 5900

ARB Coopers Plains
988 Beaudesert Road
Coopers Plains QLD 4108
Tel: (07) 3277 2020

ARB Jindalee
528 Seventeen Mile Rocks Road Seventeen Mile Rocks QLD 4073
Tel: (07) 3715 6400

ARB Mackay
9 Caterpillar Drive
Paget QLD 4740
Tel: (07) 4998 6888

ARB Maroochydore
1/127A Sugar Road
Maroochydore QLD 4558
Tel: (07) 5475 4011

ARB North Lakes
66 Flinders Parade
North Lakes QLD 4509
Tel: (07) 3491 9600

ARB Nundah
615 Nudgee Road
Nundah QLD 4012
Tel: (07) 3266 3255

ARB Rockhampton
111 Gladstone Road
Rockhampton QLD 4700
Tel: (07) 4922 7788

ARB Springwood
3355 Pacific Hwy
Slacks Creek QLD 4127
Tel: (07) 3493 3030

ARB Toowoomba
115 North Street
Toowoomba QLD 4350
Tel: (07) 4632 1122

ARB Townsville
311 Ingham Road
Garbutt QLD 4814
Tel: (07) 4728 0900

ARB STOCKISTS

Allen's 4×4
10 Basalt Street
Mareeba QLD 4880
Tel: (07) 4092 3965

Atlas 4×4
5 Simpson Street
Mt Isa QLD 4825
Tel: (07) 4743 4044

Birdsville Roadhouse
Lot 2 Frew Street
Birdsville QLD 4482
Tel: (07) 4656 3226

Coastal 4×4 and Outdoor
225 Maryborough/
Hervey Bay Road
Hervey Bay QLD 4655
Tel: (07) 4194 0833

Dalby 4×4 Accessories
89 Loudoun Road
Dalby QLD 4405
Tel: (07) 4669 0631

Goondiwindi 4×4 Accessories
8 Pharlap Court
Goondiwindi QLD 4390
Tel: (07) 4671 2153

Gulf Parts & Service
29 Iraci Crescent
Weipa QLD 4874
Tel: (07) 4030 9500

Gympie 4×4 RV Accessories
6 Kelly Drive
Gympie QLD 4570
Tel: (07) 5482 7474

Longreach Motors
33 Swan Street
Longreach QLD 4730
Tel: (07) 4658 1700

Star Tyrepower
190 Haly Street
Kingaroy QLD 4610
Tel: (07) 4162 1177

Tableland 4WD
74 Grove Street
Atherton QLD 4883
Tel: (07) 4091 3309

Tech Tune Automotive and 4×4
43 Station Street
Innisfail QLD 4858
Tel: (07) 4061 2200

UV 4×4 Accessories
21 Magura Street
Enoggera QLD 4051
Tel: (07) 3855 4444

UV 4×4 Accessories
51 Kremzow Rd
Brendale QLD 4500
Tel: (07) 3889 8555

UV 4×4 Accessories
25 Brisbane Road
Bundamba QLD 4304
Tel: (07) 3816 3344